Strategic Planning Workbook

Second Edition

Joseph C. Krallinger • Karsten G. Hellebust

John Wiley & Sons, Inc.

New York • Chichester • Brisbane • Toronto • Singapore

Library of Congress Cataloging-in-Publication Data:

Krallinger, Joseph C.
    Strategic planning workbook / by Joseph C. Krallinger and Karsten
  G. Hellebust. – 2nd ed.
        p.   cm.
    Hellebust's name appears first on the previous ed.
    Includes index.
    ISBN 0-471-58256-5
    1. Strategic planning.   I. Hellebust, Karsten G.   II. Title
  HD30.28.H43   1993
  658.4'012–dc20   92-22589

Printed in the United States of America

10 9 8 7 6 5 4 3

CONTENTS

PART 4   SUCCESS: THE FRUITS OF PLANNING

HOW TO APPLY THE
CHEM-A-LOT EXPERIENCE

PART 5   THE EVALUATION OF BUSINESS
PERFORMANCE

PART 6   THE PLANS THAT TURNED
CHEM-A-LOT AROUND

PART 7   THE CHEM-A-LOT MANAGEMENT
TOOL KIT

THOSE WHO WILL PROFIT FROM THIS WORKBOOK

*By trying, we can easily learn to endure adversity—
another man's, I mean.*

Mark Twain

Ask lenders, creditors, and consultants why businesses fail and they invariably will list the following causes:

- Management incompetency, unbalanced and/or inadequate experience of key managers.
- Death or departure of the prime leader.
- Lack of working capital (cash, accounts receivable, inventories, current accounts payable, and debts payable). Causes of most working capital problems are as follows:

  - Failure to control working capital during economic swings in profitable sales volume.
  - Significant errors in sales forecasts.
  - Inadequate cash flow, unbalanced capital asset utilization, and high amount of capital asset requirements compared to funds available.
  - Lack of control over billing and accounts receivable collection.
  - Excessive and/or obsolete inventories.
  - Poor quality of produced goods.
  - Lack of management's attention as well as poor analysis of financial and operating trends over time.
  - Technological changes obsoleting products or decreasing their unit sales prices.

1

— Excessive lead times in ordering materials or producing components (low inventory turns).

— Overspending in indirect operating and administrative functions.

• Not enough research and development to stay up with or ahead of the competition.

• Burdensome debt and debt service demands on cash.

This book proposes how each of these issues, as well as others, can be planned for so potential problems can be averted. Often, long-term planning and proper budgeting would have saved the failing businesses. Natural disasters and management fraud are the exception; they are not the basic causes of the problem. People are the problem, but they will be able to avoid failure through proper planning.

This is a book for everyone in business . . . at every level of responsibility. Why? Because this is just not another book filled with theories! It presents the real-life squeeze on business being enacted every day, now more than ever!

New material to this edition includes a section on how to critically evaluate the performance of your business and the latest information on debt financing and the increasingly key use of cash flow and working capital in strategic planning and budgeting.

The cycles of business are shorter, more violent, less predictable, and more deadly than ever. Competitors prowl relentlessly over our marketplaces. They too often grow dynamically. They come at you from everywhere. As a result, your department, your division, or your business experiences pressures on profits, demands on cash flow, and flights of good people to the competition. Under such economic conditions, planning often suffers, if it exists at all. Businesses once basic to every country find their furnaces banked, their plants significantly below operating capacity, and their shops closing. Lives are being destroyed by poor planning or no planning. Somewhere along the line, the problems of bureaucratic top-down planning caused planning to become a dirty word. Therefore, some leaders decided not to take the time to plan at all. They did not need to plan when times were good and sales were just a matter of answering the phone. Other leaders never involved employees in detail planning, considering it out of their realm of responsibility. Too bad!

Eventually, each Fad-of-the-Month book proves ineffective. Generic, large-scale solutions are difficult to apply to a specific business. Businesses evade long-term sanity by submitting to the short-term profit pressures exerted by financial tycoons and investment gurus who know nothing of how to successfully operate a business over time. Short-term thinking spells sudden death in the marketplace. Sound planning by well-trained people, led by a CEO with all of the credentials required of the leader of a business, will result in real solutions and accelerated growth in any business.

THE CHEM-A-LOT CASE

PART ONE

UNCOVERING A HIDDEN MESS AT CHEM-A-LOT

A mess is a system of interacting problems that causes a business ill health.

Adapted from Russell Ackoff's definition in Redesigning The Future: A System Approach to Societal Problems. *He defines when a problem is not a problem, but, in his exact words: "it is a mess—a system of interacting problems." In the context of Chem-A-Lot, a mess indeed describes the situation perfectly.*

CHAPTER 1

THE NEED TO SURVIVE

During his years as Secretary of State, John Foster Dulles boarded Air Force One on a tough problem-solving mission. "Where to, sir?" the pilot asked. "Anywhere," replied Mr. Dulles. "We have trouble all over."

THE PRACTICAL TACTICAL RESPONSE

Many years ago, the flight path of a two-seater Taylorcraft out on a training flight brought it through a dark prairie squall line. Upon entering the churning clouds, the instructor, a grizzled old bush pilot, took out his pocket watch and hung it by its chain above the windshield. "Why?" asked the puzzled student.

"So's I'll know which way's up!" was the laconic reply.

Today, we load the cockpits of jets with instruments to provide the pilot with the precise position and attitude of the aircraft. Most of those instruments evolved from tactical responses to real situations faced by just such early-day bush pilots. But like the hung pocket watch, those instruments simply help the pilot reach a planned destination.

Most likely, in your business, many tactical responses made to keep some earlier business on course have evolved into a part of your business control system. Yet you know that despite advanced control systems, numerous businesses continue to sputter or even crash, and that the families dependent on a crashing business get hurt. Why do these systems fail?

Often managers, intent upon the monetary minutiae that emanate from their advanced control systems, do not know which way is up or where they are going.

Plane pilots prepare flight plans; business managers should do no less. This business flight guide is about practical business planning techniques, derived from numerous business experiences, that should help you know which way is up as you pilot your business into the future.

THE COST OF SURVIVAL

All businesses are living systems that grow or decline, proliferate and evolve, to provide us with new products and unusual services. Each business attempts to survive in a climate plagued by social, political, and economic storms that are as dangerous as those faced by the grizzled old bush pilot. Survival of the fittest prevails.

The economist Joseph A. Schumpeter, talking about the need to survive, said something like this: *Profit is the current cost of survival in a world where constant innovation leads to creative destruction and replacement of products and services as well as the businesses that produce them.*

Survival costs, including environmental costs, should be, but seldom are, reflected in current records as accrued costs that must be met. Put more bluntly, if a Chief Executive Officer (CEO) doesn't use current profits to develop new and improved products and services, old products and services will most likely be creatively destroyed—that is, replaced by competitive ones preferred by consumers. For a business to survive, the CEO must be entrepreneur enough to know when to have the courage to develop new products and services through reinvesting cash generated from prior operations and through prudent borrowing from others.

Survival is the moral justification for profit, just as the surplus fat of the hibernating bear, the starch stored in the potato, or the honey in a beehive is justified by the need of the species to survive. Also as in a species, sustained losses result in the decay and ultimate destruction of a business. When our ancestors were primarily farmers, it was easy to see the connection between saving the best seed corn for future harvests and survival. Today it is not so easy to see that link!

Paradoxically, because survival depends upon the innovative uses to which profits are put over time, maximizing current-year profits simply to earn a bonus, or to issue a favorable report to impress Wall Street, is detrimental to the welfare and long-term survival of a business and, more importantly, to the people who depend on it.

Finally, in an increasingly complex world, what does survival of a business mean? Does it mean survival for the benefit of stockholders only? For management stakeholders as well? For all stakeholders, including employees and the public? Or solely for the business entity? These questions are being raised in this country because some American managers have moved large parts of their operations abroad to survive. Should those managers be censured? Or are they helping to raise the living standards in backward nations and, ultimately, our own living standards?

In response to such known and hidden questions, here is the story of a generic corporation and the very real responses made by successive managements to its challenges to survival.

AN AMERICAN CORPORATION CALLED CHEM-A-LOT

To see how important the need to survive really is, we'll follow the trials and tribulations of the fictitious Chem-A-Lot Corporation. The story of Chem-A-Lot is a composite based on real case histories drawn from many companies producing and selling a wide spectrum of products and services for many different industries. In this way, the foibles of individuals and the data used, though real enough, have been changed to protect the innocent and not so innocent.

We have chosen to portray a company involved in producing the machines and systems used by the process industries—those engaged in the production of, for example, plastic resins, canned foods, or cleaning compounds. Companies like Chem-A-Lot that supply process equipment normally face more violent fluctuations in sales than other businesses because they depend on the sporadic construction of new plants, the expansion of old plants, and the unpredictable replacement of aging or obsolete machinery and equipment. This erratic environment is ideal for demonstrating the merits of management planning and control techniques proposed here for your use in the increasingly turbulent world economy ahead.

Chem-A-Lot was founded in 1958 by two young veterans of World War II: one a chemical engineer, and the other a business major. After a somewhat frustrating record of some successes and some failures, these two men decided to cash in. They sold the company to a buddy, another veteran, Jim Dandy. The sale price was reasonable at 10 times their last year's after-tax net income. The sellers stayed on for one year to help Jim learn the business. Jim, a young, creative entrepreneur with solid mechanical abilities, employed a competent staff. Chem-A-Lot became a highly regarded source of innovative machines for the process industries.

The story opens with the problems Jim began experiencing after many years of success. By this time, Chem-A-Lot had machine sales in the $30 million range. In the United States a direct sales force covered the 25 most populous states. A network of sales representatives and stocking distributors covered the remainder of the states as well as world markets. About 10 percent of the products were sold abroad.

Fairly good profits began in Chem-A-Lot's fifth year. For the next 11 years, it was considered to be a growth company—doubling in size nearly every five years. However, two years later, in Chem-A-Lot's eighteenth year of operation, problems were evident.

There had been a recession, and Chem-A-Lot was not bouncing back as quickly as Jim felt it should. When the following conversation took place, Jim was 56 years old. Until two years ago he had been satisfied with what he had accomplished. Now he was deeply concerned.

DANDY FACES A DILEMMA AT CHEM-A-LOT

Jim: Tom, come into my office. I want to talk to you about our sales and
marketing picture for the coming year.

(Thomas Puller, vice-president of sales and marketing, notices a troubled look on Jim's face. Tom nods and steps into Jim's well-appointed office as his adrenaline begins to surge. Jim shuffles through the annual financial reports received for the past calendar year, looking for some summary figures he had jotted on a legal-size scratch pad earlier that morning.)

Ah, here are my comparison figures.

	(Dollars in Thousands)			
	Year 17		*Year 18*	
Sales	$28,000	100.0%	$28,000	100.0%
Cost of Goods Sold	17,900	63.9	18,300	65.1
Gross Profit	10,100	36.1	9,800	34.9
Operating Expenses:				
Operating and Selling	4,099	14.6	4,000	14.2
General and Administrative	4,100	14.6	4,000	14.2
Total Operating Expenses	8,199	29.3	8,000	28.5
Pre-Tax Income	$ 1,901	6.8%	$ 1,800	6.4%

Look at this, Tom. Sales are practically flat again this year at just over $28 million. Gross profit margins have dropped another percentage point. We are now at 35 percent gross profit on sales, which is down from 36 percent gross profit last year, from 38 percent in year 16, and from 42 percent in the year before that. And look here—operating expenses have not come down as much as planned during the last three years. This combination has really hurt our pre-tax as well as our after-tax profit. Your sales, Tom, are 10 percent under budget . . . and for the first two months of this year, sales don't look any better! Tom, I want you to raise the selling price of our products 10 percent across the board.

Tom: I can do it, Jim, but I think we might be in trouble with our customers. Look, as your sales and marketing vice-president, I can tell you our prices are already 6 or maybe 7 percent higher than our competitors'. And I'm afraid even our most loyal customers are beginning to believe our product quality is only on a par with our competitors', and our service not much better. Jim, I really would hesitate to implement a price increase at this time!

Jim: Well, Tom, I've made up my mind. I really do want you to raise prices now—we must get our margins up! *(Tom frowns and does not nod in agreement.)*

Tom, what do you think our problem is *in the marketplace?* Some of the other guys I know in this business at least *talk* about doing better than we seem to be doing.

Tom: Jim, I think we've got to do several things before we raise prices.

Jim: Such as?

Tom (ticks the items off on his fingers):

- Produce products with better quality than the competition's.
- Increase our inventory levels so I can respond faster to customer needs.
- Broaden our product line.

Jim, we should be a full-line producer now that we market all over the United States and worldwide. *(Tom's adrenaline really has him going now, so he rushes on earnestly before Jim can interrupt.)* And Jim, if you'd allow me to give further-out payment dates to our customers, I could get a lot more orders. Just let them pay over a longer period of time, and we'll be golden again! In addition, why not put $100 thousand into a good R&D program—then we'll continue to be known as the top innovators in the marketplace.

Jim: Tom, you know we can't do those things with sales and profits like they are!

(Once again the conversation ends like all others they've had recently about profitability: Jim wants higher margins via price increases, and Tom wants reduced prices, or at least more to work with in terms of inventory, quality, selling terms, and new products. Nevertheless, as a loyal subordinate, Tom will put a 15 percent across-the-board increase into effect next month, hoping at least an average 10 percent increase will hold. And, of course, his salespeople will scurry about telling customers to beat the price increase by placing large orders now.)

Jim (as Tom is leaving): Oh, by the way, I really think we ought to cancel those two new salespeople you were talking about until we get over this slump. And your budgeted advertising should be cut back to 10 percent below last year. Why not cut back all selling and marketing expenses 10 percent, too?

Tom: I'll see what I can do. *(To himself, as he exits hurriedly)* Gotta get out of here before he comes up with any more lousy ideas!

(Jim tilts back in his chair, clasps his hands behind his head, and slowly swivels toward the large thermoglazed window overlooking the shipping docks as he ponders what else might be done to get the bottom line up. After a while he swivels back to his desk, picks up the phone, and asks Charles Fisher, manufacturing vice-president, to come to his office.)

Jim (as Fisher enters): Hi, Charlie. I need you to get cracking right away on a cost reduction program. Our gross profit margin has been dropping, so we must get manufacturing costs under control. Let's start with the big hitter—raw materials. As you can see here *(jabbing at the figure on his scratch pad)*, Charlie, raw materials account for 55 percent of total costs to produce our products. I think it's time to use some of this modern value engineering I keep hearing about. I've been thinking it over, and I'd like you to go see that vendor we had lunch with last month. Sounds like we ought to turn over all raw material purchases for our main product line to him and save that 5 percent he promised. That will go a long way toward solving my particular problems right now.

Charlie: Okay, but I don't know how stable that vendor is. His product quality and delivery might cause problems.

(Charlie, an old hand, knows better than to protest more. All but recent hirees know that Jim calls the shots at Chem-A-Lot.)

Jim (not really hearing Charlie's protest): And, Charlie, I also want you to cut plant overhead across the board by 10 percent, starting next month. I know it's gonna be tough, but you'll get it done somehow. By combining the reduction in material costs with a big cut in your overhead, we'll readily pick up our margins and help cash flow a lot.

Charlie: Jim, I really don't think it can be done. But I'll try to get you your 10 percent, even though I don't like across-the-board cuts.

Jim: Good boy!

Charlie (hesitantly, but with determination): Jim, maybe this is not the time, but I really feel we ought to put in those new pieces of machinery I wanted last October. If I could get productivity up, we wouldn't have to worry so much about those other plant costs that concern you.

Jim (cuts Charlie short): That equipment was overpriced. You have plenty of the old stuff. It's always been dependable. *(To himself)* There's no darn merit in spending the $725 grand for those new machines Charlie wants when profits have been off for three years. *(Aloud)* Charlie, why don't we come back to the new machinery issue at the tail end of the year when we see how things are shaping up?

Charlie: Well, okay.

Jim: In the meantime, get those direct employees working harder. Charlie, your direct labor has been creeping up at about 5 percent a year. That's not bad, but it's all coming out at the bottom line on this statement. You've just got to find a way of reducing direct labor costs without spending extra money on machinery and equipment. You can do it, Charlie. I've got faith in you.

Hmmm, let's rethink what we talked about last week insofar as the new engineer is concerned. I really believe that if you spread around these guys you already have, you'll be able to handle everything pretty well.

Charlie (to himself): That means I won't be able to replace Jake, the best darn engineer we ever had! Guess there's no point arguing. Jim rarely asks my advice, and when he does, he doesn't accept it anyway.

Maybe I made a mistake coming here seven years ago. Jane never did want to move to this part of the country.

Jim: Charlie, please close the door when you leave. I want to be alone.

Charlie (to himself): You may well be!

(Dandy feels that his orders to Puller and Fisher will pretty much stop the bleeding, but there is one area left—general and administrative expenses— that is, in large part, the controller's responsibility.)

Jim (as the new, highly skilled controller, Diane Sensible, enters his office): Hi, Diane. I would like you to can that computer project we discussed and forget about hiring the chief accountant.

Diane (to herself): Well I'll be. . . . He isn't even going to ask me for my input!

Jim (smiling benignly): Of course, as soon as we are past this troublesome drop in earnings, we'll be able to go first class again in your area. I knew you'd understand, Diane. Keep up the fine work and make sure you hold your departmental expenses to 5 percent under budget. I figure your total expenses will then stay just under 8 percent of revenues. That will be tough, Di. . . .

Diane (cuts in): You know, I really did want additional computer capacity and that new software to generate more sales statistics for Tom, cost analysis reports for Charlie's group in manufacturing, and accounts payable information. But I guess we can handle things the way we've been doing them the past six months.

Jim: That's it. Good luck!

Diane (on being dismissed abruptly, bites her tongue, smiles, and walks out saying to herself): Dammit, I need this job until the kids are through college. Why, why did I leave public accounting for this so-called opportunity for advancement? It's a dead end. With a lot more information, our staff could prevent fires, but all Jim wants to do is spend time and resources putting out fires that are already burning.

Jim (to himself): Now that I've got the ball rolling, I'd better schedule more frequent staff meetings to see that everyone is responding properly and to iron out any snafus. Gotta keep the pressure up to get through this slump.

(Jim starts to pick up the newspaper on his desk but puts it down. He is late for a golf game. He leaves the office early that day. After all, now everyone has been told what to do and how to do it.)

A YEAR LATER; THE RESULTS ARE IN

(It's now just one year after Jim Dandy issued the orders to his staff that he thought would turn Chem-A-Lot around. Jim's desk is cluttered with worksheets, computer runs, charts, and financial statements as well as a yellow scratch pad on which he jots figures furiously. After a moment, he stops and stares at the chart on top of his pile of papers.)

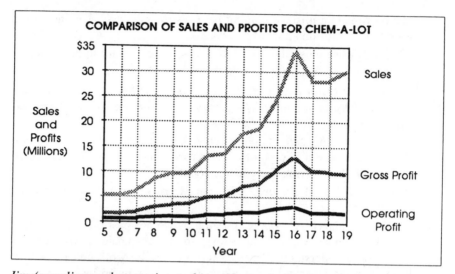

COMPARISON OF SALES AND PROFITS FOR CHEM-A-LOT

Jim (scowling and muttering to himself): Looks like I got sales up okay with that big jump in prices last year, but those increased costs of production sure ate up most of the potential profit! Things just don't seem to work out for me like they used to. (*He sighs, moves the chart aside, and studies the detailed year-end profit and loss statement as well as the balance sheet while continuing to mutter.*) Those selling and general and administrative expenses sure didn't drop like they were supposed to!

(*Jim picks up the scratch pad, tears out his summary sheets of profit and loss figures for the last two years, and places them side by side. He has rounded the figures in order to read them easily. Once more he compares them, almost in disbelief.*)

Jim (to himself again): Sales up 6.8 percent. Bottom line: a 5.5 percent drop in after-tax net income. All because of that 11.5 percent increase

| | (Dollars in Thousands) | | |
	Year 18	Year 19	Change
Sales	$28,100	$30,000	+ 6.8%
Cost of Goods Sold	18,300	20,400	+11.5
Gross Profit	9,800	9,600	− 2.0
Operating Expenses:			
Selling	4,000	3,950	
General and Administrative	4,000	3,950	
Total Operating Expenses	8,000	7,900	− 1.3
Pre-Tax Income	1,800	1,700	− 5.6
Income Taxes	808	763	
Net Income	$ 992	$ 937	− 5.5%

in the cost of production. *(After having pored over all the figures again and again, Jim still isn't absolutely sure what happened during the last year. He feels frustrated and thinks to himself):* I'm just plain tired of carrying the load, and this just about convinces me to accept that offer from Jones even though it isn't as much as it ought to be.

(Jim shuffles through his papers once more, brings the scratch pad summaries of the year-end balance sheets to the top of the pile, and places them side by side.)

| | End of Year (Dollars in Thousands) | |
	Year 18	Year 19
Current Assets		
Cash	$ 0	$ 0
Accounts Receivable	4,200	4,900
Inventory	6,100	7,300
Total Current Assets	10,300	12,200
Fixed Assets		
Property, Plant, and Equipment		
Land	300	300
Buildings	8,000	8,000
Furniture and Fixtures	1,000	1,000
Machinery and Equipment	10,700	10,700
Gross Property, Plant, and Equipment	20,000	20,000
Less Accumulated Depreciation	(13,400)	(14,200)
Net Property, Plant, and Equipment	6,600	5,800
Other Assets	500	500
Total Assets	**$17,400**	**$18,500**
Current Liabilities		
Accounts Payable	$ 2,500	$ 3,100
Short-Term Debt	700	700
Income Tax Payable	708	700
Total Current Liabilities	3,908	4,500
Long-Term Debt	5,700	5,000
Total Liabilities	**9,608**	**9,500**
Shareholders' Equity		
Common Stock	500	500
Contributed Capital	100	371
Retained Earnings (beginning of year)	6,200	7,192
Net Income (for year)	992	937
Less Dividends, Distributions	0	0
TOTAL SHAREHOLDERS' EQUITY	**7,792**	**9,000**
TOTAL LIABILITIES AND SHAREHOLDERS' EQUITY	**$17,400**	**$18,500**

Jim (to himself): Well, anyway, the balance sheet shows an increase in share-holders' equity of about a million bucks.

(After a moment, Jim slowly presses the buttons on his phone to reach Reginald Jones, the CEO at Industrial Conglomerate. Thirty minutes later, after concluding his conversation with Jones, Jim calls his staff into his office.)

Tom, Diane, Charlie, please sit down. I'd like to have a short staff meeting to talk about the results of this year's operation. I guess you all know by now that profitability is still the same old problem that it has been for the past few years. Profits don't seem to get better whether sales go up or down.

I think you know that I feel that you have all done a fine job following my lead over the years. But I'm getting too old to fight the big battle day-to-day anymore. I've just decided to accept Industrial Conglomerate's offer to buy Chem-A-Lot lock, stock, and barrel. The price isn't quite what I expected; however, our profits haven't risen to the levels I told them we would reach.

Don't worry, each of you will have employment contracts and a good benefits package for the next three years.

Tom: Jim, we're really sorry to hear that you're selling, and I'm sure I can speak for everybody on that point. Who is going to take over? Industrial Conglomerate doesn't seem to have anybody available within the company.

Jim: Well, I don't know. I'm sure they will pick someone who will appreciate all of your talents. I don't believe in hanging around because the new president has to take over in his own style and have the freedom to go down whatever track seems reasonable. We'll talk more about it later. I expect the deal to be made within the next 45 days. For now, let's all get back to the grindstone and get these numbers turned around.

(The management team is still in shock as they leave Jim. They are disappointed, frustrated, and more than a little intimidated by the unknown.

A deal was struck, and Jack Tuffitout was hired by Industrial Conglomerate to be the chief executive officer and chief operating officer. A new board of directors, which met quarterly at the parent company, was elected for Chem-A-Lot.)

THE SATISFIED MAN

The year before the sale, Jim had had reason to be concerned. Chem-A-Lot had not bounced back from the recent recession, despite the fact that, according to information Jim had, the actual markets served had recovered and were growing at a rate of 10 to 12 percent per year.

Sales for the Chem-Kraker, a machine based on a new technology, were growing at a steady clip, but the other machines in this group of products for conditioning raw materials were not doing so well. As a matter of fact, all product lines were subject to violent fluctuations, made even worse than usual because Chem-A-Lot had lost several large expected orders during the previous two years. And, of course, Jim also worried about reflecting in prices the future costs of inflation on materials inventoried as well as on plant equipment that needed to be replaced.

The company had always been regarded as the industry leader for the types of specialized processing machines it sold. Although Jim did not know exactly, he believed that Chem-A-Lot had over a 50 percent share of the markets served for his major product lines. He was satisfied that the company's machines and services were exactly right for the market but felt sure they were underpriced. And because Jim had felt that way for some time, he ordered very large price increases.

Chem-A-Lot's two major competitors sold products that had always been considered to be of lesser quality. These competitors' machines, through the years, had been priced just below Chem-A-Lot's comparable machines. When Chem-A-Lot raised prices, competitors normally followed suit shortly with a proportionate increase. On the last couple of rounds of price increases, however, Tom, the vice-president of sales and marketing, had been worried because these competitors had been slow to follow. Tom guessed then that the two competitors together might be growing at something like 12 percent per year—probably above the rate at which the served markets were growing. And when Jim raised prices, Tom knew that could mean more trouble ahead.

Jim's last big personally directed push had been into the overseas market. The travel abroad had been exhilarating for him—almost a climax to his career. He had sucessfully introduced his products in several countries. The results had been gratifying. Jim had noticed, however, during the following years that while total sales revenues from abroad were holding up, the actual unit volume was down slightly. He felt that the unit decline was a temporary aberration and that dollar revenues would also have been down if he had not insisted on raising prices modestly.

One European competitor had entered the U.S. market a few years after Jim's entry into the European market. Knowledgeable people in the industry were saying that this company had already captured a 5 percent share of the market. Jim wasn't so sure, but he had obtained a report that disturbed him: It said the competitor was growing at a 12 percent per year rate in Europe.

Jim's earlier effort in the overseas market had made him vaguely aware of the opportunities and dangers in the developing world economy. But this was just another area that Jim didn't have the energy to pursue.

As CEO, Jim, until the last five or six years, had known more about this particular industry and its product niches than any of his peers. But then markets began to shift, and Jim had not kept up. Tom and many others who had been with Jim almost from the start remained loyal. His people had always unquestioningly followed his leadership, and the company had prospered.

Founding entrepreneurs or sole proprietors like Jim often either have, or believe they have, no second level of qualified and involved managers. They become positive that they alone can make correct decisions. Finally, as in the case of Jim Dandy, lassitude combined with certitude becomes a weakness in a rapidly changing market.

Although sales had been a disappointment in year 18 before Jim had increased prices, the situation was not all that bad. Pre-tax income was only down from $1.9 million to $1.8 million. Question: Was Jim being unreasonable, and not focusing on the pertinent issues, when he insisted on large price increases in the face of Tom's objections? Did Jim's response mask his uncertainty when, for the first time, he was entering the churning clouds of a world market squall line without the benefit of a hung pocket watch to tell him which way was up?

Although your answer may be yes to each of these questions, in defense of Jim it can be said that it's sometimes immeasurably easier to fly by the seat of your pants as pilot of a $10 million business than as one of a $30 million business, even if you know the industry well. At some indefinable level of growth, more and better management is needed to handle a business. The facts concerning each business vary from industry to industry, but the scenario remains the same: Over time, new approaches are needed to satisfy customers, but one principle never changes. The customers' perceptions of your business are almost the only perceptions that matter. If you don't respond to *their* needs, *their* concerns, and *their* capabilities, someone else will.

For years Jim Dandy had known that the customer was all important. Coincidentally, on the very day of Jim's conversations with his staff about raising prices, he had left a newspaper on his desk when he took off for an afternoon of golf. It lay open to the "Letters to the Editor" page. Ironically, the headline read: "There Is No Hope for the Satisfied Man."

SUMMARY

Chem-A-Lot is at a crisis stage. Businesses all over the world face more than one such crisis during their lives. Yet many do not recognize the fact in sufficient time to avoid prolonged and measurable damage.

Periodically a checkup is in order. Preventive medicine (maintenance) should be prescribed. What is the diagnosis for Chem-A-Lot? We have not yet been given ample information; however, some obvious conclusions are as follows:

- The owner is a benevolent dictator, not a communicator. Virtually all operating decisions are made and controlled by one person.
- Management morale is declining.

- A strategy plan with alternatives is not evident or not being pursued.
- Price increases and cost cutting seem haphazard. Only in isolated cases should each product-line unit selling price or each departmental cost be increased or decreased by an identical percentage or amount.
- Each manager's program for increasing productivity, innovation, product quality, and customer service is being stifled.
- Basic financial information presented within the chapter is limited and limiting. Hopefully, Chem-A-Lot has more useful data upon which to base important operating decisions.

Sole proprietors and hard-charging, creative entrepreneurs more often than not dominate the people reporting to them. They frequently employ second-level managers who are followers, not leaders. Some dominated managers, however, possess above-average skills but remain followers due to personal circumstances that do not permit them to move on. In fast-changing markets, the total capabilities of a "one-person" show are less than those of a well-coordinated team.

CHAPTER 2

THE NEW BROOM

It is not the crook in modern business that we fear, but the honest man who doesn't know what he is doing.

Owen D. Young

ON THE FAST TRACK

Young Jack Tuffitout took over with a vengeance. Jack had visions of being able to move on from Chem-A-Lot in three or four years, after having established a good track record, received substantial cash bonuses, and earned a glowing reputation as a supermanager. Unfortunately, he was really not sold on the industry—or on Chem-A-Lot itself, for that matter.

After a general introductory meeting, the next session he held was a staff meeting with his new subordinates. They listened politely to every word, trying to analyze their new boss.

Jack (brusquely): It's nine o'clock, so let's get started. Chem-A-Lot is sick. I intend to cure it in a hurry. That's my job! Old ways are out. Chem-A-Lot is going to be overhauled and updated.

Word on the street is that Chem-A-Lot and you have been sitting on your duffs. Those days are over. We need action! *(His fist pounds the table.)* You must become more flexible in your approach to this business. I want bright people who can move with the times. Laggards and deadwood in the plant and office will be fired! Now, let's go over the situation. Tom, tell me about the sales picture.

Tom: Well the competition is tough, but we are doing better than the industry and grew almost 7 percent last year. We still haven't gotten back to the $33 million level of four years ago, but that year was abnormal due to several large contracts. I'm optimistic that last year's price increase will stick this year if we can keep our service levels up and meet delivery dates.

Jack: Tom, I want to move past last year's prices. We should be going into a boom year, so put in a 12 percent increase across the board with 15 percent on parts.

Tom: Could we wait until. . . .

Jack (cutting Tom short): Tom, let's get going on it next week. I can't see any real reason for customer complaints. We'll give them service and ship faster than ever. I'll personally meet the larger ones and do the wining and dining necessary to keep them coming back.

Now, for all personnel, I want a wage freeze, and no more hires this year. I'll approve all other spending decisions, starting today.

Diane: Our budget has some computer and. . . .

Jack (cuts in sharply): Forget the budget! I told the board of directors I cannot be held to someone else's budget. So that's out. My style of spending control is in. I'll sign every check personally. As for the increase in the computer capacity and that new software you were talking about—put it in next year's budget.

Charlie: Jack, the plant really needs those budgeted pieces of equipment and. . . .

Jack (cuts in again with an air of exasperation): We'll talk about that next quarter. Oh, Charlie, you should also cut out all but critical maintenance until I say otherwise.

Jack had taken control. He ended the meeting after less than one hour. From its tone, each manager thought Jack was going to be tough. And, as they left his office, each wondered how Jack's lack of industry knowledge as well as apparent absence of people skills would affect the people and the future of Chem-A-Lot. He seemed decisive, but could he make the right decisions?

Before the end of the second quarter of Jack's first year, it became obvious that staff relations were taking a distinct turn for the worse. Tom, Diane, and Charlie were not being asked for their input. Although that was not new to them, at least Jim Dandy had commanded their respect for his industry contacts and detailed knowledge of the business. Jack not only did not have good people skills, but he also frequently reversed his prior decisions without giving them time to be successful.

Crisis planning became the order of the day, and most of the crises were self-inflicted. Jack not only lacked a hung watch in the cockpit, but was prone to exert too much control: It often seemed as though he were trying to change direction in midflight without following any flight plan in particular.

Nevertheless, at the end of his first year, Jack made a presentation to his directors showing a much improved income statement.

Jack (with evident pride): Gentlemen, to sum up, we have concluded a very successful year at Chem-A-Lot under my leadership! *(With a flourish, he presents a chart of financial figures.)* My final chart highlights the extent of the improvement. Pre-tax income is up from $1.7 to $2.5 million. So, pre-tax income is up 47 percent for the year, and shareholders' equity is up over 19 percent.

	(Dollars in Thousands)		
	Year 19	*Year 20*	*Change*
Sales	$30,000	$33,700	+12.3%
Gross Profit	9,600	11,100	+15.6
G.P. %	32.0%	32.9%	
Operating Expenses	7,900	8,600	+ 8.9
Pre-Tax Income	$ 1,700	$ 2,500	+47.1%
Current Assets	$12,200	$14,500	+18.9%
Current Liabilities	(4,500)	(5,097)	+13.3
Net Working Capital	7,700	9,403	+22.1
Net Property, Plant, and Equipment	5,800	5,128	−11.6
Other Assets	500	500	0.0
Long-Term Debt	(5,000)	(4,300)	−14.0
Shareholders' Equity	$ 9,000	$10,731	+19.2%

(The directors congratulate Jack on a job well done, ask a few perfunctory questions, and adjourn to the country club for refreshments and lunch. All seems well at Chem-A-Lot. Jack does not feel obliged to thank his staff.)

JACK'S SWEET VINDICATION

In the second quarter of Jack's second year, the following staff conversation took place.

Jack: Tom, that across-the-board price increase we made in the first quarter should be scrapped. Instead, cut the prices on the Chem-Veyor and Chem-Lift. Go back to last year's prices on the Chem-Mixer, but raise the rest of the product lines by an average of at least 10 percent effective tomorrow. Tom, last year we increased advertising by $45,000, and I once agreed to another $60,000 increase for this year. However, I want advertising cut back to less than last year's total.

Tom: Jack, I can't cut it all now because contracts have already gone out, but I'll stop as many projects as possible.

Jack: Charlie, you're still budgeting $200,000 of capital expenditures. Forget them again this year. By the way, continue the wage freeze. If the year comes out okay, I'll give you a bonus.

Charlie: Jack, I'll do the best I can, but the equipment is getting old; it's not state-of-the-art, and deferring major maintenance is hurting us on downtime. The foremen are getting tough to handle. They want more money. After all, inflation is still going at 8 to 9 percent.

Jack: Once we get our total act together, everyone can have a raise. For now, it's out of the question. Diane, it's your turn to bring in the expense reductions.

Diane: Well, I was actually coming in to ask about the mid-size computer for manufacturing, sales, and accounting that you agreed to last month. I just placed the order.

Jack: Diane, there is no money for a computer. Cancel it. Try a service bureau for the rest of the year but don't spend more than $15,000.

Once again, the staff was confused, angry, and unhappy with Jack's unpredictable style of management.

Meanwhile, the board of directors was fairly pleased with what Jack was doing and was unaware of the growing discontent within Chem-A-Lot. But then the balance sheet became overweight: Accounts receivable days outstanding went to 60 and remained there, whereas they had been in the 45- to 50-day range in earlier years; similarly, the inventory turns in the company continued to slow down. They were now turning at the rate of 2.5, which compared very poorly with 3.5 from just a few years earlier. To counter the imbalance, Jack held accounts payable open for 55 days, much to the dismay of vendors. This net demand for substantial working capital increases caused financial pressure. Jack's responses were to stop all capital expenditures of any consequence, defer most maintenance projects, and hold wages down. For now, these kept depreciation expense and the demand for more capital down. However, Jack's approach did not help his staff attain any planned plant efficiencies. The result: an outward appearance of improvement as shown by gross profit.

Jack's second and third years showed sales increases: 3.9 percent in the second year and 3.4 percent in the third year. He also could point to slightly increased gross profit margins (34 percent). Nevertheless, those margins as a percentage were worse than any from the preceding 11 years, excluding the year before he joined the company, when they hit a low of 32 percent. The price increases at least were successful in keeping those margins up.

However, inflation was running at an average 8 percent for hourly earnings of production workers to 12 percent for prices of materials supplies and components during each of those years, according to government statistics. Therefore, unit sales were actually on the decline, though never reported. Neither the board nor Jack focused on that issue. Operating profits were in the $2.5 to $2.7 million range.

The board of directors seemed relatively comfortable with Jack during those first three years. They were placated, partly because he had inflation helping his revenues, partly because the selling price increases were holding with most long-time customers, and partly because Jack's erratic attempts at cost reduction succeeded in keeping overall spending in check. However, while Chem-A-Lot was not investing in the future, its competitors were.

At the end of Jack's third year, the directors, having heard rumors that all was not well at Chem-A-Lot, asked its independent auditors to present the financial statements for Chem-A-Lot and to discuss in detail the results of the prior three years. Here are the highlights of the financials in thousands of dollars:

	(Dollars in Thousands)		
	Year 20	Year 21	Year 22
Sales	$33,700	$35,000	$36,200
Gross Profit	11,100	11,900	12,300
G.P. %	32.9%	34.0%	34.0%
Operating Expenses	8,600	9,200	9,550
Pre-Tax Income	$ 2,500	$ 2,700	$ 2,750
Current Assets	$14,500	$15,000	$15,600
Current Liabilities	(5,097)	(5,277)	(5,398)
Net Working Capital	9,403	9,723	10,202
Net Property, Plant, and Equipment	5,128	4,410	3,692
Other Assets	500	500	500
Long-Term Debt	(4,300)	(3,600)	(2,900)
Shareholders' Equity	$10,731	$11,033	$11,494

The auditors reported that the internal controls were okay, that management had cooperated fully, and that there were no unrecorded items as of their audit date. The auditors signed a "clean opinion" in their report. They also complimented Diane by describing her efforts and accomplishments as "tops in controllership ranks."

Jack was so anxious to compare his record with the last years under Jim Dandy's leadership that he proudly displayed the following chart at the next meeting of his staff. He introduced it as his "Chem-A-Lot Turnaround Chart." Those who had worked loyally for Dandy were disgusted because it unfairly showed only the last years of Jim's stewardship without acknowledging all the high growth years prior to the downturn in year 17. The old-timers said nothing for fear of being accused of sour grapes.

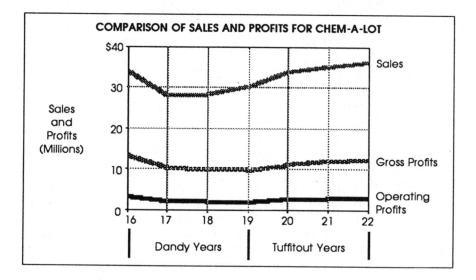

BUILDING ON SAND

Because Jack Tuffitout wanted to be able to move on from Chem-A-Lot after three or four years at most, with a good track record, he had concentrated on short-term plans. Each year, ambitious sales and profit targets were set. Unfortunately for Jack, a superlative track record was not quickly established: Gross profits hovered just over 30 percent of net sales, and operating income somehow never rose much over 6 to 7 percent of sales. So he stayed on for longer than planned—seven years in all at Chem-A-Lot.

Jack staved off outright losses in the fourth quarters of a couple of years when it became evident he wasn't going to reach set targets. To do so, *Jack first raised prices on Chem-A-Lot products*—sometimes across the board, sometimes more than once within three or four months, and occasionally more than 20 percent on some products. After a particularly large price increase, Jack would say, "I have to keep one jump ahead in the inflation game, you know." He had a deep-seated need to give the impression that he understood the detailed impact of inflation on Chem-A-Lot. In reality, he desperately wanted to make the high targets he had set and promised his directors. He knew of no other quick way to do it. For example, the year-end results for Jack's fourth year compared to budget targets looked like this, despite price increases:

	Year 22	Year 23 Target	Target Increase	Year 23 Actual	Actual Decrease
		(Dollars in Millions)			
Sales	$36.2	$41.6	+ 15%	$30.5	−16%
Cost of Goods Sold	23.9	22.0	− 8	20.1	−16
Gross Profit	12.3	19.6	+ 59	10.4	−15
Operating Expense	9.5	9.0	− 5	8.2	−14
Pre-Tax Income	$ 2.8	$10.6	+279%	$ 2.2	−21%

The price-increase strategy seemed to work well for Jack the first three years, but beginning with this fourth year, the strategy started to fail; sales actually went down 16 percent rather than up 15 percent as planned.

The second thing Jack did was to reduce costs. Because Jack lacked a thorough knowledge of the key support roles of high-salaried line and staff professionals, he chose to terminate them on short notice. The reason he usually gave was, "They're not carrying their fair share of the load." Jack thought that any salaried or hourly employee could be easily replaced by someone else at a lower cost. In fact, he found it easier to control people costs than machine costs. This approach seemed to work well in Jack's opinion because the people costs did indeed come down—he was, in this fourth year, able to reduce both the cost of goods sold as well as the operating expenses even more than expected because sales were well below target. Research and Development had been slashed, so that by now it was practically nonexistent. And Charlie, the highly qualified vice-president of production, had long since given up on machine replacements; now his goal was to hang on until early retirement or until the right company came along needing his product knowledge and industry expertise.

All through this period Jack was outwardly confident of his management capability. He felt he had all the pertinent information he needed: monthly financial statements and all kinds of statistical data that could be nicely charted for board presentations. However, he had a gnawing sense that most of his charts were for show-and-tell only. Deep down, he knew they didn't tell or show him much about the real world.

Unfortunately, Jack had a board of directors who did not give him the kind of advice and support a young manager needs; and, of course, Jack's subordinates for the most part were afraid to talk turkey with him for fear of being fired. The board simply looked at the accounting numbers at quarterly meetings. As long as those appeared okay, they asked a few perfunctory questions, and adjourned for lunch.

Tuffitout, unlike Dandy in his last few years as CEO, had a very high level of individual motive force. He had great visions for himself as a manager but lacked an evident purpose for his management career, other than the scramble for personal status.

THE DIRECTORS WAKE UP

During years 23, 24, and 25, the gross profit margin slipped steadily until it reached 32 percent. Sales dropped from the high of $36 million, when the auditors had given Chem-A-Lot a clean bill of health, and for three years stayed in the $28 to $32 million range. Spending cuts in selling and general and administrative expenses were no longer able to keep up with declining profitability, and operating profits slipped significantly.

In these years, the board meetings lasted longer, and the questioning became a bit more intense. Jack no longer looked forward to them. By his sixth year, the board was really searching for answers even though sales had improved. Jack was to become even more disturbed by the tone of the meeting held shortly after the end of his sixth year as CEO, although earlier in the year he had been encouraged because he had been able to project an upturn in sales and profits for the year.

Jack came to this meeting with a carefully planned presentation designed to defend his management record. He never got the chance to give it. The directors, for once, had their own agenda.

TUFFITOUT LOSES CONTROL

Reginald Jones: Jack, we have been experiencing an inflation rate in the economy of somewhere between 8 and 12 percent during each of the last five or six years, and yet our sales have just not kept up in dollars. Now, with this deepening recession, I think it might be time to start talking in detail about units shipped for each product line rather than just dollars.

Jason Peabody: And while we're at it, could you talk a little bit more about those competitors who seem to be out-gunning us at every turn?

Jack: Well, I can tell you things are tough out there. Personally, I think we have fared pretty well in a lousy economy, and I think we are probably making more money per sales dollar than anyone else on the street in our lines. I have tried price increases, special marketing programs, and even reduction in commission rates to the sales force, and I can tell you it has been frustrating.

Homer Williams: I for one would like to have you call in your department heads and let them answer a couple of questions about how things are going out there, Jack, if that's okay.

(Both Tuffitout and Williams glance at Jones, the chairman, who nods in agreement.)

Jack: Sure, I'll bring them in right now.

(Jack leaves the room for a moment and shortly reenters with Tom, Charlie, and Diane.)

Jones: Tom, you're our sales vice-president and I was wondering whether you might be able to shed some light on what's been happening in the marketplace. Recently sales just seem to be dropping even more than one would expect, especially after the upturn shown on the chart for most of last year. You know the chart I mean: the one you and Jack always use to show progress. Yes, that's it.

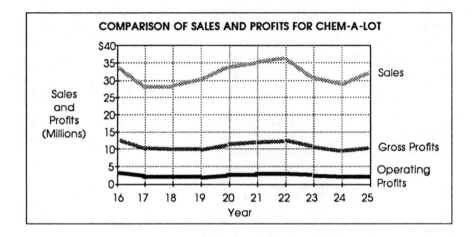

(Jack had not wanted to give the board members another look at the sharp downturn after year 22 that was evident on his progress chart, especially because sales had turned down sharply once more in the last two months. He did not want to reinforce that vivid negative image in their minds, and he definitely was not pleased that Tom had brought the chart to the meeting. Jack would have preferred to zero in on an upbeat comparison of sales and gross profit figures that emphasized the short-term increase of year 25 over year 24. It surely would have helped his digestion at the traditional board luncheon that noon if the meeting could have ended on such a note.)

Tom: Well, I can tell you that I think we're pretty much the high-priced suppliers in the marketplace. That posture doesn't help because our quality certainly isn't better than anyone else's. Second, we have had pretty erratic selling price increases that our customers are having a tough time swallowing. Third, we've missed a number of rather important delivery dates in the past few years, and that gets our customers up in arms, especially when we have little product differentiation.

Jones: Tom, do you know exactly how your unit shipments have been going over the years?

Tom: No, I've been trying to get that kind of data for years. We just don't seem to have it available in an organized, easily understood form. My guess, though, is that it's fairly flat.

Williams: Charlie, could you tell us a little about the missed delivery dates and some of the cost overruns?

Charlie: Well, I think we're hitting our dates pretty well, all things considered. After all, we have made some real cuts in personnel at the shop. Combine that with some very old equipment, and it's not easy to produce a quality product on time. I have not spent a nickel on a new machine in five years or so. I just know we could do a better job if we could modernize a bit.

Williams: Diane, perhaps you could tell us a little about some of the product costs, sales trends, and expense levels?

Diane: Well, you have all been receiving the financial reports I prepare, and you'll be happy to know that the auditors have accepted the numbers every year without any significant adjustments. Nevertheless, our receivables are getting older, and our inventory is turning a lot slower than I think it should. I have a lot of trouble holding off the vendors. They just don't like 55- to 60-day payments.

You also asked about sales statistics. I just do not have the staff available to prepare the unit figures Tom wants. In the production cost area, the volatility of sales does play havoc with overhead rates and burden absorption. Frankly, I am not sure what normal production rates we should count on to calculate manufacturing overhead costs.

Everybody seems to want more report analyses, but I can't get anybody to pay for them! The accounting department has been working overtime for the past three years, and we just seem to get further behind. I'm just as frustrated as everyone else in the search for the key to our problems.

Jones: Okay, Jack. I think you and your management team can be excused while we go into an executive session here. We'll see you at lunch.

(Jack, followed by his staff, gets up and leaves the room.)

Well, gentlemen, Jack certainly isn't turning out to be the brilliant long-term manager of people and business we thought he would be. Recently I updated an old chart that I got from Jim Dandy at the time of the acquisition. I made some copies for you. *(Passes copies to fellow board members.)* By comparing the actual sales to the sales trend line that I have added, you can see that Jack performed well as a turnaround manager . . . but now something seems to have gone awry.

Notice how Jack got Chem-A-Lot's sales back on track right after he took over. But now see how, beginning with year 23, sales dropped dramatically below the 20-year trend line. Notice also that gross profits and operating profits stopped keeping pace around year 16. I don't know why profits were not keeping up with sales. That has been bothering me for a year or so. Now, with sales off and little concrete explanation from management, we need to decide what to do.

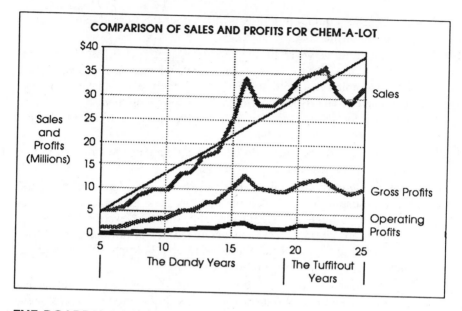

THE BOARD'S DECISION

With sales again going down during the first two quarters of year 26, the board members were deeply troubled. The responses of the Chem-A-Lot staff members to their questions had done little to reduce their worries. The sharp drop in sales for the first two quarters of year 26, compared to the same period last year, really bothered the board members. They made a fateful decision that day, one long overdue. They decided to select a management consulting firm and ask for a thorough review of the marketing, sales, and production areas as well as a review of the financial reporting procedures.

TUFFITOUT'S FAULTY TIMING

Jack had been somewhat aware of the rumbles at Chem-A-Lot resulting from his policies but had dismissed them just as he would distant thunder; that is, until now. Even so, he was surprised when Jones told him that a consulting firm was to be brought in. His first thought was: "For my career's sake, I should have left Chem-A-Lot earlier—just after my first three years." At that time, independent auditors had given his stewardship a clean bill of health, and Jack could have claimed to have turned Chem-A-Lot around.

Shortly after his conversation with Jones, Jack, too, made a fateful decision. Sensing that time had run out for him at Chem-A-Lot, he decided to accept an offer with another firm that he had not been too keen about earlier. This firm was substantially larger in sales, but Jack was less than enthusiastic about manufacturing and selling wire, cable, and related commodity type products that average 25 percent gross profit. Thus, he was able to leave with a fair record—not the brilliant record he had hoped for—but one that did, however, show an upturn in sales in year 25.

A farewell party was given for Jack at the club just a few weeks before the consultant's report was due in early November. Staff members were not unhappy to see him leave.

THE UNSATISFIED MAN

Jack Tuffitout, unlike Jim Dandy, never did feel the glow from years of real accomplishment. Also unlike Jim, he did not reach the stage of being satisfied with what he had accomplished while at Chem-A-Lot. Jack's problem, unlike Jim's lack of motivation, was a poor personal strategy for success, namely, to make a name for yourself quickly and then move onward and upward. Because Jack was unable to turn things around quickly, he felt ill-prepared to move on. And because he was unwilling, or unable, owing to a lack of interest in Chem-A-Lot's products, to change his strategy, he finally felt forced to take a position with another firm that he was even less enthusiastic about.

SUMMARY

So that's Chem-A-Lot's story so far. Will the board's hired consultants be able to save Chem-A-Lot?

Let's review the conditions Chem-A-Lot faced as a prelude to the "how to" chapters coming up. Management success will depend on a clear view of operating soundness, financial condition, and competitive position. Good managers maintain market leadership, whereas weak managers appear to be constantly behind in that race.

- The original founders of the company sold the business to an entrepreneur who employed good people at all levels in the early years. Then the entrepreneur (Dandy) aged, as did the products. He lost touch with the customers and almost stopped reinvesting in people, production facilities, equipment, product innovation, and application engineering.
- Sales and profits eventually deteriorated under the new CEO (Tuffitout), who did not recognize the existing situation. He unsuccessfully tried short-term tactics to stop the slide. He went for quick profits. A long-term, integrated operating plan either did not exist or was not used.
- The company was losing its excellent reputation for quality products, right prices, and excellent service.
- In recent years, the company lost market share to domestic as well as foreign competitors. Only the relatively new Chem-Kraker line was growing because it was technically superior to similar products.
- The team approach to management was missing. Morale deteriorated further under Tuffitout.
- The directors became concerned, more thorough in their questioning, and less pleased with operating results.

CHAPTER 3

WHAT MANAGEMENT IS ALL ABOUT

Every individual endeavors to employ his capital so that its produce may be of greatest value. He generally neither intends to promote the public interest, nor knows how much he is promoting it. He intends only his own security, only his own gain. And he is in this led by an invisible hand to promote an end which was no part of his intention. By pursuing his own interest he frequently promotes that of society more effectually than when he really intends to promote it.

Adam Smith (1776)

HOW SERIOUS IS THE SITUATION AT CHEM-A-LOT?

Before the consultants hired by the Chem-A-Lot board reveal their diagnosis in the next chapters, let's take a brief look at a few of the underlying conditions they'll be evaluating. Some managerial experts believe that knowledge of the following conditions is at least as important as straight accounting facts in determining the current health of a company:

- The level of motivation of individuals and groups within the company.
- The appropriateness of conflict-resolution techniques used.
- The competition faced.
- The degree of cooperation of individuals within the company.

After you've read the findings report contained in the next chapters, you'll want to decide for yourself how forthright and helpful the consultants have been. Remember, these consultants have been hired by the Chem-A-Lot board, a board that is not entirely blameless for any serious situation that might be uncovered. Good consultants know that most problems are people problems and that they will have to tread carefully if they are to be of real help.

The accuracy of their diagnosis will be critical to the selection of any remedial cures to follow so that realistic planning for the future can begin.

MOTIVATION: THE GLOW AND THE PROMISE

Is it enough for a manager to be satisfied with the same old-but-good products and services for customers? Is it enough for a manager to be satisfied with aging-though-not-worn-out production equipment and facilities for workers? Or enough to be satisfied with showing only patronizing concern for increasingly sophisticated staff subordinates?

It was certainly not enough for a manager of Dandy's caliber to be satisfied with expressing only patronizing concern for an employee like Diane. People like Diane do not stay as they are! They need to feel the glow of accomplishment and the promise of a better tomorrow. So what drives someone like Diane to action?

Social scientist Gunnar Myrdal's classic study on race, *An American Dilemma*,[1] says, in essence, that *the motivation of individuals separately and in groups, yes, and even in nations, is proportional to the extent of the difference between beliefs about their present life and valuations about what they want their future life to be.* Thus, the human mind is the generator of motive force, and the body, with all its technological extensions, is the motor driven.

Think for a moment what that means. Think about the mad scramble of today's youth as they incur heavy school debts or work beyond their capacities or fall by the wayside in discouragement or even succumb to drugs as they attempt to position themselves to reach the pot of gold at the end of their personal rainbows.

Conversely, think about the large number of Dandys here and abroad who have already arrived at their desired future through the free-enterprise system. That's fine for them! But for those in an organization who have not yet felt the glow of real success, the promises of the future can indeed be dimmed by CEOs who are satisfied with things as they are. Often, these CEOs give their subordinates the impression that they are men and women who sit in upholstered, tilt-back, swivel-around executive chairs issuing orders that impede progress. This image, of course, is only a partial truth, for there are thousands of individuals—like Walt Disney, for example—who do not set themselves apart from their co-workers and who pursue grand visions throughout their lives and even continue to inspire the living long after their deaths. People like Walt Disney, Thomas Edison, Martin Luther King, Robert Goddard, George Washington Carver, Carrie Chapman Catt, Edward Albert Filene, and Buckminster Fuller, just to name a few, never became satisfied with things as they were. Of course, there is a third type,

---

[1]Gunnar Myrdal, *An American Dilemma*, Twentieth Anniversary Edition (New York: Harper & Row Publishers Inc., 1962); Appendix 1: A Methodological Note on Valuations and Beliefs; Appendix 2: A Methodological Note on Facts and Valuations in Social Science.

those who want to turn back the clock to what they consider were much better times—and at least sometimes they're right!

In terms of attitudes toward planning for the future, Russell Ackoff, in his book *Redesigning the Future*,[2] has defined four types of managers:

- The **reactivist manager**, nostalgic about the past, not only resists change but wants to undo previous changes. This manager often promotes individuals on the basis of seniority, immobility, and age.

- The **inactivist manager**, perfectly happy with things as they are, is completely satisfied and does not want to rock the boat. This manager likes to use investigatory committees to delay action and substitutes words, position papers, and reports for action.

- The **preactivist manager**, unwilling to settle for mere survival or growth, wants to be a front runner. This manager likes to predict and prepare for an optimal future within the system through research and development.

- The **interactivist manager** wants to create the future. The interactivist believes that short-run gains can lead to long-run losses, and vice versa, and that the ability to see and react to the long-run consequences of a decision is the essence of wisdom. This manager further believes that *participation in the planning process is even more beneficial than the plans developed*; that to be effective, no part of an organization can be planned for independently of its other parts; that all levels of a multi-level organization must be involved; and that because both the internal and external environment change continuously, planning must also be continuous.

What do you think were Dandy's and Tuffitout's basic attitudes about the future? Did their attitudes fit any of these manager definitions? Do you think their attitudes changed during their tenures as CEO, and, if so, what specific beliefs and valuations changed? Will it be difficult for the consultants to trace the effects of these changes on Chem-A-Lot?

Like these two Chem-A-Lot CEOs, we all have a constantly updated set of beliefs about the present and valuations about the future behind our particular current mix of attitudes. Adapting Myrdal's approach, the motive force we develop as a result may be depicted as follows:

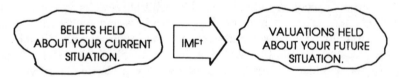

†Individual motive force available to an organization if it can be tapped.

[2]Russell L. Ackoff, *Redesigning the Future: A Systems Approach to Societal Problems* (New York: John Wiley & Sons, 1974), chapter 2, "The Self-Control Problem."

A consultant must try to understand the motive forces of the people within the client organization, regardless of his or her own attitudes. Being sensitive to a client's beliefs and valuations, even though they may conflict with the consultant's own attitudes, is a consultant's major challenge. Having understood motivations, top-flight consultants will see to it that the individuals being helped get the credit for finding solutions to problems so they look good to their peers and feel good themselves.

You might find it helpful to pause here and take the time to compare your attitudes with those of various individuals depicted in Chem-A-Lot. You might begin by comparing your answers to the following questions with those you think might be given by Jim, Jack, Diane, Charles, or one of the other individuals associated with Chem-A-Lot:

- Is your current life-style far from or almost what you want it to be?
- Which of the four defined managerial attitudes described comes closest to characterizing your attitudes?
- How much motive force do you think you have?
- Are you positive your visions for your future are based on a realistic assessment of your present situation?
- Do you waste energy on guilt trips about changes in your environment or yourself that you are not currently in a position to make?
- Do you feel your life is totally in the hands of others?
- Are you reluctant (afraid) to choose to move on to another company when you know the situation should be changed but you can't change it?

Realizing how difficult it may be for an idea to pass through your own or another's attitude screen, next try to imagine the variety of beliefs and valuations, based on both fact and fiction, that are buzzing around in the heads of all your associates. Is it any wonder that they have conflicting attitudes from which animosities and emotional hang-ups develop? All sorts of approaches have been suggested to mitigate the effect of personal problems on organizations—from the old encounter groups, which were devastating to some participants, to milder forms of therapy. But ask yourself: How often were those approaches successful in bringing about permanent improvement?

Some managerial experts say the major reason behind the lack of long-term success for those therapies was often overlooked. According to them, many conflicts arose from the fundamental nature of machine-oriented business hierarchies, in which employees were viewed as replaceable parts. Those conflicts were rarely directly addressed by therapists hired by traditional managements with a vested interest in the existing hierarchy. Meanwhile, according to these experts, a few farsighted competitors replaced their rigid hierarchies with information-rich, flexible, and more open systems. Eventually, strong competitive pressures will make it necessary for the laggards to catch up or go under.

Do you think these experts are right or wrong? How does your attitude screen affect your answer?

These same experts conclude that the larger the traditional organization, the longer the hierarchical ladder is that must be climbed to reach the promise of better positions. To climb the ladder successfully, employees must become more and more like an interchangeable part of the machine-like structure they serve. Again, unfortunately, many of those who manage to scramble to the top only have as their goal the scramble to the top and become satisfied with things as they are when their desire for status has been achieved. Some even become tired or satisfied halfway up. And some become thoroughly frustrated and leave because they have visions like those of a Walt Disney or a Buckminster Fuller that can't be satisfied by mere money or status.

Do you think the long climb to the top is or is not one of the major reasons why our traditional industries, such as the steel and automobile industries, are having difficulty competing in world markets today? What about the young highly trained professional with a master's degree or doctorate who starts near the top but lacks broad experience in the school of hard knocks? Can such narrowly focused professionals effectively compete with Japanese managers who are guaranteed lifetime employment and who, therefore, develop broad skills coupled with long-range outlooks?

A number of experts say, or come close to saying, that there is a law of motivation that operates in many organizations as follows: *The individual motive force available to be tapped is inversely proportional to the status held by the individual.* When this is true, those businesses will be or are in trouble.

If so, why? Could it be simply that a high percentage of the ideas that CEOs have about how things are in the world grow to nearly match their ideas about how things ought to be? Do they reach their personally envisioned happiness point? Do they then tend to become disenchanted and lose their drive? Do they then tend to forget about how those further down the ladder feel and begin to show only patronizing concern, as Dandy did for Diane? What do you think? If you think this law of motivation is reasonable, are you close to or far from your own happiness point? Would having reached your own happiness point affect how *you* answered these questions?

CONFLICT RESOLUTION: NEGOTIATING CONFLICTS IN THE STRUGGLE FOR THE FUTURE

Telephones, radios, television sets, computers, and data banks provide tremendously improved access to information. With each passing year, increasing numbers of people have clearer notions about their current situation and what they want their future to be like. In this process people are exposed to ideas from different cultures. Visions of the future range from that of the fanatic who wants to use modern communications to impose his or her vision upon the world to that of those who are willing to let a free world market for ideas develop. The latter group wants each individual to select from this vast smorgasbord those ideas that fit into her or his vision.

At any rate, all people around the world want to realize more of their potential; as Jimmy Durante used to say, "Everyone wants to get inta de act." With the increased demand for participation in the decision-making process on the part of more and more highly motivated people, improved negotiation methods between individuals and between organizations become an important consideration for the aspiring manager.

Both Dandy and Tuffitout issued top-down commands in a rigid hierarchy; neither really listened to the people under them. Whereas Dandy had some regard for the expertise of employees, Tuffitout had reached the point where he could coldly view people as replaceable machine parts to be used in the production process to further his own career. There was simply no room for the negotiation of conflicting ideas. He took his position with little or no consultation and sent orders down the line on how to reach that position. No wonder there were rumbles of discontent. Neither CEO fully tapped the potential of the people under his command.

Employees are becoming more informed, less dependent, and less afraid of bosses while at the same time developing highly individual sets of beliefs and valuations. Under these circumstances, don't you think negotiation must be developed to a higher art form if agreements on desirable future conditions are to be reached?

At first in the larger corporations, as the old command structure began to break down, positional bargaining by unions and management took its place. Each side would state its position and then haggle until they finally arrived at a compromise position. According to many observers, this inefficient process seldom yielded a wise agreement that met the legitimate interests of both parties. Positional bargaining often strained relationships further. Each side vehemently blamed the other whenever business began to deteriorate, and each side's preoccupation naturally became the protection of self.

Getting to Yes,[3] a book by Roger Fisher and William Ury based on the Harvard Negotiation Project, tells how to resolve conflicts between bosses and employees, between companies, and between other groups. Briefly, this book will tell you how to do the following:

- Separate the people from the problem so that people on both sides become problem solvers rather than adversaries.

- Focus on interests, not positions, so that areas of possible agreement can be explored thoroughly.

- Invent options for mutual gain so that there will be multiple options to choose from for a later agreement.

- Insist on using objective criteria so that each party to the negotiation yields to principle and not pressure.

---

[3]Roger Fisher and William Ury, *Getting to Yes: Negotiating Agreement Without Giving In* (Penguin Books Ltd., 1986, first published in the U.S. in 1981), chapter 1, "Don't Bargain Over Positions."

The Harvard Negotiation Project has found that the motivations of the parties involved in a conflict may often be found to mesh, at least in part, under appropriate negotiation procedures. In fact, the evolutionary progress that has created our amazingly strong economic system in the United States undoubtedly was helped along by the sporadic meshing of social, political, and economic motivations through negotiation. A manager, therefore, needs to know how to improve negotiating talents.

COMPETITION AND COOPERATION: TWO SIDES OF A COIN

Separate and meshed motive forces of individuals lead to both competition and cooperation. Conflict resolution through competent negotiation is often required to improve both. Competent conflict resolution was largely missing at Chem-A-Lot while Dandy and Tuffitout were in charge. Even so, their motivations, plus the motivations of all those associated with the company, had been partially channeled into the production of excellent products and services for society for many years through the operation of two dynamic, although often invisible, processes:

1. *Competition*: the supply of products and services for income by numerous businesses to intermediate or end consumers who spend their income on the products they want in a free market (derived from Adam Smith's invisible-hand concept of competition).

2. *Cooperation*: the supply of ideas and services for monetary and psychic income by each worker within a business to fellow workers and managers who select and use what they want through evolving interrelationship strategies in a free market of ideas. (Cooperation is really an extension of Adam Smith's invisible hand operating within a firm.)

So, if we allow these hidden hands to do their job unfettered, what can we expect to happen? Because viewpoints can be very complex and often internally contradictory, the viewpoint that follows may or may not satisfy you. In any event, it may provide some ideas for you to consider. Viewpoints are important. Multitudes of evolving viewpoints help create the economic storms as well as the fair weather in which your business operates.

ONE POSSIBLE VIEWPOINT

As people operate in ever larger, information-rich, flexible, and open systems for the production of goods and services, cooperation will become an increasingly important channel for an individual's motive force. Cooperation, as the internal business counterpart of external competition, is just as dynamic as competition and just as prone to conflict. If you doubt it, think of the squabbles that arise in social clubs and churches whose primary objectives are the common needs of the membership.

Needless to say, when businesses or workers operate under rigid central controls, neither competition nor cooperation is given a chance to provide the flexible and innovative responses needed today. In the modern world, competition and cooperation are two sides of a coin—neither works well without the other. Cooperation and competition are equally powerful processes that channel human energy for all types of organizations: from businesses seeking customers, to religious groups seeking converts, to athletic teams seeking victories.

To compete effectively, a business must have people who develop a long-term cooperative culture. A partial or complete business monopoly within an industry and its counterpart, an idea monopoly by an elite within a business, often cause imperfect competition between businesses and imperfect cooperation within businesses, respectively. Neither the hidden hand of competition nor the hidden hand of cooperation yet operates perfectly to dispense fair remuneration for products and services to businesses—and, in turn, to individuals within businesses—for their contributions. Laws and regulations, even though imperfectly legislated and imperfectly administered by governments, are, therefore, demanded by consumer and producer pressure groups alike to dispense justice.[4]

In this less than perfectly competitive and cooperative world, noninterference (*laissez faire*) governmental policies have not been given, and perhaps can not yet be given, a full opportunity to work. However, we now know, through experience, that regulatory bodies usually change to benefit those regulated. The simple reason is that the efforts of those regulated to support their interests are concentrated on one regulatory body. Meanwhile, the efforts of the consumers whose interests were to have been protected are widely disbursed over many areas of concern.

From an intelligently selfish point of view, the more independent people with independent judgments there are among the electorate, the less likely it is that the electorate will be stampeded into foolish action. Whereas the more concentrated the ownership of capital becomes, the more likely it is that capitalists will become an endangered species. The mounting motive force of the economically disenfranchised at the bottom will be directed toward violent change, while at the middle levels, envy and declining morals— partly caused by increasing disparity between those who have arrived at the pot of gold and those who have not—will cause white-collar crime to soar. Those who have concentrated control over property or political power will live in increased fear.

Communist theoreticians like Karl Marx predicted years ago that the coercive state exemplified by the Soviet Union would eventually wither away. It didn't. On the contrary, it collapsed because systems of unaddressed problems proliferated over the years. A managerial elite held a monopoly on both political and economic power. This structure did not have political or economic institutions through which people could enforce

---

[4]A fine discussion of what is meant by economic justice is contained in the *Capitalist Manifesto*, second edition (New York: Random House, 1958) by Louis O. Kelso and Mortimer J. Adler. This book explains why capitalism is the best economic system for a democratic society.

corrective measures. Real competition and real cooperation had essentially been eliminated.

The reaction to apartheid in South Africa, the increase in worldwide terrorist activities, the mounting rate of white-collar crime, and even the fact that the security (burglar alarm) industry has become a U.S. growth industry are all symptoms of rising pressure for change from those who feel left out. This pressure must be alleviated through efforts to improve cooperation and competition within and among all nations. Police actions, although at times necessary, do not get at the root cause of violence.

To sum up: One common-sense goal for an individual, a business, a nation, or the world would be to work for fair rules of the game that favor both competition and cooperation. Ever higher numbers of individuals must be allowed to achieve, through diligent personal efforts in a nurturing environment, what each envisions as the good life.

From this point of view at least part of the real problem shared by Dandy and Tuffitout was a failure of vision. Although Dandy moved Chem-A-Lot into world markets, both CEOs failed to visualize fully the challenges Chem-A-Lot faced because of the changing attitudes of people in the company and the world around them.

Whether you agree with this viewpoint is not the issue. It merely expresses the opinion of two individuals in a highly developed western country. What do you think the typical viewpoint might be in Japan? In Argentina? In Iran? In India? In . . . ?

The important thing is to develop with care your own integrated local and world viewpoint. Having done so, it is important to be willing to hunt for areas of agreement with others so that when conflicts arise, you can make progress toward your vision of the future on the basis of shared goals.

INTERRELATIONSHIP STRATEGY EXPERIMENT

In addition to understanding how competition develops between businesses, one must understand how cooperation between individuals can occur to produce the organizational motive force necessary for a business to survive and thrive. Frequently, the self-interest of a key individual leads to a low level of cooperation and a poorer future condition for all, as it did during Tuffitout's tenure as CEO.

Recently, the problem of just how cooperation arises has been addressed by social scientist Robert Axelrod,[5] winner of the Newcomb Cleveland Award of the American Association for the Advancement of Science. He demonstrates under exactly what conditions cooperation will emerge and continue to flourish. Furthermore, he illustrates how the anticipated future relations between the same individuals cast a shadow on the future.

---

[5] Adapted from *The Evolution of Cooperation*, by Robert Axelrod. Copyright © 1984 by Robert Axelrod. Reprinted by permission of Basic Books, Inc., Publishers.

Here, briefly, is what Axelrod did. He set up an experiment to determine the conditions under which a world full of egotists would cooperate. He based his experiment on the well-known game, The Prisoner's Dilemma, which simulates many real-world situations. Here are the payoffs for cooperation, or defection, offered to two prisoners (players), neither of whom knows what the other will do under pressure:

		PRISONER SMITH	
		Cooperate	Defect
PRISONER JONES	Cooperate	Rewards to each for mutual cooperation 3 for Jones 3 for Smith	Sucker's payoff: 0 for Jones Temptation to defect payoff: 5 for Smith
	Defect	Temptation to defect payoff: 5 for Jones Sucker's payoff: 0 for Smith	Punishment for mutual defection: 1 for Jones 1 for Smith

Adapted from Robert Axelrod, *The Evolution of Cooperation* (New York: Basic Books, Inc., 1984).

Having set up the game, Axelrod invited people from the United States and abroad to participate in a series of tournaments. Each participant was asked to submit a winning strategy after looking at the results of each round. All strategies were tested against each other by computer.

Strategies submitted used different patterns of cooperation and defection for each game, such as cooperating as long as the other prisoner did so, but never again cooperating if the other prisoner once defected. Essentially, this could be called a Holding-a-Grudge strategy.

On succeeding tournaments many strategies gradually, or not so gradually, lost out. The superior strategy turned out to be Tit-for-Tat. And what was that strategy? It was the simplest of all: You start by choosing to cooperate, and thereafter you do what the other player did on the previous move. If the other player defects, you defect; but if on the next move he cooperates, you cooperate. You do not hold a grudge, but you do not let the other player get away with anything either!

Axelrod was able to demonstrate what happened when a small group of individuals, using Tit-for-Tat strategy, was introduced into a large group of players who always tried to take advantage of others through a variety of clever strategies. The clever ones always lost out and were, after several tournament rounds, converted to the idea of mutual cooperation because it paid to do so. Undoubtedly, some of the human progress that has been made through the centuries has been due to the effectiveness of this type of response.

There was one exception, which we'll call Tuffitout's Make-a-Name-for-Yourself-and-Move-On strategy: The Tit-for-Tat strategy did not produce the highest score against an individual who was actually able, unlike Jack, to take advantage of others and then never have to interact with those individuals again. Of course, if all players operated that way, the group of such players operating in a (fortunately always ultimately limited) field of players would eventually reap a low score. How the Smiths and Joneses and Tuffitouts of the world react in short-term situations does indeed tell us something about the possible consequences of the short-term relationships of fast-track managers with co-workers in a business.

With a little imagination, it's very easy to see the dire consequences for an economy in which the bulk of the managers follow the Tuffitout Make-a-Name-for-Yourself-and-Move-On strategy. In a world made smaller by rapid satellite communication and jet travel—which puts American firms in direct competition with European and Asian firms—we are already paying a heavy price in lost markets for all of our Tuffitouts.

Dandy instinctively chose a better strategy, but ultimately lacked motivation; whereas Tuffitout had the motivation, but chose an inferior strategy for Chem-A-Lot and, in this case, for himself as well because of the shadow of the future. Both Jim and Jack were loners who were never able to trust their employees enough to allow cooperation to work for them fully.

Axelrod's work does indeed seem to offer evidence that the future casts its shadow upon present action. It seems apparent that at least as much research needs to be done on cooperation and conflict resolution as has been done on competition in the past. While recognizing that much more research needs to be done, do you think that the development of cooperation as illustrated by this game might be as essential as competition for economic progress?

THE REAL BASE FOR PLANNING

When Chem-A-Lot's people and equipment are all viewed as components of a machine-like structure, each part—such as a department—can be analyzed separately for structural problems. However, when Chem-A-Lot is viewed as a whole functioning organization, there are capabilities present that are lost when the parts are considered separately. Consider this analogy: The capabilities of a musician's hand cannot be fully understood when it is disconnected from the musician's brain. A specific problem that the musician encounters may be completely structural—his middle finger fails to move properly because a joint has become arthritic—or it may be due to a failure in some function related to the musician's brain—for some reason a mental block makes it impossible for him to use a perfectly normal middle finger.

Just as in the body, when problems occur in separate parts of an organization, the problems interact with one another. Therefore, the consultants will most likely uncover a set of interacting problems at Chem-A-Lot. Russell Ackoff has coined a new use for an old word to describe such a system of problems: a *mess*. Appropriate, don't you think? He further says: *"The attempt to deal holistically with a system of problems is what planning, in contrast to problem solving, should be all about."*[6] Good CEOs should

---

[6]Russell L. Ackoff, *Redesigning the Future: A Systems Approach to Societal Problems* (New York: John Wiley & Sons, 1974), chapter 2, "The Self-Control Problem."

strive to understand the whole organization in order to prevent major messes from arising in the first place.

While you're still wearing your critical hat, let's see what the consultants have to report to the Chem-A-Lot board of directors in the next chapter.

SUMMARY

Management involves coordinating people with differing sets of ideas about the future so that they can cooperate to compete effectively in the markets served. Accounting tables and graphs can provide clues to the correct diagnosis of an unhealthy condition. To interpret the clues, however, managers must understand motivation, conflict, competition, and cooperation.

- The motivation of individuals, groups, and nations is proportional to the extent of the difference between beliefs about their present lives and valuations about what they want their future lives to be like. The human mind is the generator of motive force, and the body, with all its technological extensions, is the motor driven.

- Conflict resolution requires the following: (1) the separation of the people from the problem so that people on both sides become problem solvers rather than adversaries; (2) a focus on interests, not positions, so that areas of possible agreement can be explored thoroughly; (3) the invention of options for mutual gain so that there will be several choices to select from for a later agreement; and (4) an insistence on using objective criteria so that each party to the negotiation yields to principle and not pressure.

- Competition is the supply of products and services for income by numerous businesses to intermediate or end consumers who spend their income on the products they want in a free market.

- Cooperation is the supply of ideas and services for monetary and psychic income by each worker within a business to fellow workers and managers who select and use what they want through evolving interrelationship strategies in a free market of ideas.

Many managers lack a thorough understanding of motivation, conflict resolution, competition, and cooperation. As a result, they are or become nonbelievers in the need for planning; they just can't see its value. A believer, on the other hand, looks at planning as an opportunity to search for significant trends, to solve existing problems, to discover previously unknown possibilities, to spark new ideas, and to develop a guide toward goals.

Planning, in contrast to simple problem solving, should be about dealing holistically with systems of interrelated, people-created problems—messes. Wherever people cooperate to compete, there are ever-changing patterns of people-created messes that usually can be untangled through careful planning.

CHAPTER 4

RATES-OF-CHANGE: THE LONG AND SHORT OF IT

*We judge ourselves by what we feel capable of doing
while others judge us by what we have already done.*
Henry W. Longfellow

THE CONSULTANTS START WORK

After interviewing several consulting firms, the directors of Chem-A-Lot hired one that seemed to have excellent operating and financial analysis expertise. The consultants spent two months reviewing prior- and current-year transactions and records. They also conducted in-depth interviews with Chem-A-Lot officers and key employees. Verbal reports on their findings were provided every two weeks; their overall conclusions were summarized in a written report at the end of their second month of work. Highlights of this report are contained in the next three chapters. In this chapter we will concentrate on rate-of-change charting techniques employed by the consultants, an infrequently used but very powerful tool. We will start by examining traditional accounting financial statements.

PRESENT MORE THAN ONE OR TWO YEARS OF OLD FIGURES

Frequently, financial statements are issued showing only two one-year periods—the current and the previous year. This practice can severely limit the reader's ability to spot important trends, turning points, and other relationship signals. Let's look at two sets of recent Chem-A-Lot income statements as illustrations. First, we will look at a two-year statement as typically presented:

COMPARISON OF INCOME STATEMENTS

(Dollars in Thousands)

	Year 24	Year 25
Sales	$28,600	$32,000
Cost of Sales	19,400	21,800
Gross Profit	9,200	10,200
Operating Expense:		
Operating and Selling	3,650	4,100
General and Administrative	3,650	4,100
Total Operating Expenses	7,300	8,200
Pre-Tax Income	1,900	2,000
Income Taxes	853	898
Net Income	$ 1,047	$ 1,102

In this type of statement, certain operating expenses may be presented in detail within the body of the income statement or in a supplementary schedule. However, rarely will you see the following statement:

COMPARISON OF INCOME STATEMENTS

(Dollars in Thousands)

	Year 21	Year 22	Year 23	Year 24	Year 25
Sales	$35,000	$36,200	$30,500	$28,600	$32,000
Cost of Sales	23,100	23,900	20,100	19,400	21,800
Gross Profit	11,900	12,300	10,400	9,200	10,200
Operating Expense:					
Operating and Selling	4,600	4,775	4,071	3,650	4,100
General and Administrative	4,600	4,775	4,129	3,650	4,100
Total Operating Expenses	9,200	9,550	8,200	7,300	8,200
Pre-Tax Income	2,700	2,750	2,200	1,900	2,000
Income Taxes	1,212	1,234	988	853	898
Net Income	$ 1,488	$ 1,516	$ 1,212	$ 1,047	$ 1,102

What different impressions, comments, or questions come to your mind as you analyze the five-year comparative income statement versus the two-year format preceding it?

Here are a few observations. In the two-year format, sales show an apparently healthy increase of $3.4 million in year 25 over year 24, an 11.9 percent gain. Year 24 was, however, the worst sales year in dollars out of the last five years. Year 25 is still $3 million lower than year 21 and $4.2

million under year 22. Surely that record is unimpressive and would lead to a series of questions about the growth of Chem-A-Lot's markets, pricing policies, and share-of-market position.

Obviously, more creative methods than the two-year comparison are needed to present otherwise mundane data so that users can more readily analyze, interpret, and manage the enterprise.

Now compare the sales and gross profit lines on the two-year statement. Sales show a $3.4 million increase, and gross profit shows a $1 million increase. The $1 million increase represents 29.4% of the $3.4 million change in sales. Given no other data, we might presume the added sales in year 25 carried a gross profit margin of 29.4 percent. Yet looking at changes in sales and gross profits between years 23 and 24 would lead one to think that the $1.9 million drop in sales was composed of products with a gross profit of $1.2 million ($10.4 million less $9.2 million) or 63.2 percent. That surely seems improbable and is! This logic could follow for each preceding year. Again, the point is to look at sufficient information over time to allow prompt and proper diagnosis so that timely and appropriate remedies can be applied.

Total operating expenses, mainly of the selling, general, and administrative classifications, show a $900,000 increase in year 25 over 24. Not bad on $3.4 million more revenues. Comparisons on the five-year income statement for these operating expenses afford a better understanding of their variability over time. On the surface, operating expenses appear to be at low levels relative to sales in year 25. For example, if total operating expenses in year 25 were more than $9.5 million as in year 22, we might also expect sales to approximate the $36.2 million for that year rather than actual sales of $32 million.

DOLLARS VERSUS PERCENTAGES

Let's concentrate on another aspect: the relationship of dollars to percentages. The Chem-A-Lot income statements for years 21 through 25 follow, unchanged from the previous statements, but this time with percentages:

COMPARISON OF INCOME STATEMENTS

(Dollars in Thousands)

	Year 21	Year 22	Year 23	Year 24	Year 25
Sales	$35,000	$36,200	$30,500	$28,600	$32,000
Cost of Sales	23,100	23,900	20,100	19,400	21,800
Gross Profit (G.P.)	11,900	12,300	10,400	9,200	10,200
% G.P. of Sales	34.0	34.0	34.1	32.2	31.9
% G.P. of Year 21 G.P.	100.0	103.4	87.4	77.3	85.7
Operating Expense:					
Operating and Selling	4,600	4,775	4,071	3,650	4,100
General and Administrative	4,600	4,775	4,129	3,650	4,100
Total Operating Expenses (O.E.)	9,200	9,550	8,200	7,300	8,200
% O.E. of Sales	26.3	26.4	26.9	25.5	25.6
% O.E. of Year 21 O.E.	100.0	103.8	89.1	79.3	89.1
Pre-Tax Income (P.T.I)	2,700	2,750	2,200	1,900	2,000
% P.T.I. of Sales	7.7	7.6	7.2	6.6	6.3
% P.T.I. of Year 21 P.T.I.	100.0	101.9	81.5	70.4	74.1
Income Taxes	1,212	1,234	988	853	898
Net Income (N.I.)	$ 1,488	$ 1,516	$ 1,212	$ 1,047	$ 1,102
% N.I. of Sales	4.3	4.2	4.0	3.7	3.4
% N.I. of Year 21 N.I.	100.0	101.9	81.5	70.4	74.1

In this table, gross profits dropped from $11.9 million and 34 percent of sales in year 21 to $10.2 million, slightly less than 32 percent, in year 25. While this approximate 2 percent decline was not large, it may be indicative of an internal problem related to the management of people and assets. The drop is not so obvious if percentages are omitted. Next look at the plus and minus deviations in number and percentages from year 21 that follow:

PERCENTAGE CHANGES FROM YEAR 21

(Dollars in Thousands)

	Year 21	Year 22	Year 23	Year 24	Year 25
Sales	$35,000	+$1,200	−$4,500	−$6,400	−$3,000
% Change from Year 21	**100.0**	**+ 3.4**	**− 12.9**	**− 18.3**	**− 8.6**
Gross Profit	11,900	+ 400	− 1,500	− 2,700	− 1,700
% Change from Year 21	**100.0**	**+ 3.4**	**− 12.6**	**− 22.7**	**− 14.3**
Operating Expense	9,200	+ 350	− 1,000	− 1,900	− 1,000
% Change from Year 21	**100.0**	**+ 3.8**	**− 10.9**	**− 20.7**	**− 10.9**
Pre-Tax Income	$ 2,700	+$ 50	−$ 500	−$ 800	−$ 700
% Change from Year 21	**100.0**	**+ 1.9**	**− 18.5**	**− 29.6**	**− 25.9**

The five-year statement and related percentage change table illustrate how the increase (3.4 percent in year 22) and decreases in subsequent years affected pre-tax income. In almost every year, cost of sales and operating expenses did not fully follow sales changes. Sales increased 3.4 percent in year 22, but pre-tax income increased only 1.9 percent. In the following three years, those operating costs and expenses did not change in proportion to sales. As a result, pre-tax income was down almost 26 percent in year 25 compared to year 21, whereas sales were down about 9 percent.

Certainly the sharp declines in pre-tax income indicate that Chem-A-Lot might be having internal cost-control problems during the five-year period. Growth, even with inflation, did not occur at Chem-A-Lot. Expenses grew proportionately more than sales, but that is not a good objective and points to the need for more analysis of the total Chem-A-Lot business.

Another point to be made here is that these percentage differences are analogous to human temperature or blood-pressure readings. Businesses in different industries will, of course, run the equivalent of a fever or high blood pressure at different proportional percentage levels. Just as a physician might ask many questions of a patient to diagnose an illness, we might ask: Were unit selling prices going down? Were unit costs to purchase and manufacture inventory getting too high? Were the plant and machinery out-of-date? Was the work force inefficient?

RATE-OF-CHANGE CHARTS GO HAND IN HAND WITH LONG-TERM ANALYSES

How logarithms can display changing proportional relationships between different series of data is not understood well by most business leaders and many business analysts. The word logarithm alone is imposing; we'll use the term *rate-of-change* instead. While not as intimidating, the semi-logarithmic (log) paper needed requires some getting used to. By employing semi-log charts, the consultants were able to spot significant turning points in Chem-A-Lot's past by charting certain statistics for 20-year periods. They also compared Chem-A-Lot sales to readily available industry and governmental statistics.

A summary of how the consultants presented the data on rate-of-change charts to the Chem-A-Lot board of directors follows. The consultants started with the usual arithmetic chart showing size, not proportional changes. It includes years 5 through 25 to provide a long-term, 20-year, perspective.

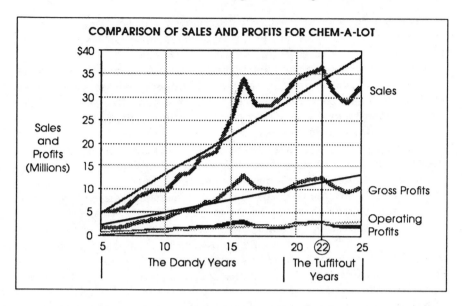

The calculated trend lines seem to indicate fairly stable growth up to year 22. After that, serious problems evidently arose at Chem-a-Lot. Frankly, this chart didn't tell the consultants much that was not already known from the earlier review of the conventional income statements.

Next, they converted the arithmetical chart to a rate-of-change chart to bring out the true proportional growth relationships between sales, gross profit, and operating profit at Chem-A-Lot.

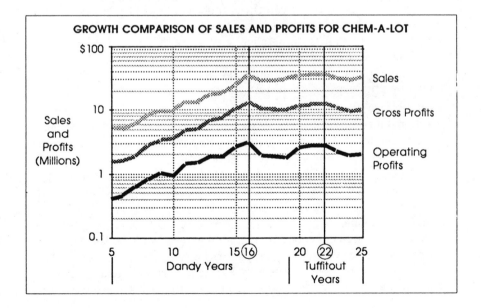

On this type of chart it's possible to show the correct proportional relationship of actual sales and profit data over many years—something an arithmetical line or bar chart that focuses on size can't do.

We think you'll agree that the last eight years now show a fairly dramatic leveling off of sales and profits. **In fact, it suddenly becomes quite clear that year 16 was the real turning point—not year 22.** This chart also clearly demonstrates that operating profits actually fluctuated more violently than sales, not the reverse.

The main point in showing you these tables and charts is this: Each type depicts identical information, from different points of view, from which very different—and often critical—conclusions can be drawn.

Accountants are "numbers driven," not "operations driven," and their records reflect cumulative, top-level, annual, or interim transactions for a conventional set of books. Rarely does the accounting department prepare analyses to highlight growth relationships within a company for operations managers, as was done in the rate-of-change chart, or between competitors for sales managers who must constantly deal with problems of market growth and decline.

No one type of display can guarantee that problems will be spotted, but visuals such as this rate-of-change chart can be of great help. Of course, an exhibit is only as valid and adequate as the data behind it.

Let's spend a little bit more time on this chart. The reason we use rate-of-change charts is that they put into perspective the exact proportional relationship of any number at any place on the chart relative to every other number on that chart. Let's compare the two chart types:

- In the usual arithmetic chart, the horizontal grid lines are exactly the same distance apart. A 10 percent change in a smaller number, such as operating profit, will barely be perceptible on the chart, whereas a 10 percent increase in a large number, such as sales, will result in a large visual increase, even though the same percentage increase in profits is at least as important. Therefore, slopes of trend lines representing sales and profits on arithmetic charts distort growth or decline comparisons.

  To emphasize, just as in the case of the percentage of sales figures used in traditional income statements, arithmetic charts are excellent for comparing sizes of accounts within a year but deceptive when used as a measure of relative growth or decline over several years.

- On the other hand, in the rate-of-change chart, you'll note that the horizontal grid lines are spaced at decreasing distances apart in repeating cycles, with each cycle being 10 times the previous one. A 10 percent change of a smaller number, such as operating profit, will now appear the same as a 10 percent increase in a larger number, such as sales. Slopes of various growth or decline lines representing sales and profits on rate-of-change charts can, therefore, be used as true indicators of relative growth. Thus, if lines have the same slope, the figures for each series are growing at the same rate. That kind of relationship cannot be shown on the typical arithmetic charts that were used by Dandy and Tuffitout.

- In addition, on the usual arithmetic chart, sales and other larger business number series will appear to fluctuate more violently than smaller number series, such as operating profits when, in terms of growth, the reverse is true.

At first blush, the difference between these types of charts would not have seemed important to Dandy or Tuffitout, who probably would have dismissed them out of hand. However, by not preparing such charts, Dandy and Tuffitout lost the opportunity to understand the effect of their price and cost policies fully.

Let's look at another way of displaying sales and profits that is even more illuminating:

AVERAGE GROWTH RATE COMPARISON OF SALES AND PROFITS FOR CHEM-A-LOT

The data portrayed on this rate-of-change chart are identical to those on the previous one, except now mathematically fitted logarithmic trend lines have been added and highlighted. (Incidentally, all trend lines used in this book have been mathematically fitted.)

The trend percentages next to each line show how much sales and profits grew annually, on average, during the stewardships of Dandy and Tuffitout. As you can see, after year 16 during Dandy's ownership, the growth rates of sales and profits dropped from around 20 percent per year to nearly 0 percent per year.

Clearly, although sales had continued to grow only at an average annual rate of 1 percent during Tuffitout's stewardship, he had managed to keep operating profits growing at a slightly better rate, 2 percent. Furthermore, these profits were, on average, larger in dollars than during the earlier high-sales growth years. However, only small amounts of these profits appear to have been plowed back to improve plant and equipment or to improve the skills of employees.

These last two charts provoke questions:

- Were prices raised without regard to specific market conditions in order to hold profits?
- Were costs also being cut in an unplanned manner in order to hold margins?
- How did management hope to cope with the current decline in sales?

Prior to this stage of their investigation, the consultants had found very little wrong at Chem-A-Lot. In fact, all the conventional accounting ratios used to evaluate the condition of a company fell pretty much within normal bounds. Only the rate-of-change chart revealed clearly that there had been a major change in year 16.

In order to find answers to their increasing number of questions without extensive market research at this point, the consultants interviewed present and former staff members. Unfortunately, those interviewed could provide very little hard data; however, they did offer opinions about what might have gone wrong and observations of how their industry had fared during the past two decades.

COMPARISONS TO INDUSTRY STATISTICS

The consultants decided to compare Chem-A-Lot's sales with the capital goods industry, using the U.S. manufacturers' new orders of nondefense capital goods industries in current dollars published monthly by the Department of Commerce in the *Survey of Current Business*.

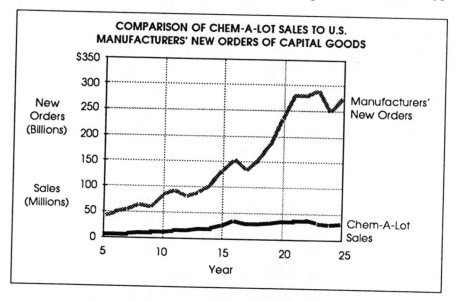

COMPARISON OF CHEM-A-LOT SALES TO U.S.
MANUFACTURERS' NEW ORDERS OF CAPITAL GOODS

Because of the great dollar size difference in these two series, and in order to make it possible to compare actual dollars on an arithmetic chart, they had to plot manufacturers' new orders in billions of dollars and Chem-A-Lot sales in millions. If they had tried to plot the Chem-A-Lot sales series on the billions scale directly, it would have shown up as a horizontal line just a hair above the zero-dollar line on the chart . . . not very useful!

Of course, they could have converted both series to index numbers with year 5 indexed to 100 on the vertical axis. However, the proportional relationship of actual dollars would have been lost in that case also. And to top that, the Chem-A-Lot sales line that represents lower dollar values would have been drawn above the manufacturers' new orders line as shown.

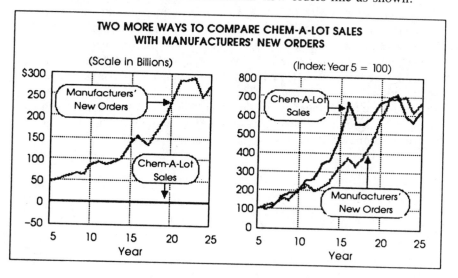

TWO MORE WAYS TO COMPARE CHEM-A-LOT SALES
WITH MANUFACTURERS' NEW ORDERS

On the chart to the left, plotted in billions of dollars, the data line had to be thickened so that Chem-A-Lot sales would not be confused with the zero-dollar line!

Undoubtedly, if you saw any of these charts alone, you would most likely obtain a different impression from each chart about the relationship between Chem-A-Lot sales and manufacturers' new orders. Nothing extraordinary appeared on any of the three charts. Now let's convert the first of these charts to a rate-of-change chart with annual average growth lines added. Here's what the converted chart looks like:

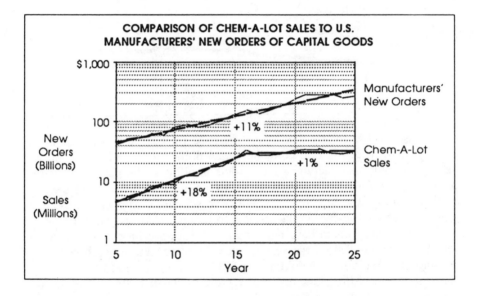

This chart simply uses the same vertical axis to show the orders for all companies in billions of dollars and Chem-A-Lot sales in millions of dollars. It's now even clearer that Chem-A-Lot ceased growing in year 16, whereas the companies in the industries Chem-A-Lot served did not. Observe that no new data were inserted. Sales never came back under Tuffitout's leadership. The consultants had to find out why.

By using the following chart it was possible for the consultants to estimate the general magnitude of lost sales and profits, assuming Chem-A-Lot had attained the same growth rates as manufacturers' new orders:

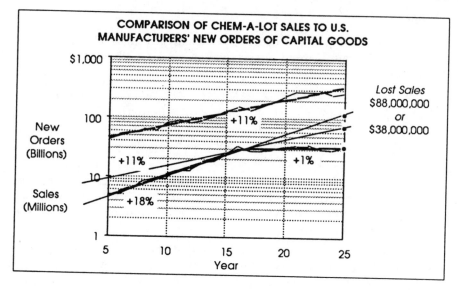

COMPARISON OF CHEM-A-LOT SALES TO U.S.
MANUFACTURERS' NEW ORDERS OF CAPITAL GOODS

On this chart, two additional lines were drawn—one continuing the earlier 18 percent average annual growth rate for Chem-A-Lot sales and another paralleling the 11 percent growth of manufacturers' new orders.

The 18 percent line shows what sales would have been if Tuffitout had been able to reestablish quickly the record for growth under Dandy. If he had been able to, sales revenue would have been about $120 million by year 25, or about $88 million more than the $32 million in actual sales recorded.

Now, if that seems a bit high, suppose Tuffitout was just able to match the manufacturer's new order growth rate of 11 percent. Then sales would have been about $70 million, or $38 million more than the $32 million actually achieved. Take your pick or make your own assumptions! No matter how you slice it, those losses are staggering!

These quick estimates of lost sales were for year 25. If you want to get a full measure of the real loss in sales, just add up the sales losses for all the years from year 16 through 25. You will be astonished.

It is important to realize that a change in a company's method of management, or its culture, has serious long-term effects. Resulting losses or gains compound in exactly the same way that compound interest does on investments.

Remember, however, that this summary of how the consultants presented the data to the Chem-A-Lot board of directors was meant only to show the magnitude of the problem at Chem-A-Lot. It does not tell us whether it was possible to do anything about the problem, either in years past or now.

This concludes the general situation analysis. In the next phase, we'll delve deeper into the causes of Chem-A-Lot's current situation.

SUMMARY

Too frequently the tables of figures in a stereotyped financial statement will be predictably limited. New perspectives are seldom offered. Several variations would be to

- *Present financial statements for several more than the usual two years.*
- *Display percentages to show both size and proportion relationships in addition to dollars.* Changes in percentages over several years, even though small, may signal underlying shifts in the business or foretell major challenges facing the business.
- *Provide rate-of-change charts.* The simultaneous display of sales, cost of sales, gross profits, and operating profits for fairly long periods will highlight significant turning points that are not normally evident. (Try them. You'll like them.)
- *Compare sales or orders to governmental or industry statistics.* See if the company's growth compares favorably by tracking it against the growth of the industry as a whole.
- *Use customary arithmetic charts for size comparisons.* Use them for sales for several years running or for different types of data—like sales, costs, and profits within a single year. Remember, arithmetic charts can be misleading because they do not relate data proportionally when different series of data over several years are shown on the same chart.

After you have read this chapter, see how many of the following questions about Chem-A-Lot's situation you can answer from the information presented so far:

1. What effect did the company culture or management style have on results of operations over time?
2. What were the life cycles of major products, and how far into their cycles were each of them?
3. There were indications of market-share loss starting around year 16. Why?
4. Was pricing used to accomplish revenue targets?
5. Were design, development, and research cut back too far to extend life cycles of current products or to introduce new products?
6. Were marketing and advertising adequate?
7. Did the company lose key people?
8. Did the company have problems with key vendors?
9. What was the ratio of orders booked to quotes?
10. How did quality, including service, compare with that of the competition during the same period?

As you can see, we still don't have a lot of the crucial answers for Chem-A-Lot. Would you be able to provide the answers to these questions for your company?

CHAPTER 5

UNIT SALES VERSUS DOLLAR SALES: A SURPRISING ANALYSIS

A decision is the action an executive must take when he has information so incomplete that the answer does not suggest itself.

Admiral Arthur William Radford

PRODUCT LINE DATA OFFERS MORE ANSWERS

The consultants' most important findings came from their detailed review of sales by product line for the past 20 years. This period of time probably seems excessive at first; nevertheless, it was crucial to the discovery of the real reasons for Chem-A-Lot's current predicament.

All too often, managers do not receive analyses of how specific product lines have been doing over the years. Frequently, they focus most or all of their attention on consolidated sales, costs, and profits. So let's start by looking at consolidated sales displayed in a rate-of-change chart:

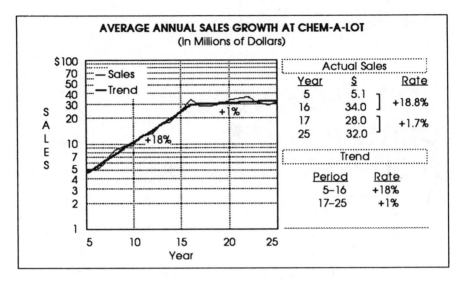

AVERAGE ANNUAL SALES GROWTH AT CHEM-A-LOT
(In Millions of Dollars)

Those average annual trend rates highlight the year-16 turning point (under Dandy). Chem-A-Lot just stopped growing.

Notice that when the actual sales figures at the beginning and end of the two periods are used, the average annual growth rates are slightly higher than when the trend end figures are used. The trend values are more representative. Trends take out the effect of end-point years that are on the high or low side for the period selected.

The income statement for Chem-A-Lot years 17 and 25 showed a 14 percent increase in sales, almost level gross profits, and a 5 percent increase in net income. Not good, but not a disaster.

CHEM-A-LOT INCOME STATEMENTS

(Dollars in Thousands)

	Year 17	Year 25	Change
Sales	$28,000	$32,000	+14%
Cost of Goods Sold	17,900	21,800	+22
Gross Profit	10,100	10,200	+ 1
Operating Expense	8,199	8,200	+ 0
Pre-Tax Income	1,901	2,000	+ 5
Income Taxes	854	898	+ 5
Net Income	**$ 1,047**	**$ 1,102**	**+ 5%**

Now look at the detail of sales for the three major products lines for the same period, first on an arithmetic chart:

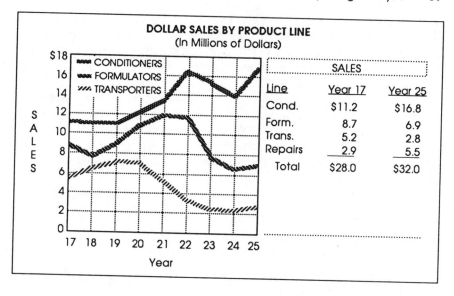

DOLLAR SALES BY PRODUCT LINE
(In Millions of Dollars)

Line	Year 17	Year 25
Cond.	$11.2	$16.8
Form.	8.7	6.9
Trans.	5.2	2.8
Repairs	2.9	5.5
Total	$28.0	$32.0

Next, the consultants prepared growth trends for each of the three major product lines and indexed these trends. For each trend they set year 17 at 100 on a rate-of-change chart. On the same chart the consultants also compared each product line trend to the combined trend for all three product lines plus repairs, which had been shown previously on the chart for years 5 through 25. For years 17 through 25, however, the consultants excluded repairs so that the annual sales rate dropped from +1 percent per year to −0.3 percent per year. This was done to obtain a truer picture of what was happening to machine sales alone.

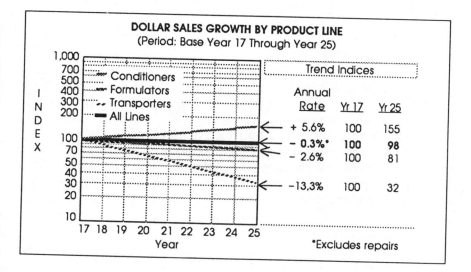

DOLLAR SALES GROWTH BY PRODUCT LINE
(Period: Base Year 17 Through Year 25)

Trend Indices

Annual Rate	Yr 17	Yr 25
+ 5.6%	100	155
− 0.3%*	100	98
− 2.6%	100	81
−13.3%	100	32

*Excludes repairs

Either at the individual product level or at the combined product line level, sales for large industrial machines are so sporadic that year-to-year sales figures vary erratically. Therefore, it's even more important to calculate average annual trend rates for these products than for those with larger unit volumes but lower prices.

Sales didn't drop much except for the transporter line. That product line is only 32 percent of what it was in year 17. Have the products in this line aged? Lost customer acceptance? Were the products overpriced?

The dollar sales chart does raise these questions. But now look at the difference between number of units shipped and their respective dollar totals:

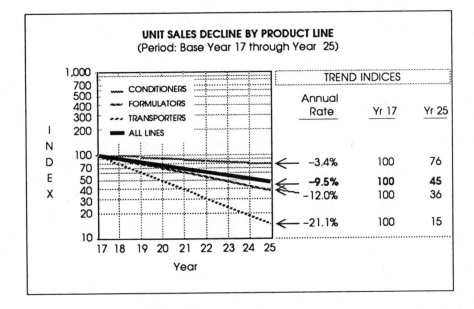

Unit sales for all lines are only 45 percent of what they were at the beginning of the period. At almost a 10 percent negative annual rate, there won't be many sales to worry about in a few years, unless the price of each unit is jacked up astronomically! That transporter line took a shellacking: Sales dollars from it dropped to 32 percent by year 25, but in terms of units, sales dropped even more—down to only 15 percent of year 17 units.

Because lumping all products into consolidated amounts is dangerous when the objective is to learn more about the business, the consultants first looked at dollars and then units. Next, they charted the effect of pricing changes:

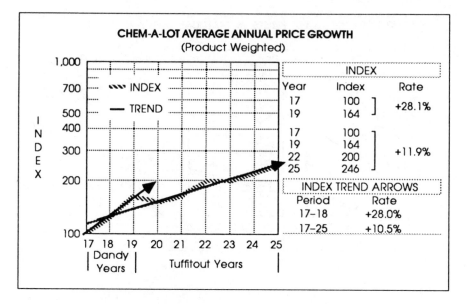

Prices were raised on the average just about the same for all product lines during the period. That 10.5 percent annual average trend increase from year 17 through 25 really was not too much higher than the general inflation rate.

The largest jumps in prices came during the last couple of years when Jim was still in charge at Chem-A-Lot. One big jump occurred when Dandy became discouraged because Chem-A-Lot had not bounced back swiftly from a recession. Some customers probably thought they were being ripped off.

Both Jim and Jack should have taken more time to learn how customers react to big price jumps. They were told that prices were higher than those of competitors, but both ignored this information.

CHEM-A-LOT PRICE INFLATION VERSUS WAGE AND MATERIAL-COST INFLATION

The consultants used the following chart to plot changes in prices, material costs, and wages:

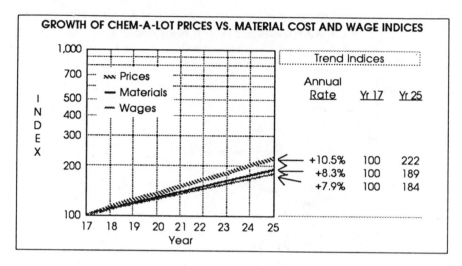

Looks like the pricing policies of both Dandy and Tuffitout resulted in prices that grew faster than the average inflation rate for wages and materials. With that trend index number of 222 in year 25, Chem-A-Lot prices more than doubled those of base year 17. So Chem-A-Lot had contributed to the general level of inflation with 10.5 percent average pricing increases versus the government index rates of 7.9 percent and 8.3 percent.

Probably the initial large increase ordered by Dandy had shocked customers the most. The impression would certainly have run swiftly through the market that Chem-A-Lot machines were expensive compared to those of some of its competitors, don't you think? Diane answered specifically:

Diane: I guess those later price hikes only reinforced the impression made by Dandy's big increase, which may have set off the chain of events that followed. That is especially pertinent because we did *not* precede or follow the price increases with quality assurance programs, advertising campaigns, better service, or other programs to pull through the unit sales.

I'll bet that, if we could see this chart for the successful innovators in electronics, the price trend would be going down, or, at least, it would be increasing below the general inflation rate—the unit sales would be way up, and the sales income would be way up too!

General price levels, of course, do not tell the whole story. We must take a deeper look at individual prices, unit sales, and promotional campaigns as well as many other factors.

The next chart demonstrates how unit sales declined at nearly the same rate that prices increased, leaving sales-dollar income from all products almost unchanged!

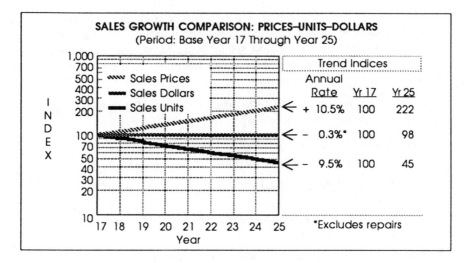

Let's hear Diane's comment on this finding:

Diane: I believe that if you checked the early Dandy years, you would discover that unit sales grew faster than prices. We know that sales dollars showed a healthy 18 percent annual growth.

From the financial statements, I knew the company hadn't grown very much for a number of years, but I didn't expect this. When I compared all those statements recently, annual net incomes looked fairly reasonable. Even the usual accounting ratios were okay.

The charts presented in this chapter demonstrate that companies often develop harmful cultures and managerial attitudes that persist over relatively long periods of time because of an inferior short-term strategy. Frequently, critical cultural shifts are obscured by traditional accounting statements as well as inappropriate graphs. It sometimes takes a major event—like a lot of red ink on the books—to change the direction of a business.

SUMMARY

Many reports generated by the accounting and sales departments start and stop with aggregated dollars for sales, costs, and profits. This is unfortunate because turning points followed by persistent business culture changes often can be understood only with much more information. Here are the critical points covered:

- Unit sales rate-of-change charts, when compared to dollar sales rate-of-change charts for the same product lines, often yield surprising results. Such charts are an important tool for identifying real success or hidden failure.

- Keeping track of a company's product-price and cost-inflation rates is as important as knowing about the general inflation rate. Rate-of-change charts showing trends for unit sales, dollar sales, and sales prices over time indicate whether customers react favorably to a company's pricing policies relative to competitors'.

Could you now answer the following questions relating to Chem-A-Lot, or if rephrased, for your company?

1. Were sales-dollar targets set unrealistically high?
2. Did customers really believe they were being ripped off?
3. Just how inflationary were Chem-A-Lot's pricing policies in the customers' eyes?
4. Did Dandy's price hikes in his final years as CEO cause good customers to look to other suppliers?
5. How critical were Tuffitout's later price increases?
6. Were Chem-A-Lot prices the crucial factor in lower unit sales, or was it general inflation?
7. Which came first: high prices or low unit sales?
8. When could higher prices lead to higher unit sales?

Although we now know a great deal more about Chem-A-Lot, we still do not have a complete situation analysis.

CHAPTER 6

INDIVIDUAL PRODUCT SALES TALE: ORDER IN CHAOS

To render an existing business entrepreneurial, management must take the lead in making obsolete its own products and services rather than waiting for a competitor to do so.

Peter Drucker

THE STATE OF EXISTING PRODUCT RECORDS

When the consultants began this project, they asked Tuffitout if he had any detailed product charts covering many years in addition to the dog-eared stacks of computer runs then gathering dust on the top of an old file. He said he had charted sales dollars for each product line. In addition, he had attempted to put all the products on one chart to see if there was a pattern of any kind, but he had found none. Here's Jack's product summary chart:

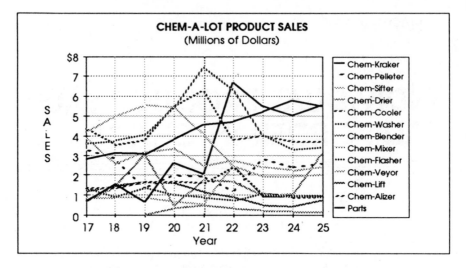

CHEM-A-LOT PRODUCT SALES
(Millions of Dollars)

Now let's listen in on the actual conversation among the consultants and the directors:

Jones: My gosh, no wonder Jack sounded confused at times! This chart sheds about as much light on the condition of Chem-A-Lot as a TV picture tube that's lost its sync.

Consultant: True, but remember, we have an advantage over Jack Tuffitout: We've already seen the end result of a sophisticated analysis in our presentation yesterday. While it is difficult to see, if you study Jack's chart, you'll find there *is* a pattern.

Jones: Really?

Consultant: Yes. Over the years you'll find just about as many lines going up as down. That's why the summary sales income line was nearly level at a minus 0.3 percent annual rate of growth on the final chart we showed you in yesterday's presentation.

If you carefully trace the line for each product through the maze on the Tuffitout chart, you'll see that Chem-Kraker is the only product with any real growth over the period.

Finally, the parts line shows the only pattern of steady, long-term growth. You would, of course, expect less violent fluctuations here because parts for all products tend to average out. More about that later.

Process machinery sales have rather wide swings compared to those in some other types of businesses we've analyzed. Wide swings were just more evident than usual in Jack's chart.

A BETTER WAY TO CHART PRODUCT SALES

Consultant continues: Next, we'll go to the unit sales rate-of-change chart to see how order was found in the apparent product growth chaos portrayed in Jack's old growth chaos chart. You will recall that whereas dollar sales were level, the real problem appeared to be declining unit sales. *(Flashes the chart on the screen.)*

So, let's find out what lies behind each line. You'll recall that unit sales trends were combined under three product lines.

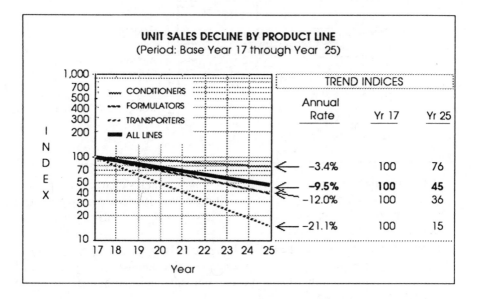

UNIT SALES DECLINE BY PRODUCT LINE
(Period: Base Year 17 through Year 25)

Now, we have dug down to the level where we can show you a chart comparable to the one Jack had but in a very different form.

It differs primarily in three ways: First, the chart represents unit sales rather than dollar sales; second, the chart has a rate-of-change scale rather than an arithmetic scale; and third, only trend lines are shown. It is, however, the same as Jack's in that it shows all 12 product lines with the exception of parts.

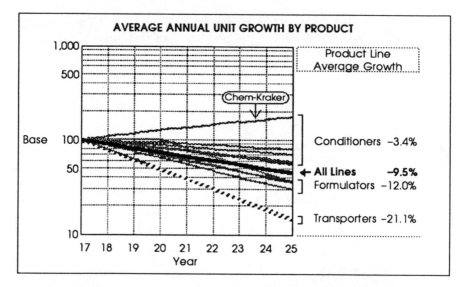

On this chart we now see that *product one* on Jack's chart actually was Chem-Kraker, a product in the conditioner line. It was the only product of any line that showed a healthy growth. We, of course, wanted to find out why.

We began by looking at rate-of-change charts by product. As you can see, Chem-Kraker had a 7.9 percent positive annual average growth rate, which was way above the 3.4 percent negative annual average decline of the conditioner line.

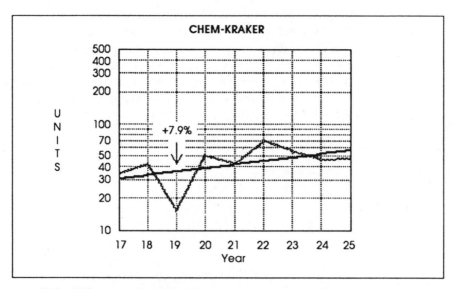

This difference immediately raised another question. Did Chem-A-Lot's pricing policies favor Chem-Kraker? A comparison of product prices obviously was called for. We made one and found that the growth rates in price of all but two products were clustered around the average annual rate of +10.5 percent for prices.

Homer Williams (director): I suppose Chem-Kraker was one of them and that it was given special lower pricing to enhance sales for some reason?

Consultant: No, to the contrary. Chem-Kraker prices were raised at a positive annual rate of 22.8 percent, compared to the average of 10.5 percent for the other products! Its technology and reputation in the marketplace readily permitted rather large increases per unit. The second product that deviated from the cluster was in the transporter line. It had the lowest unit sales as well as the lowest rate of price increase. Evidently prices were kept low on that product to encourage sales. Obviously, the general price increases ordered by Dandy and Tuffitout were modified to some degree by market pressures.

We carefully reexamined all the detailed charts of prices, unit sales, and dollar sales with rate-of-change as well as arithmetic scales for clues.

Jones: Could you show us the product lines on charts with arithmetic scales? I'll admit I'm still a bit more comfortable with those.

Consultant: Yes, of course. *(Begins to show composite arithmetic charts of products by line—the formulator line first.)* As for the formulator line, most of these machines evidently never have been too well accepted by industry, but the staff did have high hopes that the new Chem-Blender would do well in the market. Unfortunately, the engineer responsible for its design was terminated before the bugs were worked out. He was never replaced by a top-flight man, according to Charlie. So this product fizzled like a defective Fourth of July skyrocket. As a matter of fact, all products in the formulator line appear to be in a state of advanced life-cycle decline.

On the other hand, through the years, the line of material conditioners has been well received by a number of process industries—but in more recent years, other U.S. machines appear to be capturing more and more of the market. There are also an increasing number of good imports as well.

Chem-Kraker is, of course, the one exception. *(Points to the top left of the conditioner line composite chart.)* However, as we have already said, this product may now also be in serious trouble because price increases were not moderated as the product matured. Unit sales have declined rather sharply since year 22, as you can see here on this size chart. So let's examine the products in the conditioner line in some depth.

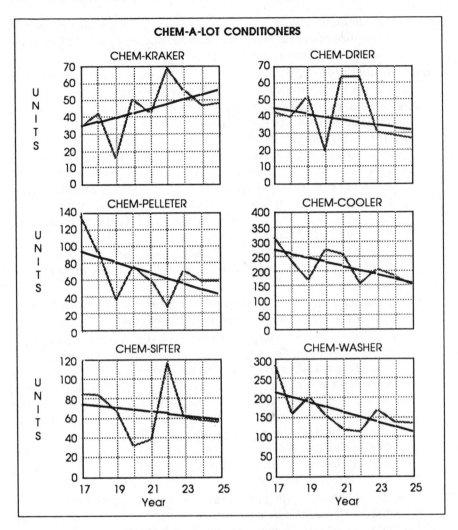

Jones: Wouldn't each of these conditioner charts be similar to the individual product lines shown on the scrambled product summary chart of Jack's ...the one we saw earlier? Of course, the separate charts you have prepared are much clearer, but with such wide fluctuations, can those trend lines really be representative of the underlying figures?

Consultant: Yes, these are similar, but Jack's charts were plotted in dollar sales, rather than unit sales, so the decline in dollar size trend lines wouldn't have been as steep because unit price increases were made in most years.

In answer to your second question, because of the length of the period covered by each product trend line, we can make meaning- ful comparisons with other products. Furthermore, in a weighted line representing a category of products, the annual fluctuations of individual products largely cancel out one another.

Both rate-of-change charts and size charts with trend lines on them were carefully studied at the product level as well as at the group level. Here, for example, we have compressed the year scales so that it's possible to compare, in detail, rate-of-change and size relationships in units for Chem-A-Lot conditioners. And for the sake of clarity, trend lines have been shown separately.

The rate-of-change lines, unlike the size lines, clearly demonstrate that all conditioners, with the exception of Chem-Kraker, were declining at more similar rates. Chem-Kraker, on the other hand, was growing at about the same rate as the other conditioners were declining.

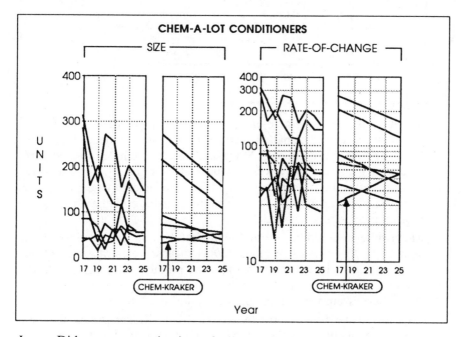

Jones: Did your reexamination of all those detailed charts tell you what actually happened at Chem-A-Lot?

Consultant: Well, no, I can't truthfully say that it did. You reach a point where the examination of numerical data comes to an end.

THE CAPTIVE-MARKET SYNDROME

Consultant continues: We do strongly suspect, however, that Chem-A-Lot had fallen prey to the captive-market syndrome. The reason: Repair part sales were not only growing steadily but becoming a larger and larger portion of total sales dollars, as indicated on Tuffitout's chart. It appears that prices may have been increased on parts as well as on all products where possible—not only to cover inflation but also to improve profits.

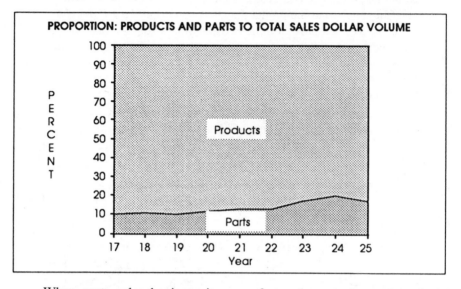

When parts sales begin to increase faster than product sales, that's frequently a danger signal. It may mean that new product sales aren't being generated fast enough. Managers are often tempted to load parts prices to make up for lower product sales—thinking that's a quick way to get well. This practice alienates customers, who must keep their machines operating. These customers then look elsewhere when replacing or adding new machines.

Meanwhile sales dollars from Chem-Kraker went up 7.8 times from year 17 to 25—a hot item indeed! During those years, it jumped from roughly 3 percent of total Chem-A-Lot product sales income to 21 percent. This product alone kept the annual average rate for total Chem-A-Lot sales from turning sharply down during all those years.

This raised the further possibility that Chem-Kraker dollar and unit sales were up only because it, too, provided income from a temporarily captive market. So, because customers obviously responded differently to Chem-Kraker price increases than to the other Chem-A-Lot price increases, we needed to find out why.

In order to discover what customers thought about the marketing policies of Jim Dandy and Jack Tuffitout, we conducted interviews with many long-time customers. One outspoken business owner summed up, quite colorfully and frankly, what most alluded to in more guarded ways. Here's what he said:

Now, Jim —there was a real live Yankee Doodle Dandy! He not only developed and sold good machines, but he supplied really innovative process knowledge to go along with 'em. Jim really understood my business, and he and his talented crew helped my business grow. And when he dropped by, he always made me feel good.

Oh, yes, you asked about Tuffitout's marketing practices. I never did get to know him as well as I knew Jim. From my observations, I guess I'd have to call him a financial manager—more concerned about the bottom line than about his company's products, services, employees, or me, his customer.

You know, the only machine worth buying from Chem-A-Lot now is the Chem-Kraker, which Dandy's crew developed. You can still get real support from a few of Dandy's old hands. As for Tuffitout, he's a cold fish. He sure ain't my kind of leader!

Although this customer is rather outspoken, I believe his opinion accurately represents the feelings of the customers we interviewed.

After analyzing all the information available, we concluded that higher prices were indeed a downward pressure on Chem-A-Lot's unit sales. Those prices, in the average customer's mind, grew to represent a big chunk of missing process knowledge, service, and leadership that Dandy's crew had at one time provided.

Customers began to believe that Chem-A-Lot's old products were overpriced for their quality. A competitive product analysis conducted by our team confirmed that Chem-A-Lot products were no longer state-of-the-art.

Williams: Could a better advertising program have changed the picture?

Consultant: Not really. Although advertising agencies can very often improve the market position of old and new products—through appeals to prospective users based on everything from economic facts to cheesecake—advertising can only go so far as a substitute for real value as perceived by the customer. And that perceived value, for commodities or machines alike, includes more than the product itself or blarney about the product.

In the early years of Chem-A-Lot, Dandy was regularly introducing innovative new products with creative installation backup for customers, which kept the overall growth rate of Chem-A-Lot exceptionally high. Do you have any questions? Mr. Peabody.

Jason Peabody (director): Your presentation has been most enlightening. I gather from your remarks that, when you get right down to it, what went wrong at Chem-A-Lot was that, in addition to the people problems, too little emphasis was placed on new product research and customer service. Is that correct?

Consultant: That's exactly right. To lend further credence to what has been said, please recall the chart shown earlier on Chem-Kraker unit sales. In it, unit sales peaked in year 22. Then, sales went down slightly during the last three years. It could very well be that competitors were beginning to make inroads. Both Dandy and Tuffitout increased the price on Chem-Kraker to as high as the traffic would bear—and, of course, the higher the price, the more lucrative and attractive a market becomes to competitors.

During a coffee break it becomes evident to the consultant that the directors now understand what happened to Chem-A-Lot. However, he also feels that the full impact of what his team has been saying has not yet been fully grasped. After the break, he decides to follow through with a restatement of the findings. He smiles inwardly when he remembers the advice of his father, who'd been a preacher: Get up, tell 'em what you're going to tell 'em, tell 'em, tell 'em what you told 'em, and sit down. Guess I won't exactly do that, he thought, but maybe I'll come close. The last session is called to order by chairman Jones, and the consultant launches into his final effort.

THE CONSULTANT'S LAST CHANCE TO TALK ABOUT CHEM-A-LOT'S HIDDEN MESS

Consultant: I wish to ask for your indulgence in this session. It'll be my last chance to summarize the findings of our team *(the directors smile)*, so here goes:

Once upon a time at Chem-A-Lot, all those old products we've been talking about were shiny new. If we had selected other time periods since the founding of Chem-A-Lot, not just years 17 through 25, against which to compare results, we would have seen many new products be introduced, grow, and then fade away—only to be replaced by others, like the flowers of summer. But during years 17 through 25, we found only one new flower, and it withered quickly. With careful observation you'll be able to identify it on Tuffitout's chart as well as the corresponding chart we made.

Perhaps, if people were programmed like computers or robots they would respond more predictably—they would introduce new products and services as regularly as the tick of the watch on your wrist. But even computers are not foolproof. Witness the 1987 stock market panic: The news media reported that at least part of the panic was caused by too many computers being programmed to respond to the market in the same way, at the same signal. Hopefully, this example is not a portent of how the computer will function in future crises. In any case, we cannot dismiss the problem of how to achieve worthwhile innovation with some rote formula.

Neither can we dismiss price inflation as a minor problem. Remember, between $38 million and $88 million of sales were lost in year 25 alone—depending on how you looked at it—not to mention the cumulative losses over the years. Price inflation obscured far greater losses. It's time to take another look at the broader economic picture.

Although it's true that Jack Tuffitout was not a brilliant leader, as a few have said, let's be fair. He was handicapped by the data available. Here are some remarks attributed to Robert Sprouse, vice-chairman of the Accounting Standards Board, in Mark Stevens' book *The Big Eight* that I think are apropos:

> If the problem (inflation) is left unchecked, our economic system will actually cannibalize itself . . .
>
> Our studies show that some corporations actually pay out more in dividends than they earn. They cannot renew themselves. This reduces the productivity of U.S. industry and further fuels inflation. It's a vicious cycle . . .
>
> Unless there is creditable financial information adjusted for inflation, we cannot manage either individual companies or the overal economy. That's because we can't really gauge where we are going. The financial reports do not present an accurate picture of where we are.[1]

So, whether we're conducting business in a period of inflation or deflation, we better have tools that tell us what really is going on.

Tuffitout, like many other CEOs, didn't know what was actually happening. And because he didn't, many people were hurt: himself and your shareholders as well as Chem-A-Lot workers and their dependents.

While remaining sympathetic to Jack, we can still reasonably ask: Even with a good set of tools, would Jack have been a good CEO for Chem-A-Lot over a longer term? For that matter, would Dandy have in his later years?

In these past two days, our team hopes that you have acquired a clearer picture than either Tuffitout or Dandy had available to them after all their years as chief executive officers of Chem-A-Lot.

We have shown how the sad decline of Chem-A-Lot, accelerated too long by inappropriate decisions, was hidden behind a veil of traditional financial statements and charting techniques that neither Jim nor Jack was able to penetrate under the press of events.

Money became a variable measuring stick that gave widely different measurements of the same amount of goods over time. This was due to price increases and cost reductions brought on by the need to keep ahead of inflation as well as the short-term effort required to show good earnings each year. Whether money inflation or deflation favors your company, you have to know what the underlying reality is in order to be in command. Furthermore, it's not good enough to know what the general inflation rate is. You must know what the specific inflation rates are for your company. To determine them, you must analyze purchases, wages, and other expenses. We believe we have demonstrated how this can be done during these last two days.

With your broad contacts, you may realize how many other American companies, from auto manufacturers to local supermarket stores, have suffered from Chem-A-Lot's malady. Each company has its own

---

[1]From *The Big Eight* by Mark Stevens, copyright © 1981. Reprinted by permission of Macmillan Publishing Company, Inc.

individual product inflation or deflation rate as well as an average rate that can bias accounting measurements and veil reality. You may well wonder how much this impedes America's ability to compete with manufacturers abroad.

Finally, all of us must help prevent the so-called hard financial facts, upon which decisions are traditionally based in America, from floating entirely free of underlying reality.

For my team members as well as myself, I wish to thank you for the opportunity we've had to serve you. The Chem-A-Lot assignment has been an exciting one for us, and we hope our findings will prove very profitable for you in the future.

The hard decision of whether to rebuild Chem-A-Lot is up to you. In the complete written report of our findings that we will now provide each of you, we have tried to provide answers to all of your written and oral questions, together with our suggestions on how to return Chem-A-Lot to an extended period of high and profitable growth. Thank you, all.

SUMMARY

The consultants struck gold when they assembled historical data by product within each product line. To sum up:

- Unit sales by three major product lines, charted for a long period of years, showed problems developing at different rates for each line. The formulator line proved to be in deep trouble.

- Unit sales for each product within each of the three lines were gathered, showing tremendous swings. Even so, when appropriately displayed on rate-of-change charts, each product pointed to similar sales problems across all lines. There was one exceptional product, however, which grew both in units and dollars despite price increases because customers found it to be worth the price.

- A disproportionate increase in parts sales relative to product sales often indicates that parts prices are being increased in an attempt to improve the bottom line. The price of a successful product may be raised unduly for the same reason. If carried too far, this practice may cause customers to feel "ripped off."

- Customers were interviewed. The technology level, product age, and pricing methods were found to be factors in customer product acceptance. Customers were not inclined to overpay for what they got despite the past reputation of a supplier . . . and certainly not for long.

- Redesign, new product development, and application engineering had deteriorated at Chem-A-Lot as perceived by potential customers.

Chem-A-Lot needed change, and Chem-A-Lot's directors awakened to this need a bit late. What should the directors do? What would you do?

CHAPTER 7

PRODUCT LIFE CYCLES AND PRICING

The measure of success is not whether you have a tough problem to deal with, but whether it's the same problem you had last year.

John Foster Dulles

CHEM-A-LOT RESTARTS

Action by the board would have been mandatory without a severe downturn in demand for the company's products. The recession that started late in year 25 continued to depress sales severely in year 26. The time was certainly at hand to change company strategies, tactics, and president.

Fortunately, Tuffitout had resigned, so the customary termination pay was unnecessary. Charles B. Fisher was promoted to president, chief operating officer, and chief executive officer as of December first.

Fisher had been better known as "good old Charlie in charge of production" at Chem-A-Lot for a long, long time prior to this promotion. Jones, chairman of the board, worked hard to convince the board to promote Fisher because he felt Fisher was highly qualified technically, knew the product lines completely, had a good feel for people, and, of course, was quickly available.

Tom Puller, vice-president of sales, was a close second choice, but Charlie's technical background carried more weight with the board. Those members who felt that marketing expertise was far more critical to the recapture of market share, in the end, went along with Jones. They finally realized that a man with Fisher's knowledge would be needed at the helm for day-to-day decision making in the tough months ahead while they began to overhaul the management structure.

The directors also did not want to risk bringing in another president from outside. They feared that a person unfamiliar with Chem-A-Lot's specific products, services, and people would probably take too long to become an effective leader at this critical juncture. The learning curve simply would require too much time, even if a qualified person were found quickly.

Charlie was delighted to take charge. With vivid impressions of Tuffitout's failures to communicate still fresh in his mind, he was determined to introduce a management team approach. He knew he worked well with Tom and Diane. He was convinced cooperation was mandatory if Chem-A-Lot were to succeed in retaking its former leadership role in its traditional market niches.

Charlie's idea of the team approach to management involved the following:

- *Communication*—dissemination of all pertinent information to each member.
- *Interaction*—provision for full discussion and testing of such information.
- *Operating decision*—selection of the best approach by Charlie.

Charlie had no intention of abdicating his responsibility to manage Chem-A-Lot properly. He was not going to manage by consensus; he was going to take a firm grasp of the controls, knowing full well that the majority was not always right. Charlie's strategy called for real cooperation, among members of his staff as well as between them and him as CEO, but he was not going to be a pushover.

A VISION EMERGES FROM UNCOVERING THE GEOLOGY OF SALES STRATA

Even before taking over in the last quarter of year 26, Charlie had had more than a hunch about exactly why Chem-A-Lot quit growing rapidly in year 16. The real reason, he had felt all along, had been a failure to envision what customers would want in the years that followed. But how had this caused such a complete departure from the 18 percent annual growth rate chalked up in the early Dandy years? To figure out just how this had occurred, he carefully studied the sales records available for all the products that had been introduced and sold by Chem-A-Lot over the years.

While unit sales records were incomplete, he was able to determine that the early products had been innovative and upon introduction to the market, had grown rapidly with rare price increases thereafter. He also noted that later, as demand had slowed and as competitors had entered the market, a long, slow decline in unit sales had usually ensued. Many product ideas and products, of course, had not gotten off the ground, but enough had in the earlier Dandy years that new products were regularly introduced and accepted by customers. There were, of course, large differences in the way the sales profiles for each product had developed.

Most of the products introduced by Dandy had achieved dominant market shares in markets that grew at a medium rate. These products had been profitable. One or two, like Chem-Kraker, were star performers that achieved overwhelming acceptance in high-growth process industries. On the other hand, Chem-Blender, introduced by Tuffitout, was a complete failure that should have been eliminated. However, Charlie knew that a blender was needed in the product mix. He felt that he couldn't just consider each product separately to understand the situation. Somehow, he had to look at all the product profiles simultaneously—not just the current position of each product on its life profile—to get correct answers.

Charlie found that during the early high-growth years of individual products like Chem-Kraker, those products often grew at over a 15 percent annual rate. However, the combined rate for all products had recently dropped to a mere 1 percent, well below the 18 percent annual average rate at which Chem-A-Lot had grown under Dandy's guidance in the early years. How could this be?

Charlie called up on his computer the rate-of-change sales chart that illustrated how the growth rate had dropped from 18 percent to 1 percent after year 16. He knew the answer was to be found in the relationship of individual product profiles to the overall record of growth on this chart, which had first been prepared by the consultants.

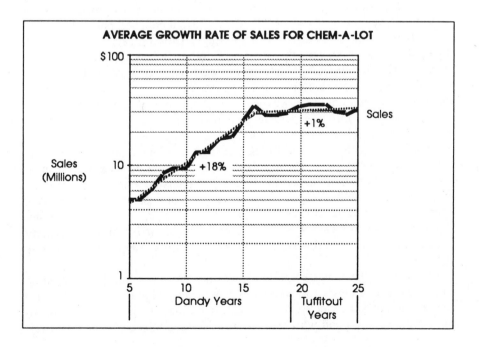

He soon realized that the answer to the question was quite simple: The actual product profiles were stacked on top of each other over time at short enough intervals to create the 18 percent annual growth rate during the early years. To check his thinking, he created a simple size chart showing actual sales stratification.

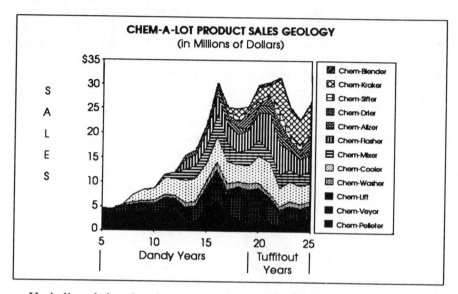

He believed the slowdown to the 1 percent annual rate was due (1) to the decrease over time in the number of new product sales profiles stacked on top of existing products or (2) to the introduction of poorly designed products in recent years or (3) to increasingly slipshod service or (4) to all three. He knew, of course, that there were other factors to be considered — such as price inflation, the state of the external economy, problems with individual machines sold, production problems, and personnel problems. But what bothered him most was that the 1 percent annual growth rate came down to about a minus 9 percent annual decline rate if prices were held constant.

Charlie met with senior staff members Tom and Diane on the same afternoon he was promoted. Charlie's explanation of how he proposed to manage Chem-A-Lot strengthened the bonds of friendship among the three and increased their mutual respect for each other's professional abilities. That afternoon they vowed to return Chem-A-Lot to its former number one position in the marketplace. Charlie was not going to make massive changes in direction; there would be no disruptive new broom approach like before under Tuffitout.

Fortunately, there was some evidence that the recession was bottoming out: Customer requests for quotations were rising slightly, though this increase was not yet reflected in orders. In addition, the personnel on board were experienced, good workers who were pleased to see Charlie take over.

Charlie presented his findings and his two charts for discussion at the staff meeting. He always referred to the stacked profile chart as a sales geology chart because it demonstrated how sales were laid down over time in strata similar to those of the earth made visible when a roadway is cut through a hillside.

Charlie (at staff meeting): Chem-A-Lot's early success was due to the regular introduction of innovative products that were accompanied by expert assistance to customers for their applications. In fact, the 18 percent growth rate through the years would have been impossible without the regular introduction of new products. The life of many a product was also prolonged through the development of an improved product version and the discovery of new applications as the result of close customer contacts.

For example, note that sales for the Chem-Pelleter fell sharply in years 13 and 14 after many years of excellent sales. Old-timers will recall that the C. A. Jones Machinery Co. came out with an improved model that lured away even our loyal customers. However, being close to our customers paid off. We got back on top of the situation when we sped up the introduction of a modified version of our own within a year. We bounced back in years 15 and 16 with help from the economy; however, increased competition, accentuated by an economic recession, again eroded Chem-Pelleter sales.

Tom: Charlie, I understand that the decline in average growth to 1 percent per year after year 16 occurred because of the failure to continue to introduce innovative new products on a regular basis, coupled with inflated prices. However, in addition, wasn't the turning point in year 16 really due to the decline in service and productivity brought on by Jim's cost-cutting overreaction to the recession that year? And don't you agree that his general state of mind at the time contributed to the problem? *(Tom feels he has to inject these thoughts for the benefit of newer members of the staff because he knows Charlie would never diminish Jim's role at Chem-A-Lot.)*

Charlie: Well, yes . . . but during this low growth period, the decline would have been very much greater without Chem-Kraker sales. And Tom, Chem-Kraker was the last product turned out by Dandy's original design team.

Chem-Blender, introduced in year 20 during the Tuffitout years, was a disaster, as you all know. Unfortunately, Tuffitout never fully understood why it failed because of his distorted notions of management. Thus, he was doomed to continue Dandy's mistakes . . . That's enough on that subject.

With the information on sales geology we now have, I believe we should be able to envision alternatives for Chem-A-Lot. We can hammer out a prime objective, create a strategy to reach that objective, and make profits that will permit us to survive and grow in a healthy fashion.

Tom, our directors have asked for a written strategy plan for the three years starting in year 28. Fortunately, the directors are letting us have a full year in which to do a good job. Before we worry too much about that, though, we simply must stop the erosion in our market share now.

Remember this fan chart? It displays the changes during the last eight years in unit selling prices, sales dollars, and unit sales for all product lines. Well, let's look at it again.

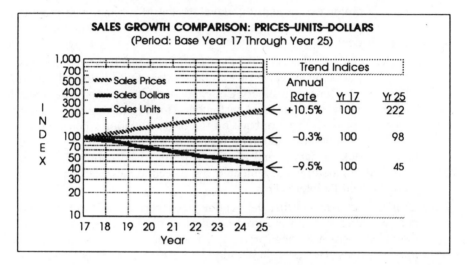

That chart really speaks for itself. It depicts what our long-time customers have been telling us. We are overpriced when compared to our competition's quality and service. Our 10.5 percent average annual rate of price increases kept our sales dollars fairly level in spite of an annual average drop of 9.5 percent in units!

Tom: And that meant that unit sales were more than cut in half during those years. So evidently the higher we raised prices, the more we lost market share to competitors who were willing to sell units almost as good as ours at a much lower price.

Diane: Tom, if we had priced higher initially and then lowered the price gradually for some machines or if we had priced less aggressively when we did have to raise prices, we most certainly would have kept some competitors out of the market as well as increased our own sales. Our pricing policies as a whole have been psychologically damaging! They've nearly killed us.

Henry Newman (Charlie's replacement as vice-president of manufacturing): If our unit sales had been increasing, our production costs per unit would have decreased as we became more efficient in producing larger numbers of units. That might also have reduced the cost of raw materials by taking advantage of larger quantity discounts.

Charlie: Henry, I agree. In recent years sales targets were set at the beginning of each year. Then, when it became evident we were not going to reach those targets, prices were raised—and sometimes competent people were terminated—to reduce costs to assure healthy-looking profits on end-of-the-year statements. And that's not to say that some excess fat hadn't accumulated, but that often the wrong people and expenses were slashed.

Tom: Our U.S. field sales force really became demoralized, and our international distributors thought we were less than rational in our pricing in the face of increasing competition.

Charlie: Tom, it's worth thinking about your comment on the loss of market share. Chem-A-Lot sales stopped growing in year 16. But we only realized the full extent of the damage after the fact, when we learned through the consultants how much manufacturers' new orders continued to grow—at an annual rate of +11 percent. If more detailed market-share information had been sought, tracked, and related to our sales figures on rate-of-change charts, the pricing policy probably would have been different.

Tom, I think we're on the right track now. We know that the lack of innovative product development really hurt us and that this, coupled with a wrong-headed pricing policy for maturing products, placed Chem-A-Lot in jeopardy from large losses in market share, which in turn led to pressures on costs and to reduced profits.

A DEEPER LOOK AT PRICES

Charlie: While our unit selling prices in recent years do seem to have been too high compared to those of our competitors, I'm still not absolutely certain if we should keep prices steady or raise or lower them now to ensure the highest future operating profits. Tom, were you able to review this question?

Tom: Sure. We in marketing have reached some conclusions about what our prices ought to be. We see a sales level of, say, $21 million for this year 26, then a much better year 27 if we take appropriate action on prices.

Charlie: We all know that when a sales manager fiddles with prices, customers call the tune with purchases, so let's look at a summary of your conclusions.

IMPACT OF CHANGING UNIT SALES PRICES ON YEAR 27 SALES
(Summary By Product Line)

Forecasted Sales at Different Unit Price Levels
(Thousands)

	Lower		No Change		Raise	
	Units	Sales	Units	Sales	Units	Sales
Conditioners (−12%,+12%)*	770	$18,300	611	$16,500	490	$14,800
Formulators (−8%,+8%)*	610	9,900	452	8,000	340	6,500
Transporters (−4%,+4%)*	83	2,800	63	2,200	41	1,500
Total Sales	1,463	$31,000	1,126	$26,700	871	$22,800

(These numbers exclude repairs and parts revenues.)

*Average price changes considered.

Tom: Based upon the evidence we have in marketing, we asked what would happen if our prices were raised or lowered for each one of our products within each line. The answers varied a great deal, but overwhelming evidence pointed to a reduction in prices. Sales in year 27 could go as high as $31 million if we take prompt action. During recessions, market shares shift as customers look for ways to become more efficient.

Charlie: So your recommendation is?

Tom: We should drop selling prices for year 27 by 12 percent on average for conditioners, 8 percent for formulators, and 4 percent for transporters as of January first. Individual products within each line will be priced differently. For example, Chem-Kraker, which is still the best machine on the market, should have a price drop of at least 18 percent.

We recommend further that an advertising campaign be mounted, starting with Chem-Kraker and emphasizing that our machines are available at new competitive prices. This will signal to the market that Chem-A-Lot is indeed back.

While this pricing tactic is being accomplished, we can study the various markets for our machines much more closely. Study conclusions can then be incorporated in the written strategy plan desired by the board.

Well, that sounds right, and I believe the directors will be inclined to go for a reasonable reduction in prices under the circumstances. However, before we go ahead, I would like you, Henry, to give us your thoughts about what that plan would do to your costs.

Henry: We have already looked into the effect on costs in some detail. The projected unit volumes were quite different under Tom's three "what if" price levels. And it took Diane and me a bit of time to analyze our costs under those different assumptions.

Charlie, you have told me how total spending was forced down by Dandy when sales dropped in year 16 and how he eventually stopped buying any production equipment for our plant. That drove up unit costs of production. As you know, a number of our key pieces of equipment are close to being obsolete, and they definitely cause many inefficiencies, resulting in higher production costs. I know I haven't responded to your exact question, Charlie, but we need to address this issue soon.

We have a long way to go before we reach full capacity in our plant. I would say unit costs will definitely come down and your gross profits, similarly, will increase if the recommended price reductions are effective in increasing customer demand, even with our old equipment. A larger sales backlog would be a big help in production scheduling. It would allow us to make better use of people, facilities, and inventories. The result would increase our overhead absorption, thereby dropping costs per unit.

Charlie: Okay. We must be very careful in this pricing area. We can't run the business profitably by selling below cost, and we don't want the sales force to go for volume rather than profit. Yet, we know our price structure is out of line.

Our calculation shows a break-even point of $27 million in revenues, assuming a normal sales mix. Let's go with the new prices starting next month. Meanwhile, please look into each cost and expense in your departments with two objectives in mind. First, we are in a recession and need every bit of cost control we can lay our hands on. Second, that will help us gear up for the new planning system we will now start to implement. Thanks for your participation and ideas. Let's close our meeting and begin making Chem-A-Lot a winner once again.

WHAT CHARLIE FACED

When Charlie took over, it was too late in the year to prevent a crash. The economic weather became more and more turbulent in the weeks that followed. Charlie found himself caught in powerful forces not of his own making, and the ship he was piloting was going down. Charlie, however, remained unflappable and used all his wits to minimize the damage to Chem-A-Lot and its crew.

At year end, after the crash, he was able to convince the board of directors that Chem-A-Lot was worth rebuilding. He reminded them that due to past managerial errors, total costs could not have been reduced sufficiently to prevent the $300,000 loss without irreversible damage. Low growth since year 16, together with the historical failure to plow back profits, he argued, had made Chem-A-Lot weak and vulnerable. Because of the work of the consultant team earlier, the board knew Charlie was right.

Charlie had told the board earlier of the price actions taken at the first of the year. Now he went far beyond an explanation of what had happened to prices and sales during his first few weeks as CEO. With a few deft strokes, he painted a picture of what Chem-A-Lot could again become.

Using a rate-of-change chart, he illustrated just how the slight differences in growth that had caused costs to exceed sales had flipped profits into losses for a disastrous year. When Charlie presented this chart to the board, he said, "Now that's what economic wind shear looks like!"

CHEM-A-LOT AND ITS CREW WON A CHANCE TO SURVIVE!

With a level of confidence that inspired the board members, Charlie concluded, "Chem-A-Lot has hit bottom, but Chem-A-Lot will bounce back higher than ever because it has so much going for it!"

The board gave Charlie a unanimous vote of confidence after his presentation. All the directors assured the management team that cash generated would be plowed back into the business as a matter of principle. Dividends to shareholders would come later. At last, Chem-A- Lot would be managed for the long-term, not just for the next quarter's profits. The rebirth would start with the quest for information needed for a detailed strategy, a business plan, and a budget. And Charlie would use the team approach to planning to avoid perishing. Henry would have what was needed in the plant, and Chem-A-Lot would finally acquire a more advanced computer system to produce, on a timely basis, those operational statistics that the staff as well as the directors needed to manage effectively.

With the primary problems pinpointed and the necessary immediate pricing action taken, Chem-A-Lot's staff launched into a series of fact-finding and planning sessions that eventually involved everyone at Chem-A-Lot. These sessions set the pattern for a three-phase planning cycle.

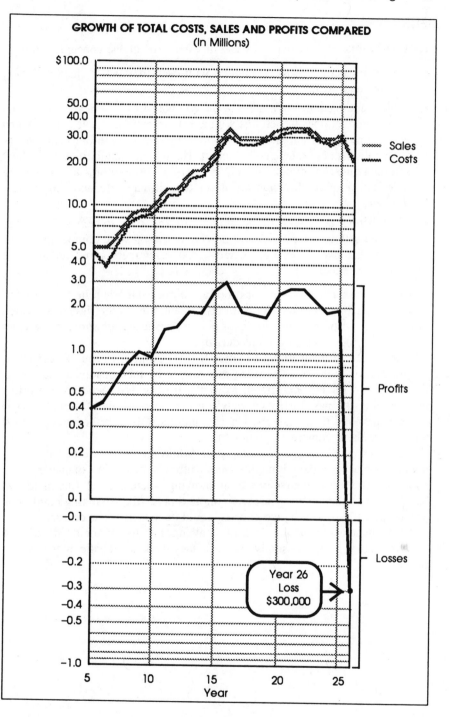

GROWTH OF TOTAL COSTS, SALES AND PROFITS COMPARED
(In Millions)

SUMMARY

As Charlie Fisher took over as CEO of Chem-A-Lot, he concentrated on:

- Establishing a good open dialogue with each member of his developing management team.

- Understanding how total sales were composed of a series of older and newer product lines—each line with a distinct pattern of sales that stacked up, one on top of another, to provide a high or low total growth rate, as shown on his new sales geology chart. He also needed to understand how setting unit sales prices, spending funds on promotion, and allocating redesign or research funds all affect the ultimate life and profits of a product.

- Establishing a better pricing policy. In the past, Chem-A-Lot often changed selling prices without knowing or caring what competitor prices were. That had to change; Chem-A-Lot customers cared about those price differences.

Despite Fisher's efforts, it was too late in the year when he took over to avoid a loss for that year. His inspired presentation to the directors, which gave Chem-A-Lot a chance to again become a successful company, was an early test of the quality of his leadership.

It is indeed difficult to get to point B from point A if you are unsure of the location of point A. The main role played by the consultants at Chem-A-Lot was to force management to revisit history. By spending real effort in analyzing the past interplays between their people, their products, their competitors, and their markets, Charlie and his staff were becoming armed with the tools to construct a better future.

However, just understanding the past, while ignoring current changes in the marketplace, is like relying on a half truth. Chem-A-Lot's managers were about to chart a firm course based on knowing where point A (the historical base) was and then astutely ascertaining and predicting changing conditions around point B so alternative courses could be selected if necessary.

Some businesses hit the wall of challenges thrust at them and do not survive. They perish—usually because they lack a realistic plan for the future.

PART TWO

GATHERING THE FACTS

CHAPTER 8

FROM MARKETING FACTS TO FUNCTIONAL PLANS

The future does not happen all at once—it accumulates routinely. Occasionally the routine is punctuated by exceptions.

Anonymous

MARKETING PLANS MUST LEAD THE WAY IN THE PLANNING CYCLE

A marketing plan necessarily shapes all other plans: manufacturing, personnel, financial, and so on. Regardless of organization structure, all departmental plans should become complementary parts of a three-phase planning cycle that consists of **(1) the strategy plan, (2) the business plan, and (3) the budget.** Underlying analyses should also provide a thorough business health checkup.

The marketing plan should be prepared by a team consisting of both marketing and sales people because, as some wit in sales accurately remarked, sales is the present tense of marketing.

Before other departmental plans can be given final form and blended into the three-phase planning cycle, the marketing plan must be agreed to in its entirety and approved by the highest-ranking marketing executive. Then it must be approved by the CEO who initially establishes the **prime objective** for the business.

OBSTACLES TO IMPLEMENTING A SOUND MARKETING PLAN

A large number of businesses do not prepare formal marketing plans because of the number of obstacles that must be overcome. These obstacles include the following:

- Management remains uncommitted to planning.
- Management has insufficent time to plan because energies are concentrated entirely on putting out today's fires.
- Individual managers dislike detailed planning, especially the associated paperwork, or prefer, for security reasons, to put nothing on paper—often a predilection of owner-entrepreneurs.
- Relevant basic data has not been kept, is not readily available, is in disarray, or data is too voluminous and irrelevant.
- Individual managers lack the ability or desire to derive growth relationships from base data.
- Management has difficulty in forecasting future time periods with reasonable accuracy.
- People in relevant operating and support functions are not involved, which lessens the effectiveness of the plan.
- The plan developed amounts to mere window dressing to impress the board of directors.
- The plan fails to distinguish between separate businesses with very different problems.

WHAT A MARKETING PLAN SHOULD COVER

The marketing plan is a written program for an individual business. No one format or writing style can possibly fit all businesses; however, here's what every marketing plan should cover:

1. **An executive summary including prime objective.** A concise overview of the plan, placed at the beginning of the document, that includes a clear statement of the prime objective for the business as a whole, not just marketing.

   For example, Chem-A-Lot's prime objective was to reestablish Chem-A-Lot as a leading producer of quality conditioner, formulator, and transporter equipment for process industries around the world.

2. **A situation analysis.** A description of both the external and internal environments in which a business operates with quantitative data on past, current, and forecasted trends from which marketing insights can be derived.

   The story of Chem-A-Lot to this point has been essentially a situation analysis. While the depth of understanding illustrated here should be available, only key points are presented in a strategy plan.

3. **Marketing goals.** Proposed goals for marketing, sales, and related support functions such as advertising flow out of the prime objective, and priorities should be established for each goal.

Here are some sample marketing goals:

— Unit and dollar sales expectations for new and old products, by major line, by territory, and by key customer.

— Market-share targets by major product line.

— Sales time allocation by product or line to maximize profits.

— Sales, advertising, and promotional program targets.

— Sales training program targets.

4. **Strategies to reach goals.** Moves designed to reach goals, such as price changes, new market penetrations, or new advertising campaigns.

You may have to consider many alternative business moves before you find the right combination of moves to help you reach the goals on the way toward your prime business objective.

5. **Tactics for people.** A series of tasks assigned to sales engineers, advertising specialists, and others to implement a strategic move.

6. **Contingency plans.** Plans for sales that fall considerably short of or exceed sales forecasts.

In brief, a marketing plan should cover where the business came from, where it is now, where it will go, and how it will get there. Before we can think clearly about prime objectives, goals, strategies, or tactics, we must first take a hard look at the past and the present. That means we must do a situation analysis.

THE MARKETING SITUATION ANALYSIS

A marketing situation analysis starts with the collection of basic information about the markets served. This data can be obtained from internal records and should go back at least 10 years. Minimally, records should include series of data by product on dollar sales, unit sales, and prices. From the relationship among these series, it is possible to derive trend information on each. Unit sales are the critical measure for both market trend and share. As we have seen at Chem-A-Lot, it is quite possible to unknowingly follow a pricing policy that saps a company's strength.

In addition to the basic information, it is helpful if good records have been kept on orders gained and lost. Ideally, records for orders lost list what competitor the order was lost to and why, whether it was because of price, quality, service, or another factor. These records provide information on market shares held by competitors.

Information on distribution, pricing trends, and individual customers is also valuable.

Once the basic information has been assembled in house, it is important to look at the market data from the point of view of growth as well as size. Some company ills can be diagnosed only by using both approaches.

The next stage of a situation analysis is a bit more difficult. The internal data should be broken down so it can be compared to external data series for leading indicators, industries, regions, and product categories.

The combined internal and external data, if analyzed carefully as at Chem-A-Lot, can provide answers to such questions as:

- What are the market boundaries? How are the boundaries changing? What are the customer location patterns? At what rate is the market growing? What favors or hinders growth? What is the projected demand for the total market and major segments?

- How many firms supply the market? What is the distribution of sales among those firms? What are the marketing, production, and financial strengths and weaknesses of each, including your own? What local, national, and international political, economic, and psychological factors help or hurt your industry? Your competitors? Your business? Are you gaining or losing market share in terms of dollars? Units?

- Are new technologies a threat? In what phase are your products and your competitors' products in the product life cycle? How much product differentiation exists now? Do your products have a special market niche? How much effort should you put into the development of new products?

When you have completed your marketing plan, you should have an accurate evaluation of the health of your business, plus an assessment of its strengths and weaknesses relative to competitors.

SOURCES OF INFORMATION OUTSIDE THE BUSINESS

Information is a growth industry; change is rapid. Therefore, no attempt will be made to provide a definitive list of sources. You will find that your public library is an excellent place to start your key fact search. Special departments devoted to the needs of businesses and computer searchable databases have been added to library services in recent years. Database protocol experts can help you obtain information from database suppliers such as Dialog, Datatimes, and OCLC (On-Line Computer Library Center, Inc.) and others that maintain hundreds of databases under such listings as markets, industries, companies, management, price indices, new products, forecasts, financial ratings, inventions, government statistics, business magazine articles, and much, much more. Because there are charges for database searches, it is a good idea to get a clear notion of what you want to know before you initiate a search.

With the advent of the personal computer, many databases can be searched directly from your desk. However, it is not advisable for the novice to do so since on-line connect-time rates can run from just a few dollars per hour to several hundred dollars per hour, depending on the nature of the database searched. Wasted minutes can be costly. In addition, there are on-line and off-line printing charges for hard copy.

Next, let's consider directories and various types of information guides. Sometimes a source of information is as close as your telephone directory. Other times, special directories—such as the *Encyclopedia of Associations*, published by the Gale Research Company in Detroit—are of help. The *Encyclopedia of Associations* provides descriptions of each association's purpose, publications, address, telephone number, and chief officer. Many such directories are now available in both book and database form. Industry trade associations often publish special directories for use by members. Sometimes they may be purchased by nonmembers who need them.

The Manufacturers' Agents National Association (MANA), located in Laguna Hills, California, publishes annually the MANA Members Directory of Manufacturers' Sales Agencies. The Industrial Distributors Association, located in Atlanta, Georgia, also publishes a membership directory. These two resources are particularly useful to new companies that wish to market their products nationwide.

The most important sources of economic data are government agencies. The ease of access and the amount and quality of information available from these agencies vary greatly. Often the data are analyzed and repackaged for resale to meet the special needs of customers of national and international information suppliers. Washington Researchers Ltd. and Information U.S.A. (publishers) are two organizations located in Washington D.C. that provide access to government data as well as to industry specialists.

The National Technical Information Service (NTIS) is the primary source of government research reports, including those foreign reports that have been translated into English. Research reports also include those prepared under contract to U.S. goverment agencies. Many publications, such as the monthly *Survey of Current Business*, published by the U.S. Department of Commerce and obtainable through the U.S. Government Printing Office, keep tabs on the growth of the economy. The U.S. Census of Manufacturers can also provide helpful industry benchmarks for the Standard Industrial Classifications (SICs). As our country moves into an ever more competitive world economy, it would be shortsighted indeed to allow these vast sources of easily accessible information to wither from lack of support.

Your library, advertising agency, or advertising manager can provide publication information on trade journals and related services. One of the best sources is *Business Publication Rates and Data*, for U.S. and international industrial merchandising professionals. Copies can be purchased from Standard Rate & Data Service, Inc. of Wilmette, Illinois.

And don't forget that local chapter members of national organizations such as the American Marketing Association can often be extremely helpful when you are seeking information sources. The American Marketing Association publishes the *Marketing News International Directory of the American Marketing Association and Marketing Services Guide*.

Moody's Industrial Manuals, Standard & Poor's, and Thomas Register are three other sources of financial and product information. The few sources mentioned here hardly scratch the surface of the huge amount of information that is as close as your telephone, your library, and your personal computer.

Finally, you might employ a management consultant for a general problem. Or, if you have a situation that requires a highly skilled specialist in a particular field, you might want to define the situation as you see it and then contract with a market research firm to find the answers. For smaller firms this can be less costly than employing or training the personnel needed for a major study.

ORGANIZATION OF INFORMATION

Until the staff at Chem-A-Lot began to contact outside sources systematically as well as develop inside sources, there had been a dearth of useful management information. But, by mid-year 27, they had begun to be overwhelmed by the bewildering array of responses to their requests for information. This is a common development that can get out of hand. Now the problem became: how to screen, store, and retrieve the information efficiently. The staff soon agreed on some general principles:

- *Internal data should be collected over long time periods to make it easier to discover the key relationships between trends derived from both internal and external sources.*

  Short-term records simply tend to produce shortsighted decisions unless considered against a long-term background. Many otherwise astute business managers do not and will not take the time to collect and analyze data for 10 or more years. They do not see the point in doing so. As a result, these same individuals tend to miss important market trends and shifts. Survival then becomes more difficult. Take the time and make the effort to inform yourself and others about the past. You will benefit from the rather small investment required.

  Longer-term data records also permit one to define business cycles, seasonal patterns, and changes in operations monitored with greater precision.

  One lesson really sank in: Whenever possible, tie unit counts to dollar amounts so price and cost change effects on unit counts can be monitored simultaneously.

- *Facts from both internal and external sources should be screened and openly critiqued for accuracy and usefulness. Then a decision must be made to keep or discard and, if to discard, whether to list the source and describe the content of the material.*

  Some outside sources that the staff at Chem-A-Lot considered were of dubious quality and difficult to assess. Other sources were excellent but, even so, were not easily combed for useful nuggets of information.

- *All information kept should be dated and filed by date so recent information is not mixed with past information.*

  Where current information routinely incorporates past information, valuable future search time is minimized.

- *Easy access that cuts across traditional departmental boundaries should be provided for any piece of information.*

  This seemed particularly important to the Chem-A-Lot staff as they struggled with pervasive problems affecting many of their functions.

HOW TO MAKE BEST USE OF INFORMATION

It is not enough to search, identify, and arrange key facts. That is only a start. The most valuable information can often be derived from examining the relationships between and among sets of data, as we have seen at Chem-A-Lot. Therefore, you will need an information system that makes it easy to track and compare series of data. Changes in your share-of-market-held in a sales territory, for example, can be derived from basic data on the size of the industry niche you elect to serve and competitive supply patterns, detailed by geographic area. Or, in another example, the ratio of advertising leads to orders received over the years can tell you much about the effectiveness of your advertising dollar.

It is important to realize that the pool of information that gradually accumulates on marketing can be useful to other departments in an organization. Keep clearly in mind how the information flows through and serves to interconnect all departmental activities. This flow can actually help promote cooperation if it is made accessible to all who might benefit. Think creatively. The departmental structure arose for the convenience of keeping records and the supervision of numbers of truly unskilled workers before the advent of large numbers of skilled professionals and electronic communication technology.

Here's an outline of essential marketing information, both basic and derived, often needed by skilled professionals in more than the accounting and marketing departments.

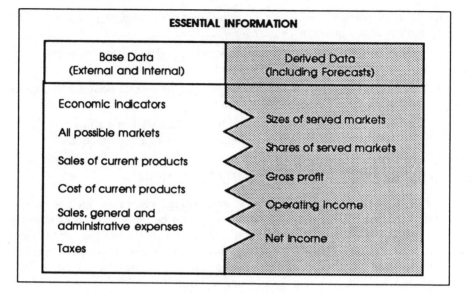

Study your data for interrelationships and seek out retrieval systems that reflect those interrelationships. Today, any piece of information can be indexed under numerous concepts, not just one name on a file folder. Through computer search programs, you can avoid wasting hours searching for the specific pieces of information you need at hand when making a decision.

At times you'll want to keep the data in your data bank—such as those numerical tables, size charts, rate-of-change charts, and percentage charts used by Chem-A-Lot—in parallel forms in one retrievable document for ease of use.

Remember, too, that all those number measurements you have in your data bank can become misleading if you don't adjust them for the internal inflation effect. The use of a general deflator is not good enough because it is a broad average and not specific to your business. You have to keep records of changes in product prices, raw material costs, labor rates, and other major items if you really want to know what's going on. Don't be lulled into neglecting those records because inflation has slowed down.

Costs should be broken down into those that are variable and those that are fixed for periods of time in order to determine contribution margins through break-even analyses.

Accuracy, flexibility, and retrievability are the names of the game for a management information system containing information for all areas of the business.

Now for some marketing illustrations of how base data and derived data were put to use in planning by the staff at Chem-A-Lot and how, at times, information from unexpected sources proves helpful.

CHANNELS OF DISTRIBUTION

Channels of distribution and sales territory structure must be tailored specifically to your business because every business is different. That is why you hear so many arguments over what the best channel of distribution is and what the optimum number of sales territories should be. Often a company can be successful with more than one approach. If you want steady sales growth and loyalty, however, it's best not to constantly threaten to change distribution channels and sales territory boundaries. This causes unrest in the ranks. When changes are made, they should be made on the basis of well-understood performance measurements that are really fair. Fairness is not easily achieved when sales territories contain cities that vary as widely in market potential as those in Illinois and Nevada.

So, rather than rehash all the old arguments, let's examine a cultural approach to sales-territory boundary determination, plus fair performance measurements for whoever covers each territory.

Because of the problems faced by Chem-A-Lot, we'll look in on them and see how they have upgraded their marketing system.

CHEM-A-LOT LOOKS AT SALES TERRITORIES

For many years Tom Puller had been concerned about the best way to cover industrial markets. Should you use a company sales force? Independent distributors? Manufacturer's representatives? He had carefully studied the literature published by associations and talked with many sales managers.

Too often Tom had seen companies switch from one approach to another, not because one was better than the other but really because of the unrecognized failure to nurture an enduring mutual trust between the company and the people within the selected channel. He firmly believed that violation of commitments in order to reap short-term benefits for the company could only lead to distrust and declining sales. Fortunately, he and Charlie agreed. Tom, therefore, saw no reason to switch from the direct sales force that had been covering the 25 states with the largest markets since Jim Dandy's time. Remaining states continued to be covered by sales representatives; Canada and other world markets, by independent distributors.

Early in year 27 Tom caught Charlie in the hallway and told him that he had developed some interesting information he thought Charlie should see. It concerned the method being developed to determine how well Chem-A-Lot's markets were being covered. Recently, Tom and Charlie had had a number of discussions about just how to do this without excessive cost. They had finally agreed upon an initial approach, so Charlie was delighted to hear that Tom was ready to talk. Charlie replied that he had time available the next morning.

Tom (next morning): Hi, Charlie. We have just completed our first run-through, comparing sales for nine North American regions during years 22 through 26, to see just how each region was being affected as we headed for the disaster last year.

Charlie: Why did you choose to start with year 22?

Tom: Remember the chart that Tuffitout didn't want the board to see because things were going sour? Well, I dug that old chart out of my files when I started this project. Here it is. It just seemed important to me to find out what happened to sales in various areas as things began to unravel and particularly to find out where we wound up at the end of year 26.

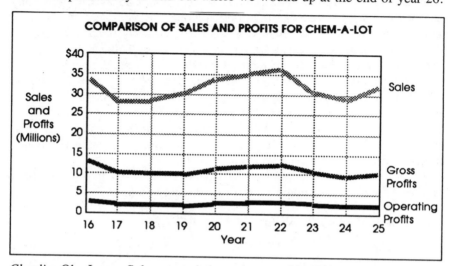

Charlie: Oh, I see. Sales started down in year 22. That's reasonable, but why nine North American regions? We have always had just six.

Tom (with a twinkle in his eyes): Well, that's a story in itself. Guess I'd better explain. Last Christmas my son gave me a book he thought I just might be interested in. Well, it turned out, I was. It hit a responsive cord since, as you know, I've been trying to figure out how sales boundaries ought to be determined. The name of the book is *The Nine Nations of North America*, by Joel Garreau, a newspaper editor.[1]

Charlie: I've heard of it—a friend recently recommended it.

Tom: Garreau starts out by saying that when you think about North America, you should forget about the traditional map. He says that new realities of power and people are reshaping the continent into nine nations— each of which is developing a unique culture.

Charlie: So what differentiates these nine regions?

Tom: Charlie, during my years as a salesman, I noticed that there were some subtle, and not so subtle, differences in how we sold products in different parts of the country. There were, of course, some obvious differences, such as the mix of our products sold into each territory. You'll want to read the book, Charlie, to really get the flavor of Garreau's conclusions and the reasons for them.

At any rate, I thought this book might contain the germ of a useful idea for how we should cover geographic areas. I started with a map of

[1] Joel Garreau, *The Nine Nations of North America* (Boston: Houghton Mifflin, 1981).

North America showing proposed Chem-A-Lot sales regions based on Garreau's general divisions as well as the names he uses. Those names on this map, I think, will give you the quickest sense of the cultural differences involved. Here's a copy.

The Empty Quarter

Ecotopia

Quebec

New England

The Breadbasket

The Foundry

Dixie

MexAmerica

The Islands

Adapted from *Nine Nations of North America* by Joel Garreau. Copyright ©1981 by Joel Garreau. Reprinted by permission of Houghton Mifflin Company.

Charlie: Interesting. Yes, I can get a sense of what the author of your book was driving at. Okay, take it from there.

Tom: The first thing we did was break out our sales records for years 22 through 26 for these nine regions. This involved a lot of conversation with our sales people to determine the states and counties that belonged in each region. The same was true for the provinces of Canada. We'll probably have to change those boundaries many times before we are completely satisfied with them.

After we settled on region boundaries, we converted the usual arithmetic dollar sales comparison by region to a rate-of-change comparison as well. Here are the two, side by side on the same chart.

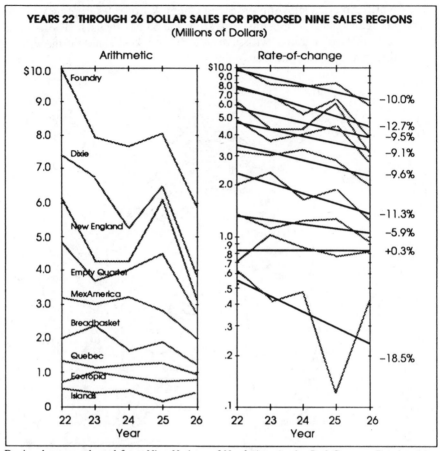

YEARS 22 THROUGH 26 DOLLAR SALES FOR PROPOSED NINE SALES REGIONS
(Millions of Dollars)

Regional names adapted from *Nine Nations of North America* by Joel Garreau. Reprinted by permission of Houghton Mifflin Company.

Since our sales normally fluctuate so much from year to year, we wanted to compare the improvement or decline in performance of regions through trend averages, rather than actual end-point sales figures for years 22 and 26. For example, in the case of the Foundry region, if you use the actual $10 million in sales for year 22 and $5.9 million estimated for year 26, you would get an annual average rate of −12.4 percent rather than the trend of −10.0 percent.[2]

---

[2] Formula for calculating rate of growth or decline over several years where N equals the final year minus the start year: $\text{Rate} = \sqrt[N]{\dfrac{\text{Final}}{\text{Start}}} - 1$

Calculation using actual sales for years 22 and 26: $\text{Rate} = \sqrt[4]{\dfrac{5.9}{10.0}} - 1 = -12.4\%$

Calculation using trend end points for years 22 and 26: $\text{Rate} = \sqrt[4]{\dfrac{6.3}{9.6}} - 1 = -10.0\%$

In the future, Charlie, when those minus percentages on the chart turn to pluses, we can use them, together with share-of-market information, as a basis for giving out fairer incentive awards for sales performance — fairer than those we have given out in the past, which were merely based on sales dollar size.

Charlie, the rate-of-change comparison between regions on the right clearly shows that the annual average percentage decline for the trend in sales hit the larger sales regions to about the same degree. You can't really tell that from the normal arithmetic comparison on the left.

You can also see from the rate-of-change chart that the gain or loss of a few machine sales has a much more drastic effect on regions with smaller total sales. That fact is completely obscured by the arithmetic comparisons, which emphasize size relationships rather than growth relationships.

Charlie: True, but it does take both to get a realistic perspective! The left-hand comparisons give me a clear picture of the relative size of sales for each region for those years.

On the other hand, as you say, the slopes of the rate trends certainly do tell you at a glance which regions were declining most rapidly during this period. And those annual average trend rate figures in the margin do pinpoint the rate differences, as you no doubt intended.

I see that only Ecotopia managed to achieve an annual average trend growth during this period, and then just three tenths of a percent. Since Ecotopia, according to this chart, was the second to the smallest region in terms of total sales, I assume that the sale of just a couple of our large machines made the difference between a negative and positive growth rate in this instance.

It does appear that most of the larger sales regions were hit about equally hard by our bad marketing practices in those years. So, Tom, it looks like we've got an across-the-board rebuilding problem.

Tom: Yes, that's true, but I would like to know more. This chart doesn't tell us what the product mix was for each region, how well each region was being covered relative to the other regions, just what the size of the market was in each region, or, for that matter, just what our market share was versus our competitors' at the end of year 26. These are things we should get a better handle on for our turnaround planning!

Charlie: Absolutely! When we discussed these needs before, you were going to see if we could purchase, or have custom designed, a market potential index for our markets—if it wasn't too costly, that is. What's the status on this now?

Tom: Before we ordered an index I felt we ought to look into several ways of determining market share and discuss them.

Charlie: Not now. Let's cover that subject at the next staff meeting.

GROWTH MEASUREMENT CHARTS TESTED IN A VARIETY OF BUSINESSES

Growth measurement charts can be customized for a variety of businesses. Here's just one example that is far removed from Chem-A-Lot's situation. This is the case of a company that mass-produced a number of components for industry in the under-$100 price range. The time depicted was during a long period of U.S. economic growth without a recession. These components were supplied to the market through independent regional distributors with which the company had developed excellent rapport over the years. Here's a facsimile of a chart showing end customer sales, sales target set by the supplier, and the cost of the components sold one such independent distributor:[3]

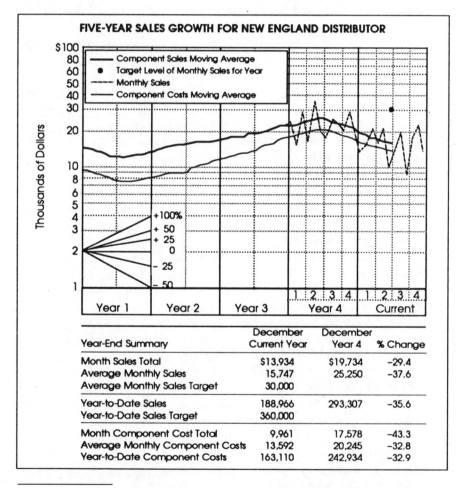

Year-End Summary	December Current Year	December Year 4	% Change
Month Sales Total	$13,934	$19,734	−29.4
Average Monthly Sales	15,747	25,250	−37.6
Average Monthly Sales Target	30,000		
Year-to-Date Sales	188,966	293,307	−35.6
Year-to-Date Sales Target	360,000		
Month Component Cost Total	9,961	17,578	−43.3
Average Monthly Component Costs	13,592	20,245	−32.8
Year-to-Date Component Costs	163,110	242,934	−32.9

[3]This facsimile chart was the first of a series combining a rolling numerical table, a logarithmic chart, and a logarithmic fan developed and tested nationwide over a period of years by Karsten Hellebust. Later, similar charts were employed in international studies.

Instead of trend lines, 12-month moving averages (the heavy black line at top) that eliminated seasonal and irregular effects were used to show the sales volume of each distributor for these components. This made it possible to compare the sales growths shown on charts for all distributors directly even though some distributors in regions of low market potential had much more pronounced month-to-month sales fluctuations. Costs to the distributors (the lighter bottom line) were the revenues actually received by the manufacturer.

The slopes on the logarithmic fan provided a quick approximate growth rate reference.[4] For example, using the fan, sales in years 2 and 3 grew at $+30\%$ estimated annual rate. For the same period, the average monthly costs to the distributor of the components grew at the much higher rate of about $+50\%$ annually.

For the last two years of the business plan period, monthly sales figures were also shown. Note that the 12-month moving averages are centered within each 12-month period to show the proper relationship of the moving average to the 12 months averaged.

If you would like to show seasonal swings around the 12-month moving average for your business rather than monthly data, you can do so by calculating a 3-month moving average. Plotted correctly, the exact quarter averages would be centered between the vertical dotted quarter lines of the chart. Both 12- and 3-month moving averages are calculated in the same manner. Here's a 3-month moving average calculation:

Month	Sales	Formula	Moving Average*	Calculation
A	$14,000	$\dfrac{A+B+C}{3}$	Month B =	$\dfrac{\$40,100}{3} = \$13,367$
B	12,500	$\dfrac{B+C+D}{3}$	Month C =	$\dfrac{\$40,400}{3} = \$13,467$
C	13,600			
D	14,300	$\dfrac{C+D+E}{3}$	Month D =	$\dfrac{\$43,600}{3} = \$14,533$
E	15,700			

*For the proper centering of moving averages with an even number of months, see a good statistics text.

The black dot centered in the current year represents the average monthly target level of sales set by the component supplier, which was not reached by that particular distributor. Why? The distributor's margin was shrinking over the years as the components faced stiffer and stiffer competition. On

---

[4]Later, a logarithmic rate-of-change protractor was created to measure discernible trends with greater precision. This was followed by regression analysis and growth rate calculations on computers, which made the comparison logarithmic fans illustrated in this book simple to create.

this rate-of-change chart, the decline was signaled by the convergence of the sales and costs moving averages. In fact, the distance between the two lines was halved between year 1 and the then-current year. A check by the manufacturer revealed that the distributor had begun to shift his efforts to other products from which he could make more money. In setting distributor sales targets for the year based on its forecasting procedure, the supplier had not taken into consideration the special competitive situation faced by this particular distributor. The solution to the problem was found by working with the distributor to find ways to meet the competition and still provide a fair margin to the distributor.

Depending on the situation, there are other useful ways of presenting this type of data. One popular method is to weight recent monthly data more heavily than earlier data in preparing a moving average. The moving average alone is then plotted. This method makes the moving average respond more quickly to a change.

HOW TO DETERMINE MARKET SHARES

At the next staff meeting, Tom Puller discussed the new proposed sales regions, together with the data he had prepared. After that, he launched into a discussion of how to determine market shares.

Tom: We're now going to discuss actual size and share-of-market determination. I have found that this is usually the most difficult and costly information to obtain. Competitors just won't tell you what their sales are.

Henry: How about government census of manufacturing statistics?

Tom: Government census statistics and interim updates, Henry, are very useful because they provide total figures for many products, often broken down geographically in great detail. However, the government does not print product totals for any area if doing so would reveal actual sales of a single competitor in the market.

Henry, you've identified the basic source for measurements of the total size of markets in this country. In addition to the government, however, there are numerous suppliers of marketing information who take government data and, by various means, make it more useful for their clients. Unfortunately, sales totals for our specific products are not available. For that reason, our supplier had to devise a tailor-made index from Standard Industrial Classification data and input from us.

Diane: But even if the supplier had been able to provide total sales for our machines, you would only have been able to calculate Chem-A-Lot's share. The remainder would consist of unknown shares split among the competitors active in a region. Correct?

Tom: Yes, that is correct, Diane.

Diane: Are you telling us, then, that there is no way for us to arrive legitimately at the market share of our competitors, Tom? I constantly hear market shares being discussed.

Tom: Not at all. It's just more difficult. Let me describe three possible ways that it can be done—a couple of ways that we can do it ourselves, one of which involves the cooperation of other manufacturers, and a third—most likely more accurate but also more costly—through market research.

First, I'll describe a method for getting ballpark share estimates that we're currently trying. I decided I would like to know more about the Empty Quarter, where we now seem to be doing quite well; and about another area—Los Angeles, which is part of the so-called MexAmerica region, where we are not doing as well. The quickest way of finding an answer we could come up with was to ask our experienced sales engineers in each region to estimate market shares. Here are the results:

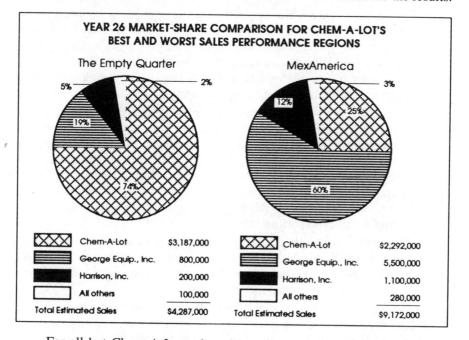

For all but Chem-A-Lot sales, these are rough estimates, but they do tell us that in the western part of the United States George Equipment, Inc. is a major competitor.

These share figures would probably be much more reliable if we had kept accurate sales-lost records through the years to compare with sales gained. We could have done this rather easily in our industry because we sell large ticket items. It might be difficult to do so in others.

Diane: Your first suggestion sounds reasonable and would be a fairly low-cost approach, Tom. What about your second approach?

Tom: Many industries have a trade association collect and publish industry sales on a confidential basis. Through the association, each data contributor can obtain market size and its own share as well as trends without having direct access to the others' sales figures. This can work well if there are a number of competitors.

By comparing your own sales with the trade association totals, you can determine whether your share is increasing or decreasing through the years. However, this method still forces you to guess how the remainder of the market is split up among your competitors. Besides, the data are often inaccurate or incomplete, because some association members fail to submit figures or refuse to cooperate with other manufacturers in the industry.

Diane: Doesn't that approach provide just about the same type of information that you might obtain through a tailored market-potential index that you can purchase?

Tom: Yes, it does, except for one thing. It's a continuing cooperative arrangement whereas the other tends to be a one-shot effort because of cost. In a very few years, our market-potential index would become out-of-date and would give misleading results if it were used to update the kind of charts we have been discussing. In the developing world economy, industries are shifting geographically faster than ever.

Now, let's go on to the last method. By using the detailed information, broken down to the county level, that we have already developed for ranking sales regions, we could select sample areas and have a detailed market-share study conducted for each. This would avoid the cost of doing a study covering all of North America. If we made the selections carefully and contracted the survey work out to a good market-survey house, we could get the information for much less than the cost of putting a survey expert on staff.

The art of constructing questions and asking those questions in such a way as to elicit unbiased responses is not an easy one to learn, so I just don't believe it would be cost effective for an organization of our size to develop this capability in-house.

I might mention that once in a while, if you are lucky, you can purchase industry studies conducted by experts from information houses, parts of which are directly applicable to your problem. Your luck will, of course, improve if you maintain a file on those houses that produce such studies. In this connection, I have found our city library can often prove helpful.

Charlie: When we do need a study, I believe that we should contract with experts who understand the culture of the region in which they are to do the work. You can read in trade journals, for example, about all kinds of major marketing mistakes American businesses have made in Japan and other nations because they simply didn't understand the culture. Even in North America, it now seems we're also dealing with cultural differences that we have not recognized in the past.

WHAT MORE THAN MARKET SHARE SHOULD YOU KNOW ABOUT COMPETITORS?

During the last month of year 26 the Chem-A-Lot staff had its attention riveted on determining what had gone wrong internally and how to fix it. Toward the end of the first half of year 27, after they had gotten a rough fix on the market shares of competitors, they began to seek answers to additional questions. Here are just a few of them:

- How do competitors define their businesses in terms of customer groups? Functions? Technologies?
- How are they segmenting the market? Which segments are they pursuing?
- How are the competitors performing in terms of current sales? Growth? Pricing? Service? Profitability?
- In the following areas, what are each competitor's strengths and weaknesses?

Product uniqueness	Product quality
Promotion efforts	Distribution channels
Marketing	Selling capabilities
Operations	Warehousing
Management	Human resources
Purchasing practices	Costs
Ownership	Financial condition
Selling prices	

- How quickly and appropriately do competitors respond to changes in the environment and marketplace?
- How are they likely to respond to specific competitive moves that Chem-A-Lot or other competitors make?
- Where are they most vulnerable? Strongest?

Pricing decisions are not easy and certainly not simple to make. In order to establish realistic prices over a series of years, you should target certain market niches, levels of market share in each niche, and types of customers. Success will probably not come to businesses that try to be everything to everybody. Instead, analyze your business culture, your product costs, and the available markets. Decide how to position or reposition your business and its products, as perceived by customers, in the following areas:

- Are you or do you want to be a price leader, a price follower, or the low pricer?
- Are you the low-cost producer, given equal quality ratings? Should you be?
- Are your products of high quality, average quality, or lesser quality in the market niches you target?

Your response to these questions must be realistic. No competitor will willingly and knowingly give you a customer. Price-cutting can destroy market profitability. Selling value is a tough marketing chore that takes long-term and consistent effort. Do not try to sell what customers do not really want—at any price.

At Chem-A-Lot, profiles backed by dossiers of collected facts were soon compiled on each competitor. One such profile, started on George Equipment, Inc., looked like this:

COMPETITIVE PROFILE OF: George Equipment, Inc.

Background: An independent company that was founded in 1965 in Los Angeles. None of the founders currently works for the company. Professional managers were first employed in 1979. Sales efforts have been concentrated on the West Coast of the United States and in Mexico. In recent years, it has moved into markets east of the Rocky Mountains. It appears to have competent as well as innovative engineering and management staffs. Growth appears to have been steady. According to Dun & Bradstreet and 10K reports, it has no financial problems at this time. Employs 25 people.

Competitive Products	Company Sales	U.S. Market Share	Manufacturing Facilities	Distribution Strengths	Perceived Strategy
Pelleter	$3,300,000	45%	Newly	Warehouses	High quality,
Sifter	900,000	35%	expanded	in Mexico	excellent
Washer	800,000	N.A.	plant in Los	and Denver.	engineering,
Cooler	400,000	N.A.	Angeles with	Use only sales	and good
Other	100,000	N.A.	30,000 sq. ft.	agents, no	service.
				direct sales	Prices are
				force.	competitive.
					Now appear to
					be acquiring
					complementary
					products and
					courting our
					customers
					with a broad
					line.

Total	$5,500,000

Note: All sales figures are based on the estimates of sales engineers by region and then totaled for the United States. We do not yet have worldwide estimates. Confidence level for accuracy of data is high.

HEED THE WARNING SIGNS OF A MARKET KEY-FACT SEARCH GONE AWRY

There are strong temptations to present "guesstimates" without any hard supporting data just because a form calls for them. Guesstimates, such as those made in the George Equipment, Inc. profile by Chem-A-Lot sales engineers, are okay as long as they are recognized as such and are replaced or supplemented with hard facts when those become available.

When preparing a form, it is easy to identify a lot of wonderful things that it would be nice to know but very costly to obtain. Some beautifully designed forms simply invite fantasy responses. Pity those who make decisions based on those responses.

After eavesdropping on snatches of discussions at Chem-A-Lot, you may react by overdoing either the planning steps or the action. A careful balance of both—appropriate to the particular business—is required. It is, therefore, important to stress that you will never be able to get all the information you might want. Information gathering can be overdone and, paradoxically, can never be finished. Risk can never be eliminated because business situations constantly change.

HOW TO USE A BROAD MARKET INDEX TO DETERMINE MARKET SHARES

So far, based upon internal records and "guesstimates" we have learned how to present, track, and compare three general market measurements:

1. The size of sales volumes over the years.

2. The rate of growth, or decline, in sales.

3. The market shares held by competitors.

Let's sit in as Tom discusses a fourth measure with the staff: how to use a market index purchased from an information supplier to determine market shares.

Tom: As you know, we recently ordered a market potential index from a marketing information supplier. Since I wanted to look at North America as a whole, not just the United States, I had previously asked Diane to break out Chem-A-Lot sales for all of North America. I also asked the supplier to break out comparable data for the other countries of North America. Fortunately, he was able to provide rough estimates for most of the other countries. The figures for Canada, for example, are felt to be quite accurate.

Charlie: Are the figures for the other countries good enough to be useful?

Tom: Not yet, but sales to countries outside of North America for the last few years have been very low, so for this go-around, we're looking at the United States and Canada only. We hope to add Mexico soon.

This purchased index uses a formula based on Standard Industrial Classifications for the industries we sell to. In the United States, combined industry indices at the county level were prepared so that county indices could be aggregated to match the nine sales regions we have been considering. This index then told us what percentage of total U.S. sales for all competitors should be obtained by industry from each region. From our prior share-of-market work, and with help from our supplier, we finally estimated that our U.S. share had fallen to about 25 percent of the total market.

Next, using the index, the total estimated U.S. market was broken down into the nine regions. Rather than compare our actual sales for year 26 with these estimates, we compared them to the year 26 trend figure for each region. These figures are more representative of the average direction sales were going in for the entire period from year 22 through 26.

Henry: Tom, before you go on, please explain to me just why you didn't use an ordinary average for several years or the actual year 26 sales figures for the regions.

Tom: Our average order is fairly large, so a few orders cause our sales to fluctuate rather sharply and differently for each region from year to year. The calculated trend figure, on the other hand, takes into account long-term increases or decreases—an ordinary average would understate sales if they were increasing and overstate sales if they were decreasing. The sales trend figure, therefore, simply provides a better measure to use. Does that make it clearer? *(Henry nods.)*

Here, then, is a table that summarizes our market share by region, based on our sales trends, the index, and the best estimate of the total market in the United States at this time.

CHEM-A-LOT NINE-REGION SHARE-OF-MARKET COMPARISON FOR YEAR 26
(Dollars in Thousands)

Region	Total Market	Chem-A-Lot Share	%	Competitors Share	%
The Breadbasket	$ 2,820	$ 1,407	50	$ 1,413	50
Dixie	22,052	4,399	20	17,653	80
Ecotopia	1,412	829	59	583	41
The Empty Quarter	6,008	3,187	53	2,821	47
The Foundry	29,716	6,329	21	23,387	79
The Islands	528	239	45	289	55
MexAmerica	14,200	2,292	16	11,908	84
New England	14,576	3,788	26	10,788	74
Quebec	2,728	1,040	38	1,688	62
Total or Avg. %	$94,040	$23,510	25%	$70,530	75%

Regional names adapted from *Nine Nations of North America* by Joel Garreau. Copyright ©1981 by Joel Garreau. Reprinted by permission of Houghton Mifflin Company.

Henry: Look at those market-share percentages; they're all over the place! Our highest, 59 percent, in Ecotopia, and our lowest, 16 percent, in MexAmerica, are both on the West Coast.

Tom: Henry, Ecotopia is one of the smaller regional markets, and we have a very good manufacturer's representative in Seattle who handles a lot of equipment compatible with ours. Also, in a smaller market, a few machine orders can make a big difference in percentage share for us. On the other hand, MexAmerica includes California and only indirectly some business south of the border. Los Angeles obviously is a very large market in which we have not done well.

Diane: Tom, from the table it appears to me that we cannot obtain market shares for each of our competitors by this method either. Correct?

Tom: Right, but I have been doing some thinking about your question. As time goes on, we could get a handle on this by arriving at better estimates of total U.S. sales for each of our competitors through our own gained- and lost-order records and through market research in sample areas. Then we could use the index to break out the estimate of each competitor's total U.S. share—at region, state, and county levels, just as for Chem-A-Lot.

But, Diane, right now I'm much more interested in using the index to target areas where we are weak than in finding out the market shares of each competitor. Remember, at best what we have is a statistical probability table like an insurance mortality table.

Our summary table does not take into account our January price change. It uses a best estimate of the total market, rather than an actual figure, and it uses an industry formula that may or may not be entirely correct. In addition, because of rapidly shifting markets worldwide, the database from which the index is prepared is constantly undergoing revision. Therefore, we will most likely have to have our index updated every few years. With all these drawbacks, it is still an excellent tool for strategic planning.

Our supplier also provided mailing lists of potential customers with addresses broken out by Standard Industrial Classification. These can be used to target prospects in market niches of choice through direct-mail programs, local seminars put on by sales engineers, and other promotions.

Charlie: Tom, you mentioned to me some other plans you had for using the index to measure advertising performance as well as sales performance. We can go into that later.

This index approach has been used by manufacturers of large, expensive process machines with erratic sales as well as by manufacturers of small components priced under $100. Because lower-priced products tend to be sold in larger quantities, the index approach works even better for companies that sell them.

Next, we are going to look at the index from a slightly different point of view. Instead of focusing on the competitive shares within each region, we're going to observe the differences in the performance of the Chem-A-Lot regional sales forces. To do this, we have proportioned Chem-A-Lot sales of $23.5 million according to the index market potential for each region.

CHEM-A-LOT NINE-REGION SHARE-OF-MARKET COMPARISON FOR YEAR 26
(Dollars in Thousands)

| | *Index* | *Performance* | | |
Region	*Proportion*	*Sales*	*Above*	*Below*
The Breadbasket	$ 705	$ 1,407	$ 702	$
Dixie	5,513	4,399		(1,114)
Ecotopia	353	829	476	
The Empty Quarter	1,502	3,187	1,685	
The Foundry	7,429	6,329		(1,100)
The Islands	132	239	107	
MexAmerica	3,550	2,292		(1,258)
New England	3,644	3,788	144	
Quebec	682	1,040	358	
Total	$23,510	$23,510	$3,472	($ 3,472)

Regional names adapted from *Nine Nations of North America* by Joel Garreau. Copyright ©1981 by Joel Garreau. Reprinted by permission of Houghton Mifflin Company.

From this table, you can see that the sales force did a better job in some regions—like The Empty Quarter, which has a lot of mineral resources—than in others. Notice also that total sales for MexAmerica were about $1.3 million below the average for a region. Performance in this region was the worst, although Dixie and The Foundry were a close second and third.

While it is not too likely, just suppose that coverage of the territories had been uniform, so that the index proportions in figure column one above exactly matched Chem-A-Lot's sales in column two.

In Case 1 we have plotted these matched figures on a comparison chart. Rate-of-change scales are used on both the vertical and horizontal axes so we can compare very large and very small sales regions simultaneously.

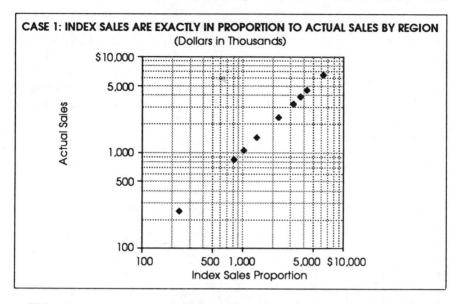

This chart assumes one extreme—a perfect positive correlation between index sales and assumed Chem-A-Lot sales. The plot points, when joined, form a straight line. All region plot points that fall on this line will have equal market shares. In this case, all the Chem-A-Lot regions were assumed to have an equal 25 percent market share.

Now let's go to the not-too-likely other extreme. In Case 2, we suppose that Chem-A-Lot sales by region had not been correlated at all, so that the co-efficient of correlation approaches zero. The chart would now look like this:

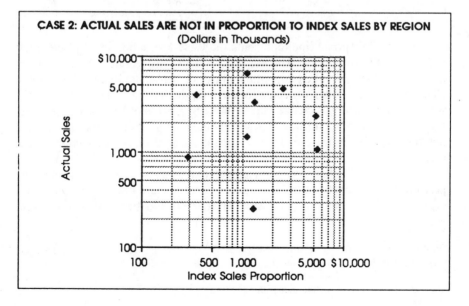

In the real world, sales performance nearly always falls between these two extremes. So let's return to the real world of Chem-A-Lot: the actual situation as it was at the end of year 26.

We simply take the nine-region end-point sales figures for year 26 on Tom's trend lines and relate them to the vertical scale. Then, by plotting the points, we compare them to the index sales on the horizontal rate-of-change scale.

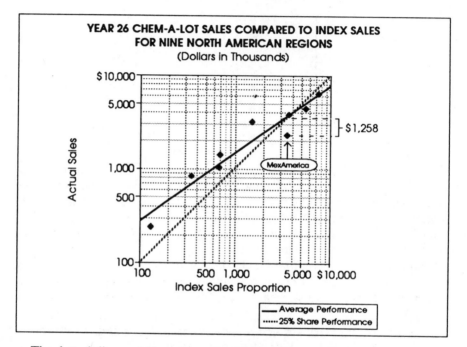

The dotted diagonal line represents the Case 1 situation and has been left on this chart for reference. The vertical distances of the sales plot point from this dotted diagonal tell us how much above or below the index sales amount Chem-A-Lot's sales performance for each region has been. For example, the worst performance was chalked up in the U.S. portion of MexAmerica. Sales there were about $1.3 million below what they could have been if all regional market shares were the same. Los Angeles is considered the center of this region.

The solid black line has been calculated to show how far the average performance differs from the average 25 percent share line.[5] It now becomes clear that all the regions with smaller markets did better than the larger

---

[5]In the following equations, Y_s is the dependent variable for sales, and X_p is the independent variable for index sales. The regression equation for the black line is

$\quad$ Log $Y_s = 1.0079112564 + 0.717788415(Log X_p)$

The regression equation for the dotted line is

$\quad$ Log $Y_s = Log X_p$

regions because this line is above the dotted line at the lower end and below it at the upper end.

With that explanation, we'll return again to Chem-A-Lot as Tom and the staff discuss this last chart:

Diane: This chart tells us that we have to do a better selling job in the regions with greater market potential. In the smaller regions, perhaps sales engineers have to work harder to make a living. Maybe we also need more salespeople, more advertising leads, and better promotion materials in the larger regions.

Another interesting thing: The three regions with the worst performance are the Foundry, Dixie, and MexAmerica according to the table shown earlier. On this chart, these three are represented by the three plot points below the dotted line. Correct? *(Tom nods.)* The odd thing is that the below-average performance of each is just a little over $1 million, yet the vertical distance of the MexAmerica plot point is the farthest from the dotted line.

Tom: Diane, you have just pointed out another advantage of this dual rate-of-change chart. Let me jot down the pertinent figures on the board here.

	Index Sales	Amount Below Index	Percent Below Index
Foundry	$7,429,000	$1,100,000	15%
Dixie	5,513,000	1,114,000	20%
MexAmerica	3,550,000	1,258,000	35%

Now, if all three of the below-average percentages had been 35 percent, all the vertical distances of the plot points from the dotted line would have been identical, even though widely different dollar amounts would be involved. As it is, the smaller the percentage, the closer the plot point is to the dotted line. What this demonstrates is that dual rate-of-change charts keep all growth relationships in proportion. You can tell how each region is performing, regardless of size, at a glance.

Henry: I suppose the low performance in the larger regions could also mean that our competition concentrates marketing efforts in the larger centers and we had better learn more about them.

Roland (an admired older sales engineer who was asked by Tom to participate in the discussion): Yes, Henry, you probably are right. Our three largest competitors are located in Atlanta, Milwaukee, and Los Angeles. As a matter of fact, I have noticed that most competitors do much better around their home-office area.

Henry: It seems to me from what I've seen since coming here that Chem-A-Lot has treated the heavily industrialized West Coast, except for the northern part, almost as an orphan. Maybe we need to put a warehouse for parts in Los Angeles and pay more attention to the new factories being built along the border on the Mexican side.

Tom: Good idea. And the beauty of this chart is that if we devise a strategy that takes appropriate corrective action soon in regions like MexAmerica, the black line will measure our effectiveness by swinging closer to the dotted line next year.

At a glance, this chart sums up dollar sales, average share of total market, and comparative regional performance; in succeeding years, it will tell you whether overall performance is improving or declining.

Diane: Tom, wouldn't this approach also be the way to measure sales performance if we decide to continue to use local distributors rather than a direct sales force in other countries around the world?

Tom: It sure would, Diane, to the extent we can get adequate indices for each country. For now, all I can say is that I feel we'd be better off if we employed native sales engineers who understand their own cultures and have established business contacts.

Charlie: Tom, you said this method could be used to measure other functions like advertising.

Tom: Yes, all we would have to do would be to keep careful records of all leads, including ad inquiries from magazines that have been carefully classified as to likelihood of being converted to sales. The percentage of total leads for each region could then be compared to the index percentage in the same way that we did for sales. We would then know which regions were getting above- or below-average numbers of leads. With the lead drought regions defined, we could ask our advertising agency to rework the ad schedule. That way we'd be more certain of an even distribution of leads among regions.

Sales engineers have one very real objection to doing all this that must be considered and overcome. Often, sales forces have found that the leads are of such poor quality that it wastes the sales engineer's time to follow them up directly. Usually this objection is loudest when the lead qualifying procedure has broken down. Fortunately, I believe our system works well. Lead quality is much more important than quantity.

Also, Charlie, we are starting to keep better track of the rate at which qualified leads are converted to orders. Now, if the rate declines over a period of time, we will be able to spot it, find out the reason why, and make corrections.

THE CUSTOMER PASSES JUDGMENT ON YOU AND YOUR COMPETITORS

In the end, it is the customer who passes judgment on your business. Will it be thumbs up or thumbs down? That is the question. To survive, a business must learn the responses needed to pass the customer's who, what, how, where, when, and why questions.

Who	• buys our product? Why?
	• buys our competitor's product? Why?
What	• benefits does the customer expect?
	• does the customer do with the product?
	• factors or people influence a purchase?
	• function does the product actually perform?
	• are the purchase criteria?
	• are the services expected?
	• distribution channels does the customer prefer?
	• is the long-term obligation to the customer?
How	• can we best serve the customer?
	• does the customer buy?
	• long is the buying process?
	• much is the customer willing to spend?
	• well will the product perform in the customer's application?
	• sophisticated is the product user?
Where	• is the purchasing decision made?
	• does the customer get information about products?
	• will the product finally be used?
When	• does the customer become aware of a need?
	• are replacement products usually purchased?
	• are services most urgent?
	• would it be best not to sell the customer a product?
Why	• does the customer need this product in the first place?
	• does the customer choose one brand over another?
	• wouldn't some other type of product be better?

When you have found the answers and can respond positively to these questions and more—and when you have discovered the patterns among numerous responses—you just may have a chance to become a growth company like Chem-A-Lot was in its early days and has a chance of becoming again.

You can discover many of the answers through good internal information systems. Occasionally, it might prove useful to employ a research house.

In the end this will all be an exercise in futility unless the knowledge gained by these methods is used to find consumer needs that your company can serve better than your competitors can.

If you can't meet a consumer's needs in a particular area, the best thing to do is to recommend someone who can, even a competitor. The consumer will remember your honesty the next time he or she requires your type of products or services. Your action now may well determine whether the consumer becomes a future customer of yours. The consumer passes economic—and yes, even moral—judgment on you and your company. Indeed, that other invisible hand, cooperation, will work for you!

With a situation analysis in hand that is as complete as possible, it's time to tackle the forecasting problem.

FORECASTING METHODS

One authority, C. L. Jain of St. John's University, says that while there is no agreement among professional forecasters concerning the classification of various forecasting methods, he has developed the following one for convenience:

FORECASTING MODELS[6]

Quantitative Models	Qualitative Models
A. Naive Models	A. PERT-derived approach
• Average absolute change	B. Judgement from the extreme
• Average percentage change	C. Delphi
• Weighted average absolute change	D. Bayesian analysis
• Moving average absolute change	E. Survey
• Moving average percentage change	F. Cross impact matrices
• Exponential smoothing	
• Trend analysis	
• Curve fitting	
B. Time Series Models	
• Decomposition	
• Box-Jenkins	
C. Causal Models	
• Regression	
• Econometrics	
• Input-output	
• Simulation	
D. Learned Behavior Models	
• Markov chains	
• Product life cycle	
E. Barometric Models	
• Indicators	
• Ratios and spread	

Note: Naive Models (item A under quantitative models above) are based on the idea that history usually repeats itself. Simple forecasting rules are devised, such as the forecast equals the current year plus 5 percent.

The Handbook of Forecasting: A Manager's Guide breaks down forecasting methods into three classes:

Judgmental. Individual opinions are processed, perhaps in a complicated fashion.

---

[6]C. L. Jain, *Understanding Business Forecasting*, edited by Al Migliaro (New York: Graceway Publishing Company, Inc.), chapter 15, p. 58.

Extrapolative. Forecasts are made for a particular variable using only that variable's history. The patterns identified in the past are assumed to hold into the future.

Causal (or structural). An attempt is made to identify relationships between variables that have held in the past, for example, volume of brand sales and that product's relative price. The relationships are then assumed to hold into the future.[7]

As you can see, one of the problems faced by forecasters is the variety of models from which to choose. Often it becomes necessary to try various forecasting models or to develop modifications that fit a particular business.

Note that, in every case, forecasts are based on assumptions that are projected into the future. Therefore, since no forecast is foolproof, simpler and less costly approaches are often the best. The success of a business is much more dependent upon the flexibility of its response to unexpected challenges than upon the accuracy of a forecast.

Growth trends such as those illustrated by the Chem-A-Lot experience can be extrapolated to provide forecasts. But since growth extrapolations as well as many other types of forecasts do not provide advance warnings of economic turning points, an approach that does so will be explained later in the chapter.

FORECASTING ASSOCIATED WITH PRICING EMERGENCIES

Plans for the future are more likely to be realized when there is a firm foundation of profitable business to build upon. With such a foundation, a good sales forecast of existing products can prove very helpful. You derive good forecasts through inputs from two sources: first, your co-workers' collective intelligence and second, any formal information recorded about sales, production costs, economic indicators, markets, and competitors.

There is a broad spectrum of business types in terms of their sales patterns alone. Businesses can run the gamut from those that have sedate sales movements with definite seasonal swings to those with violent sales swings related less to seasons than to other forces, such as the need of industrial customers to expand plants. You will, therefore, have to select your forecasting approach from among the many variations available and perhaps modify it.

One type of forecasting arises from price changes. When you set a price, you are betting on the accuracy of a quantity forecast you have in mind— whether you do it formally or not—just as both CEOs at Chem-A-Lot did. Major price changes and hoped-for quantity increases most often occur in pressure situations at critical moments in the history of a business.

---

[7]Robert Fildes in *The Handbook of Forecasting: A Manager's Guide*, 2nd ed., edited by Spyros Makridakis and Steven C. Wheelwright (New York: John Wiley & Sons, 1987), chapter 10, "Forecasting the Issues," p. 158.

During the emergency in late year 26, Tom Puller used the "what if" approach: What quantities would Chem-A-Lot sell in year 27 if the prices were raised? If lowered? Tom originally presented his findings in table form on page 87. Here we depict the results for the conditioner line of machines in chart form.

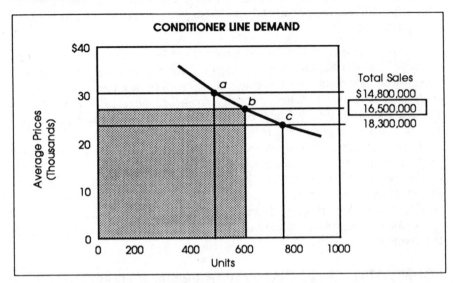

The results indicated that slightly over 600 units would be sold if the average price remained at $27,500 (point *b*) per machine for a total of $16.5 million in sales, represented by the shaded square on the chart. Total sales becomes a smaller rectangle as the price goes up and a larger one as the price goes down. At the lower price of $23,766 (point *c*), unit sales would be 770, for a total of $18.3 million in sales. Under these circumstances, demand is said to be elastic. Here are the three demand possibilities that all businesses normally face.

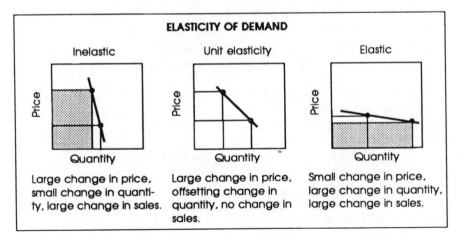

You don't have to figure out a whole demand curve when you use the "what if" approach—all that's really required are two price points for each product.[8]

Next, you use all the facts you have gathered to determine which elasticity situation you face, and there's the rub. If you don't have adequate price, unit, and sales records for all products, you're out of luck.

Recall Chem-A-Lot's situation. From year 16 through year 25, price increases almost exactly offset unit declines, so sales remained level. It appeared to be a case just like the middle one depicted with unitary elasticity of demand. Even in that situation, there lurked real danger. Remember this conversation:

Tom: The higher we raised prices, the more we lost market share to competitors who were willing to sell units almost as good as ours at a much lower price.

Diane: Tom, if we had priced higher initially and then lowered the price gradually for some machines or if we had priced less aggressively when we did have to raise prices, we most certainly would have kept some competitors out of the market as well as increased our own sales. Our pricing policies as a whole have been psychologically damaging! They've nearly killed us.

Henry: If our unit sales had been increasing, our costs of production would have decreased per unit as we became more efficient in producing larger numbers of units. That might also have reduced the cost of raw materials by taking advantage of larger quantity discounts.

It's likely that prices were raised so often at Chem-A-Lot that sales never settled down during that period; therefore, demand for all machines really was elastic, as Tom found when he used the "what if" approach. To sum it all up: Jack Tuffitout raised prices as if demand were inelastic; the record over the years seemed to say that it didn't matter since unit elasticity prevailed, but it did matter; and, finally, careful scrutiny of all the facts indicated that demand was elastic. So there you have it.

THE FUTURE WILL BE LIKE THE PAST FORECAST

If there are no major price discontinuities injected by you or your competitors, the future could be much like the present. And, if your business sails sedately through the seasons, you have an additional advantage. Your sales can be separated easily into four components: (1) long-term trend;

---

[8]In the examples used, the two-point (arc) elasticities of demand are for two points $(q_1 p_1)$ and $(q_2 p_2)$ where (q) is the quantity of units and (p) is the price. Inelastic demand is less than -1, unit elasticity is -1, and elastic demand is greater than -1. For example, for the conditioner line at the lower price, the arc elasticity of demand would be -1.70. Finally, as in the good years for Chem-Kraker, there can be an unusual positive elasticity where price and units go up at the same time. The equation for calculating two-point elasticity of demand is:

$$\text{Elasticity of Demand} = \frac{q_1 - q_2}{q_1 + q_2} \cdot \frac{p_1 + p_2}{p_1 - p_2}$$

(2) business cycle; (3) seasonal pattern; and (4) irregular events. During stable economic periods, extrapolations based on the first three components can provide useful short-term forecasts for planning. You will need to remain alert, however, to irregular events that may force modifications since this approach assumes the future will be essentially like the past. With a rapidly developing world economy, this assumption is becoming less and less tenable.

The approach does not preclude the plotting of sales and extrapolated forecasts on rate-of-change charts so you can make comparisons directly with other variables, such as costs and profits, to nip developing problems in the bud.

THE FUTURE CAN SOMETIMES BE FOUND IN A LEADING INDICATOR FORECAST

Frequently, but not always, a leading indicator can be used in sequential rate-of-change comparisons to sharpen short-term forecasts. This method takes into account changes already occurring upstream from your business. It works like this:

Step 1. Locate or develop a suitable leading indicator. You'll need to have one that will tell you what potential business is in the pipeline coming your way as many months ahead as possible. In this example, we'll assume it is simply the new orders in dollars received by your customers as represented in Standard Industrial Classification data obtained either from the government or from trade associations.

Step 2. For your leading indicator prepare 12-month moving totals of orders. Do this so that for each month, as the information becomes available, you can compare the total 12 months of orders ending that month with the total of the same 12 months of the preceding year.

Prepare three-month moving totals in the same manner.

These moving totals make it possible to calculate sequences of simple percentage changes called 12/12 and 3/12 pressures over the previous year.

The following table demonstrates the method of calculation. For example, the month 12 moving total of 1,441 is the total of the monthly totals for the first 12 months on the table, beginning with 98 for month 1. The 12-month moving total of 1433 in month 24 is the total of the 12 months beginning with 120 for month 13. Dividing the last 12-month total of 1433 by the first 12-month total of 1441 gives the 12/12 pressure figure of 99.4 percent. These percentage pressure figures can then be plotted directly on a graph. The same method is used for 3/12 pressures, except that 3 months are added at a time rather than 12 so you can compare the last 3 months with the same 3 months of a previous year.

LEADING INDICATOR
(12- and 3-month moving totals and pressures)

Month		Month Total	12-Month Moving Total	12/12 Pressure Percentage	3-Month Moving Total	3/12 Pressure Percentage
1	Jan	98	1,091	75.1	287	89.1
2	Feb	120	1,108	78.5	313	99.4
3	Mar	119	1,129	82.5	337	110.1
4	Apr	122	1,151	86.3	361	119.9
5	May	118	1,172	89.8	359	121.7
6	Jun	135	1,217	96.2	375	130.7
7	Jul	110	1,242	101.1	363	133.5
8	Aug	114	1,278	107.7	359	141.9
9	Sep	125	1,333	116.6	349	149.8
10	Oct	129	1,379	122.5	368	159.3
11	Nov	125	1,410	127.0	379	153.4
12	Dec	126	1,441	131.2	380	139.7
13	Jan	120	1,463	134.1	371	129.3
14	Feb	150	1,493	134.7	396	126.5
15	Mar	162	1,536	136.0	432	128.2
16	Apr	135	1,549	134.6	447	123.8
17	May	136	1,567	133.7	433	120.6
18	Jun	151	1,583	130.1	422	112.5
19	Jul	124	1,597	128.6	411	113.2
20	Aug	104	1,587	124.2	379	105.6
21	Sep	99	1,561	117.1	327	93.7
22	Oct	98	1,530	110.9	301	81.8
23	Nov	84	1,489	105.6	281	74.1
24	Dec	70	1,433	99.4	252	66.3

You can chart the leading indicator pressure changes coming your way in relation to the months in which they will exert pressure on your sales. The last few months charted will tell you whether the sales pressure will be increasing or decreasing and by how much. The chart for Chem-A-Lot for years 27 and 28 looks like this:

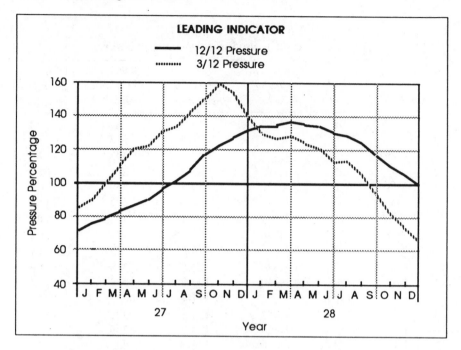

LEADING INDICATOR

— 12/12 Pressure
········· 3/12 Pressure

Example calculation:

Suppose you had data only up through March 31 in year 28, the high point on the 12/12 pressure curve. The three relevant numbers have also been underlined on the moving total table.

Year	Month	12-Month Moving Total
27	March	$1,129 million
28	March	$1,536 million

$1,536 million ÷ $1,129 million = 136%

The 136 percent predicts an upward annual pressure of 36 percent moving toward your business.

In successive months pressure percentages will rise or fall. If the orders in this example had been reversed, there would have been a downward pressure of 26 percent (100%−74%) from the previous 12 months as follows:

$1,129 million ÷ $1,536 million = 74%

For 3/12 pressures, the latest three months are compared to the same three months of the previous year. Only the latest three months are used to be more responsive to current developments. If the 3/12 and the 12/12 are plotted on the same chart, warning bells should go off when the 3/12 starts toward and crosses the 12/12. Reason: This signals an upcoming economic turning point, either up or down. In this instance, it's a downturn.

The months after March 31 in year 28 are shown so you can better see the relationship between the two series at a turning point. The 12/12 pressure indicates that sales for year 28 should be higher than for year 27; however, the rapidly falling 3/12 indicates that the reduced pressure on sales for year 29 will most likely drop sales below year 28.

Step 3.   Forecasting your sales involves a comparison between the leading indicator and your sales.

Forecast example:

Again assume your latest leading indicator pressure reading predicts an upward 12-month pressure on your orders of 36 percent for March 31 in year 28, the high point on the 12/12 pressure curve on the chart. Now, suppose your indicator provides a 6-month lead time, and it is the end of September. Your sales for the periods comparable to those for your leading indicator look like this:

Year	Period	Sales Total
Previous	Apr.–Mar.	$10 million (12 months)
Current	Apr.–Sep.	7 million (6 months)
	Oct.–Mar.	? million (6 months)

Your current 12-month forecast, based on your leading indicator, is

$$\$10.0 \text{ million} \times 136\% = \$13.6 \text{ million}$$

However, in the first 6 months of the current 12-month period, you already have received $7.0 million in sales, leaving a forecasted balance of $6.6 million for the next 6 months as follows:

$13.6 million (12-month forecast)

−$ 7.0 million (6 months, Apr.–Sep.)

$ 6.6 million (6 months, Oct.–Mar.)

You now know that the 3/12 line has crossed over the 12/12 line, so it also appears likely that sales in the immediate future will decline further.

Using this approach, just how solid would your $6.6 million sales forecast be? Well, it is definitely not set in concrete. Before that upstream pressure change translates into orders for your business, market shares can shift up or down because of a change in relative prices, new competitors and new products entering the markets served, new industrial processes being introduced at customer plants, or any combination of events can occur. Hopefully, but not always, change will be minimal and for short periods of time. You must, therefore, always remain alert so you're not caught asleep at the switch.

This approach can be expanded. For example, the short-run relationship of pressure changes among the leading indicator, sales, and inventories can be most helpful in determining inventory levels.

When pressure calculations are used to prepare rate-of-change charts showing actual sales dollar forecasts in addition to past sales, they add another dimension to your understanding of the business.

When a business is in good health, the 12/12 and 3/12 pressure methods are excellent choices for forecasting current product sales for plans and budgets. However, they may not work well if deeply rooted ills cause your sales to fail to respond appropriately to upstream pressures.

THE CUSTOMER'S PERCEIVED VALUE OF YOUR CURRENT PRODUCTS

When a business is ill, your customer's perceived value of your products becomes critical. The proliferation of new ways to measure the perceived value of old and new products, together with suggested pricing and positioning responses, is truly amazing. Fortunately, many do prove helpful. The upper limit of the variety of situations, measurements, and possible responses is probably the number of products being, or about to be, marketed. Therein lies confusion.

One common way to measure perceived value is through careful tracking of the change in orders gained and lost. This method can sometimes provide information on why your sales fail to respond to upstream pressures. Often, however, the information is incomplete, inaccurate, or both because sales people resent what they consider excess paperwork or unwarranted nosiness.

Recall how Chem-A-Lot machine dollar sales went flat in year 16, dropping to an average annual rate of +1 percent while the Manufacturers' New Orders indicator continued to grow at an annual rate of 11 percent. This signal of the customer's perceived value was the first tangible evidence of real illness at Chem-A-Lot. And remember how customers reduced or discontinued unit purchases of machines as prices rose through the years at a surprisingly negative 9.4 percent annual rate—for a 55 percent total decline before the outright loss in year 26. Was Chem-A-Lot ill? Yes! Should those long years have passed before action was taken? No!

NEW PRODUCT FORECASTS

Product research and development (traditionally called R&D) should go hand in hand with market research and development. Quite often smaller firms cannot afford to do basic research, so R&D becomes D&D—for design and development. Sadly, large sums are lost on the development of products for which there are no markets. One common reason: Marketing and engineering personnel often operate in isolated worlds. At least part of the dollars lost in these situations should have been spent up front on joint market and product research—prudent insurance against later grief. Unless your business is large enough to have competent product and marketing research staffs on board, or a very experienced management team, it is usually best to seek outside help before committing large sums to product development.

Should you desire to push ahead without research, there are numerous books on new products that cover forecasting, test marketing, market positioning, pricing for market penetration, on-site operation tests, market survey techniques, and similar topics—all of which can prove either helpful or confusing.

If you are an experienced entrepreneur with Jim Dandy's knowledge of his products and his customer's needs—and not just a fast-track financial manager—the foregoing words of caution are probably unnecessary.

Pricing of a new industrial product involves determining what the product is worth to the buyer in terms of how much your product will save him or her in time and money during production. When choosing a price, you should take this point of view rather than rely on a fixed markup policy. What kind of competitive situation may develop must also be considered.

Forecasting sales for a new product must be an integral part of a team effort that includes the marketing department from the very beginning. This type of forecasting involves:

1. Finding out what customers really need through reports from field sales forces, service staffs, and market research or just plain knowing what customers will eventually need through extensive entrepreneurial experience. (There is indeed a growing concern that we are educating creativity and initiative out of our young people.)

2. Screening identified customer needs for those that can be met by your business.

3. Determining the extent of the potential market for each selected need through market studies.

4. Selecting those needs that can result in profitable products and that fit into your business strategy.

5. Setting up the product development project so that the R&D teams have enough customer input to keep them on the right track.

6. Introducing the product to defined markets with preliminary test marketing if necessary.

Since new product development involves the strategy of the whole company, the details of scheduling for any project will be discussed further in the chapters on integrated business plans.

THERE ARE MARKETING PLANS AND CONTINGENCY MARKETING PLANS

When you have completed your marketing-situation analysis and prepared your sales forecasts, you are ready to prepare a marketing plan. Since much of the information gathered to prepare a marketing plan will be coordinated with the manufacturing plan and other plans in our example strategy package, we will not prepare a separate marketing plan. Be aware, however, that it should contain:

1. An executive summary including prime objective.

2. A situation analysis.

3. Marketing goals.

4. Strategies to reach goals.

5. Tactics for people.

6. Contingency plans.

The world being in the state that it is, you are better off with two contingency plans: the first, a fallback position; the second, a forward position. Businesses have been known to stumble as easily with too much business as too little.

THE MARKETING PLAN AFTERMATH

Now the task of coordinating your marketing plan with other plans in order to come up with a strategy plan for the entire business must get underway. For example, the marketing sales forecast becomes the input for cost and gross profit forecasts in the manufacturing plan.

SUMMARY

Many questions must be answered as well as one can during the development of a marketing plan. Ultimately, however, it is the customer who passes judgment on the effectiveness of all plans through his or her perception of the product value created. In this chapter the following planning concepts were reviewed:

- The marketing plan can be seen as the foundation of a pyramid of business plans for all departments that must be coordinated at the apex to form a company-wide **strategy plan, business plan, and budget.** All other departments need the marketing plan to kick off their own efforts.

- Analyses underlying all plans should also provide a thorough **business health checkup** that makes it possible to compare the vigor of the business with that of its competitors.

- There will always be obstacles to planning that must be faced. When these obstacles have been overcome, a written marketing plan should be prepared that includes:

1. **A prime objective** that everyone can understand.
2. **A situation analysis** that has at least some depth.
3. **Marketing goals** that are rational.
4. **Strategies** to reach goals.
5. **Tactics**, so that people know what they are to do.
6. **Contingency plans**, in case something changes significantly.

- Good sources of information from outside the company and good records from inside are vital to the development of an accurate situation analysis. Useful information should be easily accessible to all departments involved.

  Minimum essential data for past periods with forecasts derived from both internal and external records should include the sizes of markets served, the shares of served markets, gross profit, operating income, and net income.

- The correlation of leading economic indicators to sales through 3/12 and 12/12 pressure percentage calculations can help managers anticipate future economic changes that will affect sales.

- In order to understand the true situation that a company is facing, one must know much about sales performance by region. Rate-of-change charts are useful when comparing sales over time in a number of territories with diverse market potentials. Performance (log–log) charts are useful for comparing sales dollars to advertising leads or to market potential for a number of territories in a single accounting period.

- Competitor profiles with as much current detail as possible should be kept. This information will provide the basis for assessing relative strengths and weaknesses of competitors.

CHAPTER 9

FROM MANUFACTURING FACTS TO PLANS

Selling products and services below cost and making a profit on volume is generally accomplished unintentionally—and always for a short time. Don't try it!

Anonymous

MANUFACTURING STRATEGY ELEMENTS

The manufacturing strategy must be an integral part of the overall business strategy. Unless it is tailored to accommodate the planned needs of customers as well as other departments and functions, the company's strategy is doomed to fail. The overall manufacturing strategy plan is only a composite of the plans of the individual manufacturing centers or units, some of which may be located at other sites. An integrated plan must be implemented to allow the total business plan to be successful. Modern communications technology also makes this cost-effective.

In virtually all parts of a business, timely and adequate communications are needed to keep employees informed so that the prime objectives of the business and the goals of the manufacturing plan will be met successfully. Although manufacturing plans will evolve over time, the best way to get them started and keep them going is to maintain constant communications.

Basic operating principles and practices must be agreed upon and included in the manufacturing strategic plan. These include the following:

- The customers' service and quality requirements must be recognized. Maintain inventories at minimum, but acceptable, levels to meet the customers' needs. Standard versus nonstandard products affect costs. Unrealistically tight lead times may cause delivery problems. Built-in flexibility in production may be expensive, but the increased costs can be offset to an extent by allowing higher selling prices or increasing customer loyalty.

- Manufacturing facilities can be operated at maximum capacity or highest profit levels; these may be different.

- Improvement in technology, level of integration, age of machinery and equipment, and the systems used in the manufacturing processes affect efficiency and thus costs and cash flow.

- Improvement in relationships with vendors will affect manufacturing costs and efficiency.

- Improvement in employee relationships and total compensation, including benefits and incentives, are important pieces of the manufacturing puzzle.

MANUFACTURING PLANS MUST BE GEARED TO MARKETING GOALS AND FORECASTS

Receipt from marketing of two reports starts the three-phase planning cycle in manufacturing: (1) sales forecasts for existing products plus (2) information on goals for new products and markets. The manufacturing plan, together with other functional plans, becomes a part of the overall strategy plan, the business plan, and the budget.

WHAT A MANUFACTURING PLAN SHOULD INCLUDE

The manufacturing plan should include the following:

1. **An executive summary:** a concise overview placed at the beginning of the document stating clearly how the plan supports the business prime objective.

2. **A situation analysis:** a description of the past, present, and expected manufacturing environment for existing products, together with associated costs and cost forecasts derived from sales forecasts.

3. **Manufacturing and engineering projects:** manufacturing and engineering projects designed to support new marketing goals; projects might involve:
   - A new product for a specific industry.
   - The modification of an old product.
   - The establishment of an assembly plant, new warehouse, and service center in a remote region or change in existing facilities.

4. **Project milestones:** anticipated completion times for project phases.

5. **Personnel requirements:** for both existing business and new projects, a description of manpower requirements in terms of numbers and capabilities.

6. **Contingency plans:** plans in the event actual sales either fall considerably short of or exceed sales forecasts.

THE NATURE OF THE MANUFACTURING OPERATION, THE PRODUCTS, AND THE SERVICES

In year 27, marketing information requirements for strategy planning were not the only subjects being discussed extensively at Chem-A-Lot. Manufacturing dug down to bedrock with such questions as: Just what is, and what should be, the nature of Chem-A-Lot's manufacturing and customer service operations?

Some expressed the opinion that Chem-A-Lot was little more than a glorified job shop that built complete machines, integrated machine systems, and machine components.

Others believed that the factory should move more heavily into integrated process systems composed of machines with more standardized parts. These individuals, in many instances supported by field sales engineers, argued cogently that, in the future, processors would be looking for complete packaged process systems backed up by good service anywhere in the world.

The cost and manner of manufacturing machines, the cost and extent of customer service, and how those costs tied into planning were of deep concern. It was soon recognized that Chem-A-Lot, by the very nature of its customized products and the markets it served, could not become a true mass producer.

Manufacturing, engineering, and service people began to look at base information and derived data much as their counterparts in marketing had. Operations and engineering documents, of course, dominated the mix. They, too, wanted an information system that was easy to use, that would grow in usefulness, that would encourage habitual use, and, above all, that would make it natural to spark new ideas across departmental boundaries.

Clearly, the type of information sought by businesses differs according to the nature of the manufacturing operations, products, and services rendered. Businesses usually supply customers with the following:

- Raw or finished materials that are either batched or continuously processed.
- Components, complete machines, or systems that are either custom-built (job shop) or mass-produced (process).
- Consumer or industrial products that are produced for consumption, for short life, or for durability.
- Various separate or product-related services.

KEY FACTS NEEDED FOR PLANNING

Costs of production and costs of services rendered must be known for individual products and for material, direct labor, and manufacturing direct and indirect overhead costs. Fixed or periodic versus variable cost components should be identified and tracked separately. These separated costs should be not only related to current production volumes but also estimated for the whole range of your plant's capacity. The future of your business survival may depend on it.

Each cost accounting record for materials and supplies purchased should include the vendor's prices and quantities purchased. Records of cost summaries for major purchases should be kept for at least 10 years. Why? Whereas in marketing strong emphasis is put on tracking selling prices to measure internal sales-price inflation, the emphasis in the manufacturing area is to record inflation costs controlled or caused by external suppliers.

Additionally, manufacturing data from external sources should be collected and updated annually to find out: Are you, or one of your competitors, the low-cost producer? How do your facilities and equipment compare with others in productivity and unit costs?

You also must determine your manufacturing or service capacities to plan for expansion or contraction in physical facilities and the need for related funds.

Both internal and external data should be collected over long enough time periods to permit comparison of any trends and proper evaluation of temporary swings. When you do this, key relationships can be derived from the data collected that will permit you to measure performance—productivity, cost effectiveness of expenditures, and value added. Therefore, you will want to maintain records that do the following:

- Summarize internal quantifiable data in tabular form in your database.
- Summarize pertinent external data also in tabular form (some sources: Strategic Planning Institute, Chase Econometrics, trade associations, and data from quarterly and annual reports of publicly held companies).

Using this tabular data you can prepare size and rate-of-change trend charts quickly for comparing manufacturing cost trends between your business and similar businesses, as was done for Chem-A-Lot.

HOW YOUR FACTORY COSTS PUT A BRAKE ON YOUR PRICE REDUCTIONS

Factory costs put a brake on too low prices. You can't reset prices without taking unit costs into consideration. And you may have little control over the prices set by others for most of the factors of production, although careful selection and close cooperation with a few quality suppliers can reduce costly waste due to inferior supplies.

Recall how Jim Dandy forced down total dollar costs after sales went down in year 16 by postponing the purchase of necessary equipment; recall how, later, Tuffitout also felt forced to cut costs in whatever way he could: by using inferior materials, by continuing to postpone the purchase of necessary equipment, and even by finding excuses for terminating valuable people. Finally, recall how by year 26, it was impossible to keep total costs where they belonged, below total dollar sales. So, you see, it becomes critically important to understand what a specific change in price will do to unit costs.

Let's suppose your factory has been operating at or near full capacity, and that the unit costs of production are high owing to excessive overtime expense, production scheduling inefficiencies, or other problems that could force costs up. Capacity might have to be added to bring unit costs back down again. Sometimes it is wise to add capacity even before existing capacity is fully exploited in order to remain competitive or take advantage of an expected upturn in orders.

At Chem-A-Lot, they had a long way to go before reaching full capacity. Unit costs for them would definitely come down if more orders came in. A reduction in prices should never be ruled out on the basis of present costs.

As more and more of plant capacity is utilized, unit costs approach a low point, reach it, and then gradually increase again as the production pace puts strains on people and equipment. At this point, unit costs begin to act as a brake on the downward movement of prices by reducing profit margins.

You should track and analyze the relationship between variable costs and periodic costs over the years to determine when to expand your plant and what the major influences on costs are. Periodic costs are those that stay fixed for periods of time. Manufacturing plants normally represent a cost that stays fixed longer than most. If a company experiences healthy growth over a number of years, rising unit costs related to plant-capacity utilization provide a signal that one should begin thinking about the feasibility of a plant expansion.[1]

HOW A CUSTOMER'S COSTS CAN INCREASE OR DECREASE YOUR COSTS

Your customer's cost of using your product puts the brake on your price increases. If a customer can't afford your products in his or her production line because they bump total cost close to, or over, the final selling price, you may be replaced as a supplier. If your prices are too high for many customers, your unit sales will drop. If your plant then operates near optimal capacity, your factory cost will come down and you may be encouraged to reduce

---

[1]Elasticity of supply is normally negative if a manufacturing facility is underutilized, and positive if operated near capacity. Cost (c) replaces price (p) in the arc elasticity of demand equation as follows:

$$\text{Elasticity of supply} = \frac{q_1 - q_2}{q_1 + q_2} \cdot \frac{c_1 + c_2}{c_1 - c_2}$$

prices again. On the other hand, if your plant is operating below capacity, your costs will go up and you most likely will not be encouraged to lower sales prices. Neither response may be appropriate.

The declines in unit sales over years 16 to 25 in all those Chem-A-Lot products were caused by the customers' cost brake gradually being applied. The attempt to maintain the dollar sales level was an irrational response, yet many American companies have acted in a similar manner in the face of increasing competition. With unit sales at Chem-A-Lot finally lowered by 55 percent, manufacturing costs were necessarily high. The customers' brake was most effective. Unfortunately, this was not recognized early enough; Chem-A-Lot lost millions of dollars in potential sales. That brake, called competition, can kill off a single product or an entire company or reduce a nation to second-rate status.

SOME MANAGERS HAVE NO CONTROL OVER PRICES AND CAN ONLY ADJUST COSTS

In some industries such as agriculture, it is very seldom that one supplier among the vast number can throw enough of a commodity on the market to raise or lower its price. Adjusting costs often becomes the only immediate option open. Likewise, the individual consumer of bread or shoes can have little or no effect on prices paid for nationally branded goods. So, at any given time, a small consumer often faces a flat price at any quantity purchased.

In these situations, prices are dominated by the sheer volume of a few buyers or sellers of raw materials and processed goods. Some small agricultural producers have gotten around their lack of price influence by advertising organically grown vegetables to differentiate their products. Others, such as the Amish farmers, have kept their costs below other producers' by not going in for high-cost farm machines. For a number of larger agricultural growers, price influence has increased. But, generally, "what if" pricing alternatives are reduced to zero or near zero for multitudes of small consumers and suppliers.

That's why small farmers, laborers, shopkeepers, and consumers have often banded together to influence prices or have asked the federal government to exercise essentially "what if" price selection and control on their behalf. Such situations are complex combinations of evolving elements of nearly perfect competition, imperfect competition, cooperation, and government attempts to find solutions to vexing problems.

The other extreme is to have nearly complete control over price, as in the case of Chem-Kraker when the machine was first introduced. But that is not an unmixed blessing either; we saw how the braking action exercised by the market began to affect unit sales even for a unique product when price was escalated unwisely.

The majority of market situations fall somewhere between these two extremes. For this reason, a vast body of theoretical mathematics about imperfect competition has developed. Imperfect competition is said to exist when the purchases made by a buyer or sales made by a seller are large enough to give them some influence over prices. In all these instances, managers are faced with the "what ifs" of pricing. Rarely, if ever, has the ideal of perfect competition, where neither buyers nor sellers could exercise any degree of price control, existed; and if it did, would all concerned really think things were perfect? Hardly.

COST ACCOUNTING AND ITS OBJECTIVES

One definition of cost accounting is that it is a method of accumulating actual or estimated costs properly associated with the physical activity that caused the costs to be incurred. Fundamental objectives of cost accounting include the following:

- Accomplish product costing for financial statement purposes.
- Allow effective cost control.
- Permit planning and projecting costs of future operations.

Product costs are most typically used to assign generally accepted accounting values (and realizable values) on inventories for financial statements, including both those inventories consumed (cost of sales) and those remaining (balance sheet current assets) at the end of a period. Product costs are also used to evaluate selling prices to determine profitablity of products, and to permit make-versus-buy decisions.

Cost control is vital to all businesses, but it requires detailed accounting systems analysis. Cost information may be provided by the systems in place and may be accurate, but it is worthless if not used properly.

Planning and projecting costs for the future is important because future costs will become today's costs with the passage of time. Projections are best if founded on a knowledge of past costs as well as what drives those costs. Typically, personnel, materials, facilities, and equipment for the future are more easily estimated if past and present costs are well understood. When was your company's cost accounting system last changed? Should some changes be made? Does it need a complete overhaul? If the costing system has been in place for four years or more, it more than likely needs revision.

COST ACCOUNTING SYSTEM CHARACTERISTICS

Although the objectives of all cost accounting systems are the same, manufacturing businesses use different systems depending on the nature of the manufacturing functions. Among those systems are

- *Process costing*—accumulates costs by manufacturing department or process.
- *Job costing*—accumulates costs by job number or customer.

- *Operation costing*—accumulates costs by particular operation being performed.
- *Mixture* of those listed above.

COST ACCOUNTING ALLOCATIONS CAN BE DEADLY

Cost accounting and affiliated costing control systems are an integral part of the manufacturing process. Accurate annual planning and long-term planning depend greatly on strong manufacturing cost-tracking systems and procedures. Feedback reports emanate from such procedures and systems. In order to maximize the value of a costing procedure and system, all responsible key manufacturing personnel should thoroughly understand the way in which costs are assigned to products being manufactured.

Some controllers and cost accountants have limited expertise in cost accounting and the assignment of costs and expenses to products, processes, or departments. They are not good at either "responsibility accounting" or "responsibly accounting"! Yet, when such accountants issue reports on the profitability of specific products and product lines, their reports are regarded as accurate. Too often management will make important decisions based on those estimated profit reports. Too often such decisions will be wrong! Why? Let's review the types of costs and expenses that are incurred by a typical manufacturing business such as Chem-A-Lot in order to see where problems may arise in cost accounting.

In the process of manufacturing most products, the following costs are normally incurred:

- *Purchase costs of materials* (often the major portion of such costs are directly related to products being manufactured, but part may only be indirectly related to such products).
- *Direct labor* (service and/or manufacturing labor directly related to such products and services).
- *Operating expenses* (may or may not be directly relatable to specific products). These include indirect labor and administration of manufacturing (material handling and warehousing, repairs and maintenance, security services, cost estimating, order entry, purchasing, plant accounting, supervision, personnel and related employee benefits, insurance, utilities, rent, taxes, depreciation, and so forth).

The way in which such indirect costs are assigned to products, processes, or departments will almost always have a major impact on interpretations of product line profitability, inventory turnover, and other vital issues.

COST ASSIGNMENT IN COST ACCOUNTING

Inventory is one of the larger assets on most balance sheets. It usually is the largest cost included in the cost-of-sales section of the income statement;

SPECIFIC PURPOSES FOR WHICH FIRMS USE
FIXED AND VARIABLE COSTS

Purpose	Number of Citations*
Budgeting	12
Capital Expenditures	3
Special Orders	3
Variance Analysis	5
Direct Costing	4
Breakeven Analysis	5
Pricing	12
Profitability Analysis—New Products	7
Profitability Analysis—Existing Products	10
Other	1

*Number of citations totals more than 25 because some firms cited more than one purpose.
Source: Maryanne M. Mowen, *Accounting for Costs as Fixed and Variable* (Montvale, NJ: The National Association of Accountants, 1986), chapter 5, p. 35.

strategic planning and budgeting must therefore include inventories in such plans. Of course, the quantity of inventories is the biggest single factor in the total dollars involved. However, the ways by which the inventories are costed can have a dramatic impact on the dollar balances and on management's decisions on pricing those inventories for sale, paying sales commissions, and retaining or dropping certain products in the sales lines.

One key to understanding costs involves segregating fixed costs from variable and semi-variable costs. The National Association of Accountants issued *Accounting for Costs as Fixed and Variable*, which contains the following statement:

> The distinction between variable and fixed overhead is extremely useful in control and in formulating managerial policies. Responsibility for excess fixed costs usually rests with general or major production executives, whereas the responsibility for changes in variable costs falls upon minor production executives.

> Because we segregate all fixed and variable costs, we gain the advantage of being able to advise management quickly and easily the dollars of sales required to break even and the unit volume needed plus other key figures, per year, month, week or day! . . . Any accountant who has been asked to supply similar figures and has not segregated fixed and variable expense in his cost system can verify the headache involved in trying to develop these data after the fact.[2]

The study referred to above was based on responses from 25 businesses ranging in size from less than $5,000,000 in sales (9 companies) to those with more than $100,000,000 in sales (also 9 companies). Specific uses of fixed and variable cost accounting were summarized in the above table.

---

[2]Maryanne M. Mowen, *Accounting for Costs as Fixed and Variable* (Montvale, NJ: The National Association of Accountants, 1986), chapter 1, p. 1.

METHODS OF COST ACCOUNTING

Three major cost accounting methods are in use today: absorption cost accounting, direct costing, and activity-based costing. Too often only one cost accounting method is utilized. Yet management has many decisions to make at various times during the year, and other ways to view product costs might change management's decisions on how to act on a particular issue. Following is a description of the major costing methods.

Absorption Cost Accounting

Most companies use absorption costing exclusively. This method assigns all manufacturing costs, and possibly some warehousing and handling costs, to the production units or batches on an actual cost basis or on an estimated actual basis called "standard costing."

Direct costs, such as raw materials and direct labor, are assigned to specific production units or batches, whereas indirect costs and overhead expenses are assigned or allocated to products based on the volume of production, direct labor hours or dollars, machine hours, raw material costs, or some other arguable allocation method. Some companies allocate the overhead costs on a plantwide basis (direct labor for the entire plant divided into the total overhead to obtain an overhead rate). Other companies assign such costs on a departmental basis (direct labor for the department divided into the total overhead to obtain a departmental overhead rate) or based on machine hours to obtain a rate per machine. The concept is to assign all manufacturing costs to the products and services produced. The method of allocation can and often will result in materially different total product and service costs when overhead costs are large in comparison to direct costs.

Direct Costing

In order to match the cost of a product with its sale, direct costing makes a distinction between period costs and those costs that can be associated directly with products and related sales transactions. Period costs describe those costs that vary with time rather than with the rate or volume of activities. Again, as in the case of absorption costing, direct costs, such as raw materials and direct labor, are assigned to specific production units or batches to which these direct costs directly pertain. Certain marketing costs, such as commissions on sales and shipping supplies, may also be related to specific products and classified as direct costs. Indirect costs and overhead expenses that are not rationally related to specific products are not assigned to products. The difference between sales revenues and such direct costs is commonly referred to as "contribution margin" or profit left to cover all other costs and expenses and allow for net income from operations.

Activity-Based Costing

Activity-based costing (ABC) differs from conventional cost accounting and allocation methods. Under a typical absorption accounting system, high-volume production is assigned more of the overhead expenses than low-volume production. This assignment occurs regardless of the complexity of the products produced and their underlying need for disproportionate services from overhead departments such as purchasing, engineering, and production scheduling. ABC derives its thrust from associating costs with the specific activities that generate those costs.

The ABC system is often far more complex than the present cost accounting system used by many companies because of the different way of allocating indirect costs. ABC assigns direct costs (raw materials, direct labor, and so forth) to specific production units or batches. Generally, indirect costs and overhead expenses are assigned to products based on the activity demanded of the indirect costs and overhead expenses by the products. As a result, complex products requiring more engineering, more purchase orders, and so forth are assigned more of those expenses, as opposed to an allocation based only on direct labor hours or volume of production.

As an example of the impact of variations in assigning costs of a common department, look at a purchasing department. Assume two different product lines requiring direct labor of $50,000 each, or $100,000 in total direct labor for the month. Also assume the entire cost of the purchasing department for that month to be $10,000. Traditional cost accounting systems allocate the purchasing function costs (overhead) for the month to the two products by dividing that department's costs of $10,000 by the $100,000 of total direct labor, which results in a 10% overhead rate to cover the purchasing function for the month. Therefore, 10% of direct labor ($50,000) for each product manufactured, or $5,000, is assigned as indirect overhead expenses to the individual product lines.

On the other hand, suppose the number of purchase orders and/or detail records for the two product lines were heavily weighted to one of the lines, so that 80% of the purchasing effort that month was devoted to Line A, whereas only 20% of the effort was required for Line B. In this case, 80% of the cost of the purchasing function, or $8,000, should have been allocated to Line A and $2,000 to Line B. Yet $5,000 was allocated to each line using the traditional method of allocating overhead costs based on direct labor hours or dollars. Magnify that for all other overhead departments, and you can see how pricing based on cost allocations might materially distort costs of manufacturing and product line profit margins. Would erroneous pricing policies result? Detailed analyses of overhead by activity is well worth the effort even if the analysis supports the currently used allocation of overhead dollars.

An excellent book on the subject was written by Peter B. B. Turney, entitled *Common Cents: The ABC Performance Breakthrough*, which includes the following:

There are three steps to improving activity performance. The first step is to analyze activities in order to find opportunities for improvement. The second step is to look for factors that cause waste (the cost drivers) and for ways to remove them. The third step is to encourage and reinforce the right kind of improvement by measuring the important elements of performance.

Activity-based management is quite different from old-fashioned accounting approaches to improvement. Accounting focuses on meeting cost targets. Costs are cut by eliminating staff and other resources without reference to the underlying work.

In contrast, activity-based management focuses on restructuring the work to *achieve lasting cost reductions*. This involves the following steps:

- Reducing the time and effort required to perform activities,
- Eliminating unnecessary activities,
- Selecting the lowest cost activity to perform the work,
- Sharing activities wherever possible, and
- Redeploying resources made available by improvement efforts.

These efforts are as likely to improve quality as they are to reduce costs. Activity-based management and quality management go hand-in-hand in any improvement program.[3]

The ABC accounting system is not a panacea; it is another tool a business can use to further analyze its operations. Because of the potential benefits resulting from the "bottom-up" style of accounting, in which specific activities are related to a higher-level activity or cost accumulation or assignment. Businesses with diverse operations should at least consider the ABC costing system. In the process of learning more about the costs, more important management decisions can be based on the data accumulated or exposed by the process.

COMPARATIVE INCOME STATEMENT—ABSORPTION VERSUS DIRECT COSTING

The following income statement presents absorption costing results of operations compared to direct costing.

---

[3]Peter B. B. Turney, *Common Cents: The ABC Performance Breakthrough* (Hillsboro, OR: Cost Technology, 1991), chapter 7, pp. 193–194.

Absorption Costing		Direct Costing	
Net Sales	$60,000	Net Sales	$60,000
Cost of Goods Sold		Direct Costs	
Raw Material	11,000	Raw Material	11,000
Direct Labor	3,000	Direct Labor	3,000
Overhead	10,000	Variable Mfg. Overhead	7,000
Total Cost of Goods Sold	24,000	Total Direct Costs	21,000
Gross Profit	$36,000	Contribution Marginal	$39,000
Other Operating Expenses	15,000	Period Costs (including $10,000 of fixed or indirect manufacturing costs)	25,000
Operating Profit	$21,000	Operating Profit	$14,000
Percent of Net Sales	35%		23%

The difference in operating profit is due to fixed costs being carried in the inventory under the absorption costing method as follows:

Assuming no inventory at the beginning and 1,400 units carried in inventory at the end of the period in each case above, absorption costing has indirect overhead of $5 per unit more in the ending inventory than under direct costing, where those fixed or indirect costs were expensed in the month incurred. However, direct costing is not as yet a generally accepted method of accounting for inventories in the United States; thus it is used primarily for analysis and decision making rather than balance sheet accounting.

THE COST METHOD USED CAN BE AN OBSTACLE

The following quotation from a book by John Y. Lee vividly indicates that cost accounting, improperly used, can be a hindrance to proper reporting. (JIT refers to just-in-time inventory management.)

> Taiichi Ohno, the developer of JIT, has reportedly mentioned that cost accounting has been his biggest obstacle to the implementation of JIT at Toyota [Fox, 1984]. According to Fox, Ohno stated that cost accountants in Japan, like their Western counterparts, believe in high efficiency, low-cost operations, and adherence to traditional cost accounting principles, none of which would explain why JIT was so successful. Ohno reportedly had to keep the cost accountants out of the plant, and had to "prevent the knowledge of cost accounting from entering into the minds of" his people.[4]

Each business must examine its costs in different ways and at different times for different purposes. One particular method should not be used to the exclusion of another.

---

[4]John Y. Lee, *Managerial Accounting Changes for the 1990s* (New York: Addison-Wesley Publishing Company, Inc., 1987), chapter 6, p. 63. Reprinted with permission of the publisher.

JUST-IN-TIME (JIT) INVENTORY MANAGEMENT

In recent years, a new concept called "just-in-time" (JIT) has been put into practice in the area of inventory control and management. Basically, JIT management principles are based on eliminating as much waste as possible from all areas and functions of business, such as the time of people and operating assets, and the amount of equipment, material, and supplies. Time is a cost-generating factor, starting with purchasing material with which to produce inventories, getting customer orders, and ending with delivery and billing to the customers. Non–value added steps directly and indirectly affecting manufacturing are reviewed and revised or eliminated. The entire manufacturing process is simplified and streamlined.

The lead times involved in accomplishing all manufacturing tasks are attacked and minimized while efficiency is maximized, all at the least cost. The quantity of qualified vendors, inventory storage areas, engineering change orders, employees, different stockkeeping units, and reworked production are reduced, all with the view of eliminating time and waste from the manufacturing cycle. Both time and waste translate into costs. Although a portion of the business can be studied and JIT principles and practices installed there, the major benefits of JIT usually require these practices to be installed throughout the manufacturing process and across all related departments. The following areas are most often worked on:

- *Suppliers.* Fewer are used but with proper quality products and total service.

- *Quality.* A balance exists between the cost of quality built into the production and service cycles and the costs of rework, scrap, and customer satisfaction.

- *Inventory types and turns.* In general, most manufacturing businesses have a material cost of 40 percent to 65 percent or more when measured against total manufacturing costs. Control over this large cost factor can result in lesser total cost of manufacturing.

- *Direct labor.*

- *Indirect labor and supervision.*

- *Production plant and equipment utilization.*

- *Warehousing and distribution facilities and methods.*

- *Administration.*

The traditional accounting system is changed to an easily understood responsibility accounting and management reporting system when JIT is implemented. The goal is to creatively reduce or eliminate costs rather than merely account and report them. JIT is not only an inventory control system; inventory control is only a part of the JIT system, which concentrates on procedures and attitudes to maximize value-added to the customer while reducing costs to the minimum amount consistent with the company's strategic objectives. Non–value-added steps and activities are minimized. The accounting and financial personnel are trained to understand and relate to the manufacturing, engineering, and research functions. This training gets rid of the barriers to straightforward communications between operating and accounting personnel.

Together, the operating and accounting employees study, discuss, and finally understand the basic cost and expense generators within the business. This mutual awareness of how and where costs are being generated and the related impact on profitability and customer satisfaction leads naturally to integrated attacks on unnecessary costs. Direct costing or activity-based costing is then implemented in order that questionable cost and expense allocations may be eliminated.

OBJECTIVES OF JIT MANUFACTURING

The general objectives of JIT manufacturing are well described in a recent book by Richard T. Lubben entitled *Just-in-Time Manufacturing:*

1. To integrate and to optimize every step of the manufacturing process.
2. To produce product quality.
3. To reduce the cost of manufacturing.
4. To produce product only on demand.
5. To develop manufacturing flexibility.
6. To keep commitments made to customers and suppliers.[5]

Those objectives or others tailored to your business should be incorporated into your strategy plan for manufacturing if JIT is adopted. A number of good books are available on the subject, including the one cited.

Other inventory control and management techniques and procedures are effectively employed by profitable businesses. The basic objective of inventory management is to keep inventory levels at, but not higher than, levels needed to service the customers with the products they want at the prices a business can afford to sell them and at the time customers want them. Designing the balancing routines necessary to reach this objective poses difficult problems. Many books that offer valid and practical solutions are available at local libraries.

HOW COST AND PRICE LEVELS ARE DETERMINED BY SUPPLY AND DEMAND

Sorting out the exact price and cost situation you face can be confusing; indeed, so confusing that it has no doubt contributed to the mental blocks

---

[5]Richard T. Lubben, *Just-in-Time Manufacturing* (New York: McGraw-Hill, Inc., 1988), chapter 4, p. 82. Reprinted with permission of the publisher.

often encountered when we get beyond accounting ratios. So, let's take a brief look at where it all started—Adam Smith's original insight, now rarely used except as a beginning explanation of pricing. From there we'll go on to a practical shortcut for forecasting costs and profits.

First, put on your marketing hat. Suppose you were to list a range of "what if" prices for one of your products, together with expected market responses. It is most likely that you would show more units purchased as the price declined, even though it would be difficult to arrive at precise amounts.

Second, put on your manufacturing hat. You probably would show a willingness to supply more units of the product produced by your plant as the sales price went up because the business would be more attractive. Next, plot both your demand and supply price levels with the associated quantity "what if" estimates on a plain arithmetic chart. Your demand and supply estimates at various prices tell you at what level to plan production.

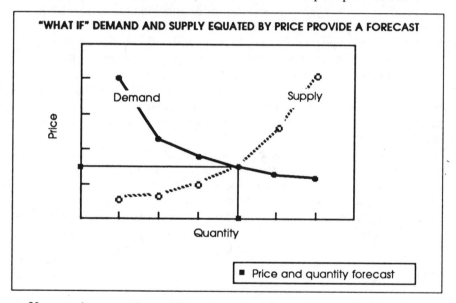

"WHAT IF" DEMAND AND SUPPLY EQUATED BY PRICE PROVIDE A FORECAST

Price

Demand

Supply

Quantity

■ Price and quantity forecast

You now have one "what if" version of supply and demand from the many possibilities. Of course, the slopes of the curves, and where they really would intersect, depend on the accuracy of the information you have and on likely customer purchases as well as your own and your competitors' costs. Any good economics text will list dozens of typical supply and demand curves for different businesses and industries. The confusion often begins with trying to learn what your type of market is.

In all supply and demand situations, prices, unit sales, and dollar sales can be tracked only when you have actually set a price by whatever method and the customers have responded with orders over a period of time. And the deviation of the quantity purchased from what you expected depends on your ability to read future conditions.

In any pricing exercise, don't confuse your lists of "what ifs" with reality. They are only informed guesses of future market conditions. Only the actual units exchanged for a specific price are real. The curves are but mathematical figments of the imagination, albeit sometimes useful. And even the specific price may be real for just that moment in time because of inflation, deflation, and competitive forces.

Instead of trying to develop complete "what if" supply and demand curves to determine a sales forecast, it is often simpler to concentrate on paired "what if" prices and quantities related to the immediate situation confronting a product. Once you have reached a decision, you are in the position to do cost and profit forecasts for the product. Here again we have a practical method for doing so—the break-even chart.

SALES FORECASTS AND THE BREAK-EVEN CHART

The break-even chart provides a useful approximation of the real relationship among costs, sales, and profits. It assumes the total cost curve of a plant to be an upward sloping straight line. This approximation is fine as long as you don't compare volumes that are widely different in size on the same chart. It's easy to overlook the economies of scale at low plant volumes and the diseconomies at high plant volumes. So, for widely different volumes it is best to reestimate your costs and make additional charts to compare with the first. In other words, the percentage of plant capacity at which you operate *does* make a difference in total costs.

In a break-even chart total costs are segregated into fixed and variable costs. In most plants variable costs change nearly in proportion to the output quantity—if you double one, you double the other. Once you have stacked the total variable cost approximation on top of your total fixed cost approximation to get your straight line total cost picture, your chart will look something like this:

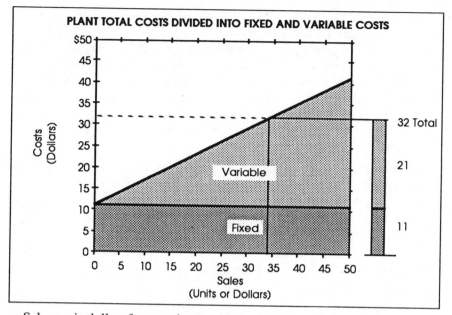

Sales are in dollars for a product mix but may be in units for a single product. A helpful aid is to show a cost bar to the right of the graph to indicate what the size of fixed and variable costs will be at certain levels of sales.

To your straight line total cost picture, you next add a size line for total sales. The point where the total sales size line crosses the total cost line is the break-even point. You can then find the costs and profits (or losses below the break-even point) related to any point selected on the size line from zero to maximum production. Here's what a complete chart for current sales might look like:

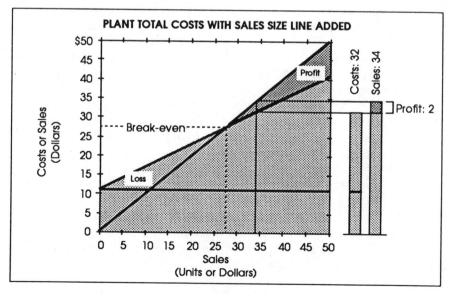

Remember, when you do your sales forecast, the further out your "what if" sales forecasts are from the current level of sales and associated costs, the less accurate your cost and profit forecasts will become. If you must go way up or down on your forecast for some good reason, the effect of underloading or overloading your plant should be considered seriously.

Generally, the relationship between variable and fixed costs of product determines overall flexibility or response to changing market conditions. The proportion of multipurpose to single-purpose production equipment plays a secondary role in determining flexibility.

- Operations with high variable unit costs often have a high safety factor and can respond to major sales declines with less danger.

- Operations with high fixed unit costs normally cannot tolerate large declines in sales—the break-even point (that is, the point at which a certain sales volume will absorb all operating costs at neither a profit nor a loss) is reached quickly.

Examples of two operations producing the same number of units are compared in this chart:

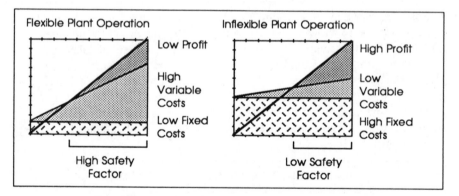

To determine break-even points, all costs need to be analyzed historically to find out which costs in the plant, or related manufacturing facilities, do and do not vary significantly regardless of the size or pace of operations. For example, depreciation, taxes, and lease expenses generally are fixed (predeterminable), even if the volume changes substantially. In contrast, direct labor and direct material costs vary and are often proportional to volume produced.

Segregating costs takes insight, an excellent knowledge of the production processes, much questioning, and some compromising. It is not always clear to what extent a particular indirect cost may increase or decrease in differing scenarios. Then, too, some people may be transferred back and forth between direct and indirect cost tasks. Keep in mind that you do not need precision; you need approximations. Actions will not take place because of the decimal point accuracy of your assumptions.

Multi-product-line plants make break-even point determinations difficult because individual sales by product have specific associated fixed and variable costs. The sum of each product's break-even points would equal the consolidated break-even point.

BREAK-EVEN POINT CALCULATIONS IN FORMULA FORM

Here's one formula for calculating a break-even point:

$$\text{Break-even} = \frac{\text{Fixed costs}}{\text{Contribution margin rate}}$$

where: *Fixed costs* means all fixed costs, including those portions from sales, selling, and administration.

Contribution margin rate means sales less variable costs as a percentage of sales.

Sample calculation:

$$\text{Break-even} = \frac{\$11,000,000}{\dfrac{\$50,000,000 - \$30,000,000}{\$50,000,000}} = \frac{\$11,000,000}{40\%} = \$27,500,000$$

where: Total sales are $50,000,000.
Variable costs are $30,000,000.
Fixed costs are $11,000,000.

Note: Compare break-even figure to one illustrated in chart form on page 153.

Break-even points are just one measure, but a valuable one, of tolerance for economic downturns in your business. Companies with low gross profit margins have a low tolerance for adversity. Those businesses blessed with unique products like Chem-Kraker or with special services often command proportionately higher unit prices and can withstand cyclical or longer-term shocks without giving up to the bankruptcy courts and creditors.

Normally, a clear trade-off exists between the size of the safety factor (risk) and the size of the profit that can be obtained through the investment in more per-unit, cost-efficient, specialized production machinery.

A similar trade-off exists in the employment of individuals at a low skill, high skill and multi-skill levels. For example, highly skilled people are usually more difficult to employ and cause higher losses in efficiency when laid off. They also tend to cost more per unit of production. The temptation to view people who have developed special skills over the years as merely replaceable machines, as Tuffitout did, can also cause serious efficiency problems.

Cost and revenue trade-off considerations are important in planning strategy and tactics. They become of major importance when you are planning a new business or reviving an old one. The risks involved in balancing a high or low selling price against the need to absorb fully the fixed and variable costs under existing competitive conditions are considerable. As we have seen at Chem-A-Lot, an error in judgment by Jim Dandy, perpetuated by Jack Tuffitout, led to millions of dollars in lost sales.

STEPS FOR EVALUATING MANUFACTURING TRENDS

(Charlie Fisher meets with Henry Harris, his replacement as vice-president of manufacturing, and Diane Sensible, the controller, to set the stage for assembling the manufacturing part of the strategy plan.)

Charlie: Good morning! Thanks for being on time. This is our strategic planning period when we will analyze every significant aspect of Chem-A-Lot's operations and its environment. I've asked you to be here, Diane, to help Henry as he and his staff look at our manufacturing capabilities for the next three years from a strategic standpoint. Tom is meeting this week with our sales and marketing team members. We will have several joint meetings later on when you and they are ready to exchange the preliminary ideas and plans upon which we will construct an integrated plan.

Henry: Charlie, I've never worked on a formal strategy plan before, so I welcome all the help I can get.

Charlie: Before you can complete the plan, you will need to know our sales projections by product line. We are a week or so away from those numbers. In the meantime, I think you should dig into the manufacturing costs with Diane's help so we know where our fixed and variable costs tend to be at different volumes.

Diane: I have brought along several analyses of costs by manufacturing cost center using both the last five years' operating statistics and those estimates you and I agreed to on last Thursday, Henry. As you remember, we reviewed each department's personnel and expenditures in great detail, by function and by department. Then we estimated which costs were generally fixed at different production levels and which tended to vary. Of course, some costs are partially fixed, or semi-variable. We did our best to be accurate in our classification, yet we know the level of precision is not 100 percent; it rarely can be in such an exercise. Charlie, we believe the results of our study are accurate within reason and thus quite adequate for the purpose of this strategy plan.

Charlie: What does the break-even study show?

Henry: Well, we have the numbers in several forms. Let's look at this chart for a bird's-eye view.

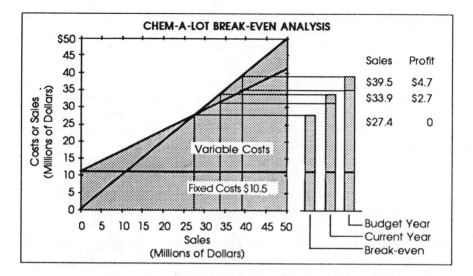

As you can see, after completing the time-consuming analysis of costs, we plotted a series of "what if" sales volumes at expected product-line mixes. Granted, our profit varies a lot by product line, but I think the chart is close to the mark on average.

When we are geared up to do $39.5 million in shipments, the zero-profit (break-even) point is about $27.4 million, give or take a few hundred thousand. That's probably close since we budget profit or operating income of around $4.7 million at $39.5 million, but only $2.7 million at $33.9 million in the current year, dropping disproportionately faster for every $1 million falloff in sales.

It's interesting what happens if the plant is operated at a lower percentage of capacity. The break-even point goes up sharply, by $2.7 million to about $30.3 million if we do not cut back on people costs or other costs, and if we only achieve 85 percent of budgeted sales—about $33.6 million versus $39.5 million. That increase of $2.7 million in the break-even level is 46 percent of the drop in sales of $5.9 million from the budgeted $39.5 million to $33.6 million. We could have quite a problem if we ignore that message!

As a result, my managers are now working on an action plan that we can implement if customer orders do not come up to expectations. We won't be caught napping. I've been that route before in a business that went out of business because they lacked a crisis plan.

Charlie: Henry, how do you think we compare to our two top competitors at the manufacturing cost level?

Henry: Good question, Charlie. You probably have as good a feel for that as I do since you ran our plant for years. I don't know for sure, but I think we are a higher-cost shop by about 5 or 6 percent. They pay the same basic labor and fringe rates per hour. We know that because we have hired a few people away from each of them in recent years. Raw material costs have to be comparable. Well, except for that one big competitor who did some interesting value engineering to take some costs out.

But, Charlie, I think we lose the low-cost edge mainly because our equipment in the plant is pretty old. You know how you tried for years to update our production machines to eliminate some bottlenecks—like the boring mill, the lathe shop, and even the storage areas—and increase the production pace. Several equipment vendors told me that our competitors' average age of equipment is around 7 years. Ours is over 10 for sure. That's got to make a difference.

Finally, I've talked to Tom in sales. He gets around, and he said the quotations from those two competitors seem to be under ours by 5 percent.

Charlie: Okay. Let me know how we can correct that situation. To compete effectively, we simply have to take some costs out. I don't mind spending some money up front to get there.

Diane: Henry, maybe you might tell Charlie what we found out as a result of our trade association study.

Henry: Good point, Diane. Well, the association periodically compiles data from all of us on a "no-name" basis and compares it to governmental and third-party consulting work. The most recent results are sitting there in that thick report. I've only breezed through it so far, but it confirms our beliefs that our operating margins are a bit on the low side. Also, the inventory turns—cost of sales divided by inventories—are averaging 3.3 times per year in our industry. Well, Diane tells me our turns are not much better than 2.4. An improvement of 0.3 turns, to 2.7, would take about $833,000 out of our inventory at our current level. That should be our goal for next year. Better vendor deliveries and prices, along with the new material requirements procedures being installed, should get us there. I need to study the report some more, but it does pass the smell test.

Charlie: Okay, thanks for your time. Let's continue with this until we've nailed down a well-thought-out strategy, a good workable business plan. Then we can build up a reasonable, tight-yet-fair budget for next year. If you can produce the results you are talking about, we'll be on the track to becoming again the company we once were, or even better! See you at lunch.

Henry: Diane, I appreciate all the analyses you've made to help me get a firm handle on the numbers. If you can produce those other schedules we discussed earlier, I'll be able to finish my section next week. My next effort will be on people needs, major maintenance projects, and capital expenditures to maximize capacity at minimum costs. We will project future costs of sales using fixed and variable cost allocations at the sales levels by product lines—Tom is preparing that report.

Diane: Sure enough, Henry. The schedules will be on your desk next Tuesday by 8:30 A.M. Happy planning!

THE RELATIONSHIP OF PEOPLE TO COSTS

The major emphasis in this book is on business planning of several years' duration; in this chapter the emphasis is to show how records of existing costs are used as inputs for plans. We have not thus far discussed just how jobs for people relate to costs or how each worker can play a significant role in reducing production costs. The best way to understand the relationship of people to costs is through the amazing contribution of one American to the revitalization of Japanese industry after World War II. The highest award a Japanese business can receive, The Deming Award, is named in his honor.

W. Edwards Deming described the relationship of people to costs in what is called the Deming Chain Reaction:[6]

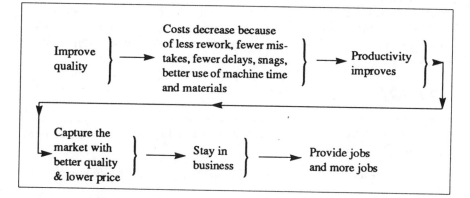

Improvement in quality starts the Deming Chain Reaction. Deming was able to convince Japanese business leaders that an entirely new business culture would have to be created in Japan, a culture in which the individual worker was given the responsibility for producing products of ever-improving quality under an appropriate production system. He was able to demonstrate that about 80 percent of production problems were due to the production system being under the control of management and not due to the workers themselves.

Under Deming's tutelage, the search for excellence became every worker's job in Japan. Workers were shown not only how to perform their assigned tasks but how to improve the quality of their work through simple but

---

[6]Reprinted from *Out of the Crisis* by W. Edwards Deming by permission of MIT, Center for Advanced Engineering Study, Cambridge, MA 02139. Copyright 1982, 1986 by W. Edwards Deming.

effective statistical controls that they could apply themselves. To make this all happen, Deming had to cause a massive shift in Japanese management attitudes. It's an inspiring story!

There is one less obvious lesson to be learned: The timing of a major shift in management attitudes in a country, just as at Chem-A-Lot, can seldom be planned. The time happened to be right in Japan for Deming to make his contribution. Such a shift can occur only when there are enough uncertain or dissatisfied leaders and workers who are open to new ideas—enough to form a critical mass desirous of change. And even then the shift only opens the door to worthwhile change. It can easily be slammed shut again.

In this book, in the context of American democracy, we have also focused on the shift in attitudes required of the CEOs and workers at Chem-A-Lot in order to survive. Although we have talked about specific techniques, it is clear that none of those techniques will be of help if leadership is uncertain and worker morale is low.

Although we are concerned primarily with the tools necessary for long-term planning, here's a list of some of the powerful but simple tools that Deming gave to Japanese workers: cause-and-effect diagrams, flow charts, Pareto charts, trend charts, histograms, control charts, and scatter diagrams. Descriptions can be found in most current elementary statistical texts. When taught to workers in a healthy business culture, these tools can dramatically reduce costs.

SUMMARY

A well-conceived strategic plan always integrates manufacturing plans with those of other departments. In this chapter certain key manufacturing strategy concepts were reviewed.

- The manufacturing plan should be in writing and should include the following:

  - An executive summary.
  - A situation analysis of the past, present, and expected environments.
  - Manufacturing and engineering projects needed to support the marketing goals.
  - Project milestones.
  - Personnel requirements.
  - Contingency plans covering shortfalls in or increases over planned sales.

- Key facts needed to plan manufacturing are as follows:

  - Cost of production/services by product line and by cost element (material, labor, and overhead).

— Determination of your position as a low-cost, average, or high-cost producer.

— Analyses of physical manufacturing or service facilities in comparison to forecasted need for capacity.

— Summary of external influences on your business.

• Your factory cost level directly affects your ability to reduce selling prices.

• Your customers sell into various markets, which will affect your ability to obtain higher prices from those customers.

Business conditions in certain industries severely restrict suppliers' abilities to increase prices in significant amounts. This is particularly true for commodity products.

• Supply versus demand for products and services influences most prices fairly dramatically, except in governmentally regulated or monopolistic sectors.

• Determining operating break-even levels is not only a useful exercise; it may be critical to surviving large downturns in demand.

Businesses with comparatively high fixed operating costs will experience more pressure than those that have much lower fixed costs during periods of slackening demand.

A simple break-even formula is

$$\text{Break-even} = \frac{\text{Fixed costs}}{\text{Sales less variable costs as a percentage of sales}}$$

• The relationship of people to costs in a business is given by the Deming Chain Reaction:

Improve quality → Costs decrease because of less rework, fewer mistakes, fewer delays, fewer snags, better use of machine time and materials → Productivity improves → Capture the market with better quality and lower price → Stay in business → Provide jobs and more jobs.[7]

The chain reaction is started when workers themselves can help change the production system to improve quality in a healthy business culture.

---

[7]Reprinted from *Out of the Crisis* by W. Edwards Deming by permission of MIT, Center for Advanced Engineering Study, Cambridge, MA 02139. Copyright 1982, 1986 by W. Edwards Deming.

CHAPTER 10

FINANCIAL MANAGEMENT

My friend, you still have time to join a circle of the chosen few. Just give me your life savings and my troubles will be over.

Anonymous

FINANCIALLY MANAGE YOUR WAY TO SURVIVAL

Without financial stability, a business either wastes effort fighting fires or creditors—and therefore is less than successful over time—or fails. Long-range plans will not succeed if they do not deal appropriately with the major financial needs of the business. Having cash available at the right time is crucial to the success of any business. Cash and the other elements of working capital (receivables, inventories, trade payables, and other currently due liabilities) are the first line of offense and defense in the fight for financial survival. Appropriate physical facilities and equipment are the longer-term assets needed to stay in business and produce the quality products and services customers need efficiently and at acceptable prices. The need for cash to fund these net assets can be planned well in advance and should result in borrowing at the right time, in the right way, and at the right cost. These needs are discussed below.

- *Cash flow—the key to survival.* No single concern is more important to a business than the availability of cash to meet its needs. Bankers could certainly confirm that many businesses fail because they lack sufficient cash at the right times. Small- to medium-size businesses have the most problems. They may be undercapitalized, and they are more dependent on bank financing than public financing (the stock market).

The importance of cash flow is well described in Joseph C. Krallinger's recent book, *How to Acquire the Perfect Business for Your Company*. Krallinger states:

> *Consistent, predictable cash flow is not just something; it, rather than earnings per share, is everything over the long term.* Earnings per share cannot be consumed, spent, or paid as dividends until converted to cash. Cash flow may well be the best single tool or measure to judge the value of the company—its past and its future values.
>
> *Unrealized appreciation* in the value of a company or in the value of a share of common stock is nice, but unrealized appreciation does not buy the bacon and eggs for the table. Eventually, value must be converted or be convertible into cash or cash equivalents.[1]

Cash balances and availability are impacted most by the profitability of the goods and services produced. These goods and services are of no real value unless sold and converted into accounts receivable. However, accounts receivable must be collected in full and as rapidly as possible. The longer the delay in collection, the less profitable the sale will have been. Time is money . . . earned or lost!

- *Inventories—a major cause of cash flow problems.* The shortest distance between two points is a straight line. The way to increase cash flow is to have the shortest possible time between the placement of customer orders or production and payment by the customer. Excessive inventory costs money and may eventually lead to write-off of the inventory as not saleable due to its condition. That is, inventories become obsolete or worthless due to technological changes, excessive cost, or for other reasons. Ways to keep inventory levels commensurate with customer demand and satisfaction are presented in Chapter 9.

- *Control over billing, collecting the accounts receivable, and managing trade payables—integral parts of cash flow.* The terms of collection often are stated as payable upon delivery or within 30 days, but other terms may also apply. Regardless of what the terms are, many customers do not pay in accordance with them. Rather, they frequently pay after 50 to 65 days. They are using late payment as a means of managing the cash flow within their company. Probably, they are collecting their receivables late, too. Customers blame computers for the delay. We all know computers are not the cause. The credit crunch is the problem. Despite the expense, more and more customers are "borrowing" from their suppliers as well as their banks. "Borrowing" from suppliers is cheaper (frequently no interest is charged) and less complicated (there are no loan agreements) than borrowing from banks.

---

[1] Joseph C. Krallinger, *How to Acquire the Perfect Business for Your Company* (New York: John Wiley & Sons, 1991), chapter 8, pp. 81 and 82.

Strategy plans, business plans, and budgets must account for pricing, billing, returns, and allowances as well as collection policies. If collection policies are to be taken seriously, they must be enforced. Cash flow will be markedly better if someone is delegated to follow up on billing and collection routinely.

- *Borrowing (leverage)—abuse and good use.* In the old days companies and their lenders were conservative. The normal debt to equity (shareholders' net worth) ratios were in the range of one dollar of debt to two dollars of equity. That changed . . . for the worse.

The late 1980s and early 1990s were filled with horror stories of business after business borrowing too much (over leverage) from banks, insurance companies, and the public. Frequently, the borrowed funds were used to buy other businesses or to fuel unwarranted growth of the borrower. Financial tycoons from Wall Street and other avenues around the world came into the arena and bought businesses without any understanding of them. They leveraged their and their clients' investment dollars by borrowing amounts of 5 to 15 (or more) times greater than their own capital. Later, the operating results came in well below expectations, and the creditors were not repaid. "Junk" bonds abounded in the junk yard!

Now, many businesses really need working capital and are good credit risks, but cannot get a loan. Lenders have withdrawn into the trenches, leaving such businesses exposed to the forces of competition without the firepower to stay in the fray. The lenders are overreacting, no doubt. Strategy plans must include all the long-term financial needs of the business—working capital, facilities and equipment, and repayment of debts. Sounds easy. It is easy. Yet, some do not believe they can plan so far in advance. They will be casualties! Strategic planning, when properly done for each major operation and function in a company, is not a waste of time and energy. It is necessary for survival and profitability. Strategies must involve all levels of the business, down to the lowest, and that includes the assets used in business.

The impact of leverage on return on investment is well illustrated from the book by Joseph C. Krallinger entitled *How to Acquire the Perfect Business for Your Company* as shown below.

IMPACT OF LEVERAGE ON ROI

	Case A: Pay all cash	Case B: Borrow 50%	Case C: Borrow 80%
Purchase price	$10,000,000	$10,000,000	$10,000,000
Equity paid in cash	10,000,000	5,000,000	2,000,000
Borrowings	0	5,000,000	8,000,000
Earnings before interest and taxes	2,000,000	2,000,000	2,000,000
Interest on borrowings at 14%	0	700,000	1,120,000
Income before taxes	$ 2,000,000	$ 1,300,000	$ 880,000
Less Income taxes @ 40%	800,000	520,000	352,000
Net Income after taxes	$ 1,200,000	$ 780,000	$ 528,000
Rate of return on investment (Pre-Tax)	20%	26%	44%
Rate of return on investment (After tax)	12%	15.6%	26.4%

Source: Joseph C. Krallinger, *How to Acquire the Perfect Business for Your Company* (New York: Wiley & Sons, 1991), chapter 8, p. 94.

Thus the more one can borrow, the less personal assets are exposed to creditors, and the more leverage is brought in from third parties, who will presumably receive less in income than the business that is financed. Borrowing based on the assets and future cash flow of the business is not a bad idea. It is simply an idea that has been exploited in some cases to an extreme—with poor results for both the lenders and the owners. Many, if not all, businesses could benefit from using some leverage to attain their objectives more quickly and more completely—if they approach borrowing conservatively and obtain a properly executed loan with acceptable terms.

FINANCIAL COMPARISONS

To provide owners and management with a balanced view of how the business is doing, some managers compare their operations with those of similar businesses. Businesses may be similar in terms of product lines, industry segments, size, or financial stature. Trends may be compared for:

- Working capital as a percentage of sales.
- Leverage (liabilities compared to shareholders' net equity), sales, and profitability growth.
- Return on investment.
- Growth in value of the business.

- Inventory turns.
- Receivable collection periods.
- Operating efficiency (sales or production divided by employees and administrative expenses per employee or per sales dollar).
- Other items.

Some ways to accomplish these comparisons are to assemble data from the following sources:

- Trade industry statistics.
- Publicly available information on publicly traded corporations as contained in the annual reports to shareholders and in filings with the Securities and Exchange Commission.
- Standard and Poor's Corporation Value Line and Dow Jones & Company, Inc., data.

In these ways the standards set by the company in its strategy plan can be related to those of other companies. Reasons for significant variances should be plausible and explained.

MEASURING THE COSTS OF SURVIVAL

Return on investment is one measurement of the income obtained from the ownership of assets managed over one or more accounting periods. This return, as the economist Joseph A. Schumpeter pointed out, is in reality a cost of survival that remains after all the normally recognized costs of doing business have been met.

Owners in our society may use this return on investment as they see fit—for the long-run survival of the business itself, for their own survival upon retirement, for the start of a new business, for the support of the arts, for medical research, often reluctantly through taxes—for the education of the young, for the protection of the environment, and for the highways and other necessary infrastructure costs of conducting business—and living life.

Unfortunately, this return on investment also can be wasted by owners who unknowingly live beyond their means or by managers who act imprudently. As a nation we have at last begun to worry about this mounting improvidence as our national debt and trade deficits soar.

RETURN ON INVESTMENT (ROI): A FINANCIAL YARDSTICK

Shareholders of publicly traded corporate securities have several ways to evaluate their position. They can obtain quoted market prices for current holdings. For securities held, they can decide whether, on the basis of cash dividends, those securities are attractive enough to risk future price fluctuations. Public shareholders also judge the relative risk/reward benefit of investing in public businesses versus private security positions. Private businesses, by definition, are not as easy to evaluate and compare with other businesses.

Furthermore, directors and managers of public and private business make frequent decisions relating to different types of investments and disinvestments, such as the purchase of capital equipment, facilities, and other businesses or the disposal of assets.

You can bet on having more investment opportunities than available resources. How can you decide which ones to select? One good financial tool used to measure and compare investment risk and reward is return on investment (ROI).

ROI measures the income obtained from assets managed over one or more accounting periods. ROI long-term trends in a business depend upon the nature of the business objective, socioeconomic conditions, rate of technological change, efficient use of assets, and the capabilities of managements as compared to their competitors.

ROI calculations are not immune to short- and long-term distortions. ROIs may or may not represent true returns for any one or even several annual accounting periods. What are a few of the pressures causing these distortions?

- America's rapidly aging production facilities. In many industries ROIs have been overstated for years because of lack of facility replacement and expansion. Some railroads, steel plants, and chemical facilities are unfortunately great examples of this short-sighted approach.
- The pressure exerted by financial markets to show a good return, sometimes called the tyranny of Wall Street.
- The pressure to show a high annual return because managerial bonuses are often tied to ROI.
- Distortions in the underlying data from which ROIs are calculated caused by reaction to spiraling inflation.
- Pressures to show premature returns on the new product or new market investments.

HOW IS AN ROI CALCULATED?

The ROI is expressed as a percentage derived by dividing income from the investment by the cost of it. Sounds simple. Yet ROIs can be calculated in a number of ways as is illustrated here, using figures from the following abbreviated financial statements:

BALANCE SHEET

Working Capital	$ 5,000	Debt	$ 5,000
Plant and Equipment	14,000	Other Liabilities	5,000
Other Assets	1,000	Shareholders' Equity	10,000
	$20,000		$20,000

INCOME STATEMENT

Sales	$20,000
Operating Income	3,500
Interest Expense, etc.	500
Pre-Tax Income	3,000
Net Income After Tax	1,500
(Assume 50% rate)	

ROI generally is computed in one of the following ways:

$$\text{ROI \#1} = \frac{\text{Operating income}}{\text{(pre-tax and pre-interest income/expense, etc.)}}{\text{Shareholders' net equity}}$$

$$= \frac{\$3,500}{\$10,000} = 35.0\%$$

$$\text{ROI \#2} = \frac{\text{Operating income (pre-tax and pre-interest income/expense, etc.)}}{\text{Shareholders' net equity plus long- and short-term debt}}$$

$$= \frac{\$3,500}{\$15,000} = 23.3\%$$

$$\text{ROI \#3} = \frac{\text{Pre-tax income}}{\text{Either denominator in preceding examples}}$$

$$= \frac{\$3,000}{\$10,000} = 30.0\% \text{ or } \frac{\$3,000}{\$15,000} = 20.0\%$$

$$\text{ROI \#4} = \frac{\text{Net income after taxes}}{\text{Either of the preceding denominators}}$$

$$= \frac{\$1,500}{\$10,000} = 15.0\% \text{ or } \frac{\$1,500}{\$15,000} = 10.0\%$$

$$\text{ROI \#5} = \frac{\text{Net income after taxes, after adding back interest expenses, net of tax benefits}}{\text{Shareholders' equity plus long- and short-term borrowings}}$$

$$= \frac{\$1,500 + (50\% \times 500)}{\$15,000} = 11\%$$

Return on assets (ROA) is sometimes used in investment return computations. Commonly, ROA is the percentage derived by dividing the total gross assets, with or without reserves for depreciation included into one of the above numerators. Here's an example using total assets and net income after tax:

$$ROA = \frac{\text{Net income after tax}}{\text{Total assets}}$$

$$= \frac{\$1,500}{\$20,000} = 7.5\%$$

Pre-tax income would also have been acceptable in the calculation of ROA.

COMMON PITFALLS IN USING ROIs

- The ROIs can be calculated differently.
- The balance sheet, shareholders' net equity, and net investment (equity plus debt) do not usually approximate current fair values. And these net numbers were surely derived in different periods and at various levels of inflation, making it difficult to compare most businesses.
- Optimistic forecasters may receive more funds than conservatives, yet produce worse financial returns over time.

THE ROI CONNECTION TO STRATEGY PLANNING

Each business should adopt an objective and establish strategies and detailed tactics to attain that objective. In the process, the option of alternative investments, lesser investments, or no investment should be studied. Rarely is there only one way to go. Hopefully, a long-term vision will be the guide. From time to time, a project with a purportedly lower ROI should be approved. It may deter competition or increase market share, although these hard-to-measure benefits may not have been obvious, or even measurable, at the time of investment.

ROIs do focus planning on excess or idle assets, levels of working capital, and leverage—all of which should be included in a strategy plan. In the final analysis, if consistently measured ROIs are not acceptable, shareholders, vendors, and lending parties will take action. That action is rarely in our strategy plans.

SUMMARY

Return on investment (ROI) is one important tool used to evaluate and compare income over time to net assets employed. Confusion abounds as to how to calculate ROI and how ROI relates to return on assets (ROA).

CHAPTER 11

UNLEASHING THE TALENTS OF PEOPLE

The concern for man and his destiny must always be the chief interest of all technical effort. Never forget it in your diagrams and equations.

Albert Einstein

The subject of management is man; the objective of management is the moving of man's mind and will and imagination.

David E. Lilienthal

MEN AND WOMEN ARE NOT ROBOTS

In many company cultures, the creative talents of individuals are stifled by their unspoken fear of being different, criticized, or fired. A few managers even attempt to brainwash individuals into being similar cogs in the gears of their own pet image of the company machine. Innovative ideas are lost in a miasma of fear and ridicule. In such an atmosphere, only safe responses to problems are considered: Rational planning for the future seldom occurs, while the motivation to do so declines.

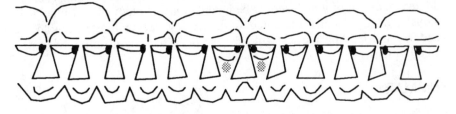

The Ridiculed Creative Cog in a Company Machine

THE MANAGEMENT OF TIME

Managers sometimes stockpile raw materials as an attempt to buffer a firm against the uncertainties of supply. Today we are just beginning to learn the true cost of this practice as we compete with Japanese firms who have developed what we call "Just In Time" inventory policies. In Japan such policies have reduced costs dramatically because they were built on a solid foundation of mutual trust among management, workers, and suppliers of materials and services that had developed over many years. Note that a healthy business culture comes first. There are no shortcuts. In view of our competitive experience with the Japanese, we have reason to ask what the true cost of a file drawer full of unused innovative ideas or a warehouse of stockpiled resources is.

Unlike raw materials and ideas, work time cannot be stockpiled: The CEO, the department head, the supervisor, the production worker, and the janitor all have the same allotment of just 24 hours in a day. Therefore, costs for stockpiling time have been automatically eliminated from our consideration. However, time used unwisely can be just as costly as the destruction of a warehouse full of raw materials.

Everyone in a company is faced by demands on his or her precious time allotment. And anyone in management has:

- *Tasks directly assigned by his or her supervisor or indirectly imposed by insufficiently trained subordinates.* Time on assigned tasks can be well spent. Too often, however, people problems arise when supervisors do not train workers adequately or leave training to co-workers who have not been trained properly themselves. Then, because of a lack of trust in the workers, such novice supervisors wind up doing much of the critical work themselves. They often appear harried and are prone to stomach ulcers. Their workers, on the other hand, are usually disgruntled. The traditional organization chart shows how task assignments are supposed to flow from the CEO down through the branching chain of command. Sometimes, however, the task assignment flow stops, reverses, and flows upward because of incompetent supervision.

- *Tasks indirectly imposed by routine business reporting, coordination, and control systems.* These tasks are essential to the coordinated control of departments; however, many companies operate an unnecessary paper mill. Frequently, complex reports prepared jointly by several departments continue to be produced long after they have lost their usefulness. With turf to protect, people can make it very difficult to prove that a report is unnecessary. Analyses of report preparation and associated paper-handling activity can sometimes cut unnecessary paper-flow expenditures by as much as one-third to one-half. However, such analyses treat the symptom and not the cause; thus, the paper flow regenerates quickly. It should never be underestimated in our fear-ridden business culture how much time-consuming, nonproductive, defensive paperwork is being squirreled away in each individual's desk.

- *Tasks that are valuable to the business, self-imposed, and competently self-directed*. These tasks represent the ideal work time that produces the astounding results of the best companies. Motive force can be greatly amplified when all individuals spend most of their time in self-imposed tasks, coordinated informally with their peers, to support a clearly stated company objective that includes a demand for excellence. Self-imposed tasks become possible only when a supervisor delegates both authority and responsibility to a worker and the worker is professional enough to anticipate the detailed work of the tasks required to reach the objective.

  The pride generated by self-imposed tasks can be felt and indirectly charted through success rates. And supervisors who hold workers accountable to a planned schedule now have the time to create and consider innovative ideas.

- *Tasks, self-imposed and self-directed, that waste business time.*[1] Such time may be great for the individual, especially if he or she uses it wisely to prepare to move on. The extent of this type of activity can tell us whether a company is in decline.

  The lack of morale can also be felt and indirectly charted through failure rates and resignations.

Human dignity requires a work day with an increasing content of self-imposed and self-directed tasks rooted in perfected skills in a nurturing business culture. Such a culture encourages the release of Individual Motive Force (IMF) useful to the company. A good leader coordinates the IMFs of all the individuals in the company to provide the ultimate Organization Motive Force needed to make the company successful. Performance improves when individuals:

- Can visualize a personal stake in reaching the business prime objective.
- Have participated in the strategy development needed to reach the prime objective.
- Are, therefore, motivated to do the tasks assigned that they themselves have helped create within the guidelines they have agreed upon.
- Have perfected skills required to do the work, assigned or self-imposed, that benefits all stakeholders in the business.
- Are not frustrated by overdirection from supervisors or overburdened by authoritarian reports and controls.
- Are capable of understanding, using, and even setting up their own simple, statistical control techniques on the jobs they are performing. (Be-

---

[1] One of the authors of this book first heard time allotment definitions similar to those given here in a presentation made over 20 years ago by William Oncken, Jr., a New York consultant to management.

lieve it or not, if the business culture is right, pride of workmanship will make them want to do this.)

- Are rewarded appropriately for jobs well done.

LEADERSHIP AND MANAGEMENT

Most of us prefer working environments where there is a participative atmosphere—an open sharing of information with a number of participants covering one or more job functions. In fact, business planning will rarely be effective with anything less.

Professional services, production facilities, and finances are of no consequence unless people bring them together properly in the production of an excellent product. Orchestration under a CEO is required to ensure good results. The CEO has two primary functions: (1) the leadership of people and (2) the management of material and financial resources. In order for the company to provide a product that customers want, the CEO must see to it that the people associated with the company are motivated, compensated, and capable of planning their work and working their plan.

Leaders must be alert to the need for quick plan shifts, whether temporary or long-lasting. Managers can be most effective when they explain changes to their associates and provide support as those changes are made. Team building, not dictatorial commands, usually wins in today's world. Highly motivated individuals are the key to profitable use of the otherwise dormant potential of production facilities, natural resources, and finances. Employee turnover, voluntary or involuntary, is costly, but the cost is even higher when it occurs unexpectedly during a period of rapid change.

INFORMATION ABOUT PEOPLE NEEDED IN PLANNING

Personnel records can provide invaluable clues to the alert manager about the changing culture of a business. Too often the personnel department is dismissed as being simply "those people who hire and fire, set wage rates, and look after the employee benefits package."

All departments should be able to draw upon the personnel department for expertise in human relations. Serious long-term problems are usually people problems. (In this book we have tried to emphasize the importance of people problems by looking at Chem-A-Lot through the eyes of the people directly involved.)

In order to manage change, you need measures to estimate and forecast that change. Therefore, personnel statistics should be accumulated over a series of years and include, as a minimum:

- Number of employees by skill and responsibility level.
- Rates of employee turnover.
- Wage and salary levels.

- Employee benefits.
- Evaluations of employees.
- Number of grievances. (Why? To identify new problems that could become messes.)

When a business is ailing, personnel records are one source of information that should not be neglected. They often contain information on what has gone wrong. For example, one question to be asked is: As unit sales declined, did prices go up? An equally important one is: Were necessary but highly compensated support people in operations, sales, service, or administration retired or terminated to reduce costs? The latter is what Tuffitout did at Chem-A-Lot.

WAYS TO EVALUATE TRENDS

Having data and using it in a meaningful way are not synonymous. To measure productivity, spot problems, and sense opportunities, pertinent human resource data should be summarized and analyzed. A couple of approaches might be:

- To prepare summary profiles, updated regularly, for each employee. (These profiles can then be reviewed by employee skill for use in strategy planning, job promotions, and transfers. *En masse* they can also prove helpful in identifying positive or negative changes in the business culture.)
- To prepare tables of quantifiable data—such as wages, salaries, promotions, and absenteeism—over several years and to obtain comparable data from external sources for similar businesses so that trends may be calculated to identify problems and reveal opportunities.

PERSONNEL POLICIES

Personnel policies should respond to problems identified in actual records. For example, an extraordinarily large number of problems can arise from an irrational promotion policy. A business's promotion policy should make it clear when to promote from within and when to go outside for fresh talent.

Some companies have a stated policy that a supervisor cannot be promoted until he or she has trained a fully qualified replacement for himself or herself who has been approved by his or her supervisor. In the long run such a policy can prevent delegated critical tasks from reverting to the supervisor because of incompetent subordinates. Such a system can be formalized in the personnel records by showing in the manager's file that the manager has no trained replacement. A penalty should be placed on such a manager who has not trained a competent replacement within a specified period of time.

Other policies could relate to a suggestion award system. Some companies share the rewards from an idea for increased production with the worker who contributes the idea. The reward is not just a token amount, but a significant share, based on an accounting judgment and paid to the individual periodically as the suggestion becomes productive. In those companies that strive for excellence, cooperation between the worker and the company is recognized as a two-way street.

QUESTIONS TO ANSWER

- Are our wage and salary pay rates competitive?
- Do we have the right people in the right positions for both the company and the people?
- When should we hire from outside? When should we advance people from within the company?
- What should our rules for eligibility for promotion from within be?
- Do we have good training programs and centers with facilities for training programs, discussions, and customer presentations?
- Is creativity encouraged? Are incentives needed? Should they be revised? Do we reward what should be rewarded?
- With or without a union representing workers, are general grievances handled fairly?
- What may stop or hamper resolution of grievances?
- What critical people problems will surface in the future?
- When necessary, how will we handle termination of individuals and general layoffs?
- Is our business socially responsive to its employees and its community? Can it be? Should it be?
- How do we best foster cooperation between individuals and departments without overdoing formal meetings?
- What should the role of our company publications be?

If you are positive there are no serious personnel problems facing your business then you may be the problem! Perhaps it's time to pick up several good books on personnel management at the library. Good human resource plans, actively pursued, are very important. In business, people are the single most important asset you have.

Plans of your people, by your people, and for your people are essential. Where have we heard that line before? It's not enough to give lip service to this concept in a glossy annual report!

SUMMARY

- People are individuals whose creative talents can be stifled by poor supervision, unnecessary paperwork, and a machine-like business culture.

- The proportion of each individual's time used in productive and nonproductive activities is critical to the success of a company.

- The personnel department must be involved in more than hiring, firing, and wage setting. Creative personnel policies should be based on good long-term records that provide clues to helpful and harmful changes in the business culture.

PART THREE

PLANNING CYCLE: THEORY AND PRACTICE

CHAPTER 12

THE PLANNING CYCLE

Plan ahead—it wasn't raining when Noah built the Ark.

General Features Corporation

EFFECTIVE PLANNING IN THREE PHASES

Every function of a business should be included in planning: manufacturing, customer service, marketing, advertising, sales, product development, and administrative functions. To be most effective, a top-down and bottom-up team effort, with interactive lines of communication among all functions, is required.

A number of planning tools used in coordinating separate business function plans are described in subsequent chapters. Both the method and the tools were developed from years of experience and represent seasoned, successful, and sound approaches to good planning. Once again, Chem-A-Lot's newly adopted planning approach is used to illustrate how a useful strategy plan, a business plan, and a budget are constructed; integrated to form a complete action plan; and oriented to attain a prime objective. The suggested planning cycle described in succeeding chapters is composed of three phases.

Phase 1: *The long-range strategy plan (new or revised), to be completed in the first quarter of the year prior to the planned period of years, should include the following:*

- One inclusive prime objective, three to five years or more out, selected from alternatives, together with the reasons for its selection.

- A strategy selected to move the business from its current situation to that objective.

- Tactics embedded in the selected strategy, defined as essential projects for new products, production equipment, or information systems needed to support the strategy.

175

- Costs, revenues, persons needed, and timing will be roughly estimated at this time. (See Chapter 13 for the theory, Chapter 14 for the practice.)

Phase 2: *The annual business plan, to be completed by the third quarter of the year prior to the planned period of years, should include the following:*

- Detailed descriptions of tactics to be accomplished during the two years ahead. Descriptions should include more exact estimates of revenues as well as capital needs to cover equipment and personnel costs.

- A summary of the expected progress toward the long-range objective to be made during the next two years. (See Chapter 15 for the theory, Chapter 16 for the practice.)

Phase 3: *The annual budget, to be completed by the end of the fourth quarter of the year prior to the budgeted year, should include the following:*

- The final estimates of revenues and costs for tactics to be implemented during the coming year. These are then added to updated forecasts of the existing base business.

- Financial statements for the budget year based on forecasted revenues, expenses, and other applicable information.

- Contingency plans to be used in emergencies. (See Chapter 17 for the theory, Chapter 18 for the practice.)

SMALL BUSINESS PLANNING IN TWO PHASES

Although medium- and large-size businesses generally use the three-phase planning cycle discussed above, smaller businesses may obtain similar benefits by condensing the business plan with the budget and preparing them together in an integrated planning document. The result would be a strategic plan and a combined business plan/budget. The contents of each plan and that of the budget would remain basically the same as those shown in subsequent chapters.

Larger companies tend to schedule Board of Directors' meetings around the three-phase planning cycle for at least two reasons. First, larger companies must coordinate at least one additional level of management. The planning cycle is a logical basis in such coordinating. Second, board discussion of the overall long-term strategy early in the planning year allows time for a change in the direction and thrust of the business if the stategic plan as presented by management is not acceptable. It gives management sufficient time to make revisions in strategies and tactics in the long-term business plan that are normally completed by the end of the third quarter of the planning year. The annual budget, prepared in the last month or two of the fourth quarter, can then include more accurate estimates of revenues and departmental expenses based on the revised tactics in the business plan.

Whether your business has a three-phase planning cycle or uses the two-phase version is not important. What is vital is how and when the planning is done, who is involved in it, what is planned, and how the plans are used to gain the support of the people to manage and control the business. Going through the exercise of planning is valuable in its own right, but using the plans is the most important issue.

ROLLING BUSINESS PLANS

To further enhance planning effectiveness, the strategy plan and the business plan should be prepared by deleting the first year and adding another as each year passes. In that way, planning documents become real operating tools used on a day-to-day, month-to-month, and year-to-year basis. Such plans do not gather dust. They are not merely the product of some isolated annual event with no connection to the everyday transactions, opportunities, and pressures of the business. Planning in this way will be routine, not time-consuming, and never out of date.

CHAPTER 13

PHASE 1: THE STRATEGY PLAN (THEORY)

We know in our hearts that we are in the world for keeps; yet we are still tracking 20-year problems with 5-year plans, staffed by 2-year personnel working with 1-year appropriations. It's simply not good enough.

Harlan Cleveland in The Futurist

WHAT IS A STRATEGY PLAN?

- It's the planned movement from an always partly understood present to a desired possible, as well as probable, future—the objective that lies several years out. To be successful, a CEO must be able to develop the necessary Organizational Motive Force to so move the business.

*OMF is the total Organizational Motive Force that the Chief Executive Officer is able to muster among all the employees of the company.

The strategy is broken into annual segments, and as the years progress, each year in turn is detailed in annual business plans and budgets.

WHAT IS THE REAL PURPOSE OF A BUSINESS?

- Customers, through the marketplace, cast dollar votes for products and services that they feel best serve their needs. The businesses that work to meet those needs thrive.

- A free economy rewards each business whose purpose for being is providing a product or service that enhances the future of its customers. Paradoxically, although the reward is profit, annual profits cannot be the sole reason for being if a business is to survive.

- Only profits extended over time, kept in line with resources, will allow survival.

WHAT DO MANAGERS NEED TO KNOW TO PREPARE A STRATEGY PLAN?

- *An understanding of the past.* You can't really know where you want to lead your business unless you know where your business has been and how it arrived where it is today. Understanding the past of a business involves the understanding of the following:

  - Human resources (like Charlie, Diane, and Tom).
  - Products (competitors' products versus yours).
  - Markets and market niches (in the United States and abroad).
  - Manufacturing (production technologies).
  - Research and development (of markets, products, and systems).
  - Investments (the return on alternative investments).
  - Public and governmental relations.

- *An understanding of the present.* Looking at the present is like watching a video tape. For planning and accounting convenience, we press the pause button to freeze a moment at the end of the current fiscal year to give us time to make a projection for the following years.

  The present, then, is simply the last image of a real-time movie, represented by the end points of the combined trends of the past. In a business plan, this present is represented by the latest estimates of actual figures for the current year, which are then used as the base year from which figures are projected for the next year. If we concentrate too hard on these frozen fragments, we may miss the real movie.

  It is critically important to realize that the present is constantly changing and cannot be captured in any static balance sheet or year-to-date income statement.

- *An understanding of alternative possible futures.* To choose an objective is to choose from among alternative possible futures for the business.

Just because the objective chosen can be attained does not mean that it will or should be. What resources are available—or how to acquire the resources needed—must be considered.

WHAT CHARACTERIZES A SUCCESSFUL BUSINESS STRATEGY?

- The strategy actually moves the business toward the objective for the planned distance.

- The planning procedure places an acceptable burden on personnel, based on their perception of how they will benefit from the results.

- Procedures evolve prudently to give managers time to begin to appreciate the value of being forewarned of possible opportunities and problems. When this happens, these managers will not view the procedures as a burden that interferes with current activities. Preventing fires by adequate planning is much more effective than putting out fires later.

- Routine tables and charts developed for strategy planning are accurate, user friendly, and easy to update by computer. Data collection, retrieval, and analysis programs are designed to provide in-depth data only when needed. Neither pounds of computer runs nor reams of uncorrelated charts and tables clarify issues.

- The data collected and analyzed for strategy planning are also needed for ongoing corporate operational analyses.

WHAT IS A BUSINESS PRIME OBJECTIVE? HOW DOES IT RELATE TO A STRATEGY? TO TACTICS?

- A *prime objective* is a clearly defined, decisive, and attainable future for a business that is rooted in customer needs. A prime objective must embody a purpose that infuses all activities of a business. A single business must have a *single* objective at any one time—like a ship or plane, a business cannot travel in two directions at once.

- A *strategy* is the course of action laid out to reach the prime objective. It may cover several years. It requires careful coordination of a multiplicity of variables, only some of which are given in balance sheets and income statements.

- *Tactics* are series of planned actions that make up a strategy. Many tasks may be involved. For example, one group of individuals might lay down an advertising barrage to obtain sales leads for salespeople assigned to sell a new product, while another group busily sets up a display of the new product for a local trade show.

- A *sales goal* (or secondary objective) describes a planned event as a military tactical unit might describe the capture of a hill. Since competitors in a market, like the enemy in a military engagement, may have selected the same target to defend or attack, the outcome is by no means certain.

- An *engineering or manufacturing goal* involves the creation of a new product or facility required to reach the prime objective. Positioning of the new product relative to competition or the facility relative to market geography may later determine the degree of success or failure of the strategy.

- A *completion date* marks the expected point in time at which the goal of a related group of tactics should have been reached en route to the prime objective.

- Formal planning methods, such as Program Evaluation and Review Technique (PERT), distinguish between activities and beginning or ending events. Activities involve a period of time, events do not. In computerized planning programs, events are often called *milestones*.

- A *corporate objective* is a *single* objective that coordinates and sets the limits on the objectives of subsidiary businesses. Each subsidiary should have no more than one objective for each separately defined business in which it is engaged.

WHY DOES THE PROCESS OF SETTING A PRIME OBJECTIVE OFTEN BECOME CONFUSED?

Confusion 1:   The business has not been properly defined.

Confusion 2:   Short-term tactics are mistaken for long-term objectives. To make matters worse, a number of uncoordinated or conflicting tactics are often set up as an objective.

The following are examples of tactics that have been raised erroneously to the status of objectives:

- *To increase unit sales of a product in the northeast region of the United States by 10 percent over the previous year's total.* This goal involves only a part of the business, so it is not a prime objective. It could, however, be a valid tactical maneuver.

- *To increase ROI (Return On Investment) by 5 percent over the previous year's total.* This goal is not an objective or a tactical maneuver. It is a hoped-for accounting result based on one or more tactics. It gives no indication of the actions required to increase the ROI, but it does indicate the state of a company's health as it moves toward its prime objective. Exception: It could be an objective for an investment company.

- *To improve morale.* This goal is not a business prime objective either. It is, however, a desirable goal because it makes it much easier to reach the prime objective of the company.

Confusion 3: Stereotyped or textbook responses are made to unique problems and opportunities. This confusion has become prevalent in recent years because of the notion that an academically trained manager can manage any business effectively without experience in relevant industries.

WHAT ARE SOME LOGICAL PRIME OBJECTIVES?

Here are a few. Obviously, to pursue several at once in a single business would be the route to disaster.

*   *To be the technological front-runner for defined products and markets in a specified number of years.* Many Japanese businesses have obviously held this as an objective since shortly after World War II.
*   *To become an industry's low-cost producer of mature products.* This certainly has been an objective of businesses in underdeveloped nations with low labor costs.
*   *To carve out a market niche for a high-technology product based on R&D conducted.* The computer industry has many companies with this objective.
*   *To reorient a business to another industry or product niche from a declining or unprofitable one.* This must be a hidden or explicit objective in the cigarette and steel industries as they attempt to diversify under social and economic pressures.

HOW DO YOU SET AN ACTUAL OBJECTIVE?

Setting the objective for a business requires a great deal of knowledge, common sense, and imagination. The real world is complicated. Management is not a cut-and-dried science in practice, but rather a challenging, messy, serious, and at times even humorous art involving the interplay of many disciplines—all of which are constantly evolving.

The scenario describing the adopted objective should include reasons for its selection. These reasons should be clear, whether for the retention of an old objective or the establishment of a new one, and should state why alternatives were discarded.

HOW DO TACTICS RELATE TO THE PRIME OBJECTIVE?

Suppose, like Charlie, your prime objective is to reestablish your business's leading position in the market. By using your personal computer, you can quickly prepare simple or complex strategy charts (critical path charts) like the one shown here for Chem-A-Lot, which has three strings of tactics:

A SIMPLE STRATEGY PLAN

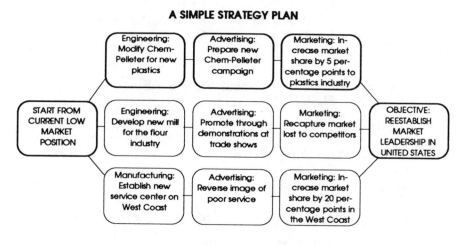

HOW DO YOU DEFINE A STRING OF TACTICS?

Tactics are those groups of planned actions or tasks that are necessary for attaining a prime objective. The critical path string of tactics at the top of the chart is the path of critical tasks that put a time limit on completion. It might look like this when written up for the strategy plan.

Goal: To increase market share by 5 percentage points to the plastics industry by modifying and repricing the Chem-Pelleter.

Time: Over the three-year period of the plan.

        Primary Responsibility: *Marketing.*

Task 1: Determination of product modification required by the market.

        Responsibility: *Marketing.*

Task 2: Product modification.

        Responsibility: *Engineering and manufacturing.*

Task 3: Determination of the price of the modified product.

        Responsibility: *Marketing.*

Task 4: Mounting an advertising campaign to reach plastics industry people who influence purchases.

        Responsibility: *Advertising.*

Task 5: Meeting the production schedule.

        Responsibility: *Manufacturing.*

Impact Statement: Estimated cost: $85,000 for the first year of the plan and $93,000 for the second year. Revenues expected, at the earliest: the last quarter of the second year.

This description of a string of tactics, however, is not detailed enough to act as a day-to-day guide for action.

Later, in the business plan, we'll show you how you can elaborate on a strategy chart and make it a dynamic working tool for carrying out your strategy.

HOW DO THE RESULTS OF THESE PLANS TIE INTO THE BASE BUSINESS?

Additional revenues and costs are simply shown as additions to the projections of the base business accounts, which have been modified to reflect expected economic conditions to arrive at forecasts. The new business portion of a forecast, however, is always more difficult to make than the old business one, which has an established record.

WHAT STEPS ARE REQUIRED TO PREPARE A STRATEGY PLAN?

Step 1: Define the business as it is right now.

Step 2: Envision the possible alternative futures for the business.

Step 3: Select the best futures envisioned and fashion prime objectives that make sense for each.

Step 4: Consider possible strategies and the resources required to reach each objective.

Step 5: Select one future with its prime objective based on risk, reward, attainability, and the breadth of enthusiastic participation that you can generate.

Step 6: Decide by which year you expect to reach the prime objective selected.

Step 7: Obtain the participation of all individuals in the business in developing the overall strategy and specific tactics needed to reach the prime objective. At this stage the tasks required for a tactics string need not be spelled out in detail.

Step 8: Ensure that the entire organization agrees to the prime objective. Do not take for granted that plans will be universally accepted. Maintain momentum. It generates enthusiasm.

Note: Steps 9, 10, and 11 are shown for clarification although they belong to the business plan and budget plan phases of the cycle.

Step 9: For the business plan, define in detail only those tactics that can be accomplished during the next two years.

Step 10: Estimate in the business plan how much additional sales will be brought in and how much additional costs will be incurred by using the tactics defined for each of the years.

Step 11: In the first budget year, add the new estimated revenues and costs to those projected for the ongoing business.

CHAPTER 14

PHASE 1: THE STRATEGY PLAN (PRACTICE)

YEAR 27 CONDITIONS AT CHEM-A-LOT

Sales began to bounce back dramatically early in year 27. Business was looking up despite the excessive prices customers had been charged in the past. Those prices had resulted in the sharp 55 percent unit-sales decline from years 17 through 25, followed by a further decline in the disastrous year 26. In addition, many good workers had been terminated during those years to keep costs down. Now they were missed. New people had to be trained. How had this rebound come about?

Soon after taking over as CEO, Charlie urged that machine prices be reduced based on a gut feeling he had developed over the years. Some staff members opposed this and countered with another idea: Let our prices stay put and allow the competitors' prices to catch up to ours. His opponents were certain that Chem-A-Lot would run the least risk by following such tactics. This do-nothing approach bothered Charlie. Finally, he asked George Newhouse, the consultant, what he thought about it.

Newhouse responded:

First, based on our earlier sales/units/price studies for Chem-A- Lot, demand would probably be fairly elastic for some time to come for most of your machines.

Second, market shares often shift during recessions because customers search for ways to reduce their own costs through the purchase of machines that either cost less or produce more.

Third, the gathering momentum of a recovery would counter lower unit profits because of rapidly increasing volume.

Fourth, morale would improve as everyone becomes busy and less worried about their own futures.

Finally, taking these four likely developments into consideration, I would not rule out a judicious reduction in prices at this time.

Charlie wanted further clarification of the first point on elasticity of demand for himself and his staff. Newhouse was called in to lead a discussion on the subject in one of Charlie's training sessions.

After the staff and others attending the session thoroughly understood the problem, Charlie made the decision to lower prices but tailored his action to each product, based on market and manufacturing information.

Rapidly increasing sales during year 27 quickly validated the insights of George Newhouse and Charlie's gut feeling. By the middle of year 27, Chem-A-Lot was a beehive of activity unmatched at any time since year 16—just before that long decline in unit sales.

During the early growth years, Chem-A-Lot had necessarily expanded production capacity to keep pace with demand. At its peak, year 16, it was operating at about 85 percent of capacity. During the following years, 17 through 25, price-weighted total unit production figures fell an average −9.4 percent annually for a total decline of 55 percent. The decline in units of equipment produced would be another way to look at the decline in capacity utilization. At any rate, by the end of the loss year 26, the factory was operating at about 30 percent of capacity.

FORECASTING THE BASE BUSINESS

Shifting market shares, shifting price levels, and increasing international competition during and after this recession made forecasting difficult. Charlie was sure the forecasts on which Tom Puller had based the strategy plan would most likely have to be altered later for the business plan.

Tom, meanwhile, neither pushed nor opposed price reductions, for as a professional sales manager, he believed that a good sales team ought to be able to sell its products regardless of the competitors' lower prices. However, he and his men pulled out all the stops in their efforts once the decision was made.

Tom was responsible for providing the sales for the base business on which growth through strategic planning rested. In order to achieve healthy growth, beyond the already established business, he also had to be concerned about the developing new products and new markets to produce sales revenues over and above base sales for existing machines. Because of these responsibilities, it was Tom who coordinated the entire strategy plan. Excerpts from the strategy plan report submitted to the board at the end of the first quarter in year 27 follow.

Excerpt: The Prime Objective of the Business

Reestablish Chem-A-Lot as a leading producer of quality conditioner, formulator, and transporter equipment for the process industries in the world.

Our objective is subdivided into first- and second-priority goals:

Priority 1: Turning the base business around through a combination of moves such as improved pricing practices, needed but overdue product modifications, and development of new markets for old machines. Since these goals have required a minimum of funding, they are already well under way.

Priority 2: Developing entirely new products to sell to existing and new markets. Since many of the talented engineers who developed our original machines are no longer here, we must recreate this capability—no mean task. In addition, we can only work on a few new prototype machines at a time.

Details were provided about alternatives that had been considered for the prime objective as well as the major alternative strategy strings being considered to reach the two goals. The risks involved in each of these strategies, such as the risk that had been taken in reducing prices to break the harmful pricing policies of the recent flat dollar-sales years, were also discussed.

Excerpt: The Markets Served

Our serviced markets are not yet mature and will not become so during this three-year period. Our old customers and potential new customers do not appear to face unusual or insurmountable competition for their products. Substantial optimism abounds in their circles.

Our lost market share in North America in virtually every product line must be regained, and we must reestablish ourselves as the leader in our market niches. We fully intend to stay and compete successfully and profitably in the conditioner, formulator, and transporter product lines.

Excerpt: Competitors

We have three major competitors in North America. They are Harrison Inc., Johnson Machinery, and George Equipment, Inc. All three are based in this country. The competitors moving in from other countries (see page 312) are not an immediate threat, but will present a formidable challenge to the marketing of our machines outside North America.

There followed a detailed description of all competitors, their products, and their estimated sizes and shares of market.

Excerpt: The Three-Year Forecast for Base Business

Because of the price level change, our forecast is based primarily on the sales for each machine since the first of the year, plus customer plans reported by our sales engineers in the field. We believe the rapid recovery rate experienced during the first three months of the year will slow down next year. For the balance of this year, we believe sales will continue to grow but at a reduced rate. This information has resulted in a sales forecast, which has been used to prepare a rough forecast of profit levels for years 28 through 30 using the fixed and variable cost data now becoming available. We needed to make these preliminary cost and profit forecasts in order to evaluate how rapidly we could push our second-priority goals of developing new products for existing and new markets.

In the next few months, as work proceeds on the business plan, and later on the budget, we believe these forecasts will need revision. For now they are conservative; hopefully, they will have to be revised upward.

CHEM-A-LOT
YEAR 28 STRATEGY PLAN
SALES, COSTS, AND INCOME BASE BUSINESS FORECAST
FOR PLAN YEARS 28 THROUGH 30

(Dollars in Thousands)

Year	Sales	Fixed Costs	Variable Costs	Operating Income
27	$33,000	$ 9,800	$21,100	$2,100
28	38,300	10,000	23,800	4,500
29	40,600	10,700	24,800	5,100
30	46,000	11,400	27,600	7,000

To this base forecast we anticipate additional sales, costs, and profits from our planned strategy initiatives as follows:

CHEM-A-LOT
YEAR 28 STRATEGY PLAN
BASE BUSINESS FORECAST PLUS
STRATEGY INITIATIVES FOR YEARS 28 THROUGH 30

(Dollars in Thousands)

Year	Sales	Fixed Costs	Variable Costs	Operating Income Amount	% of Sales
27	$33,000	$ 9,800	$21,000	$2,100	6
28	38,300	10,100	24,000	4,200	11
29	44,000	10,900	26,900	6,200	14
30	49,800	11,700	29,900	8,200	16

Excerpts: The Strategy Goals Selected

We have developed a plan for the next three years, primarily for the United States, to concentrate on three strategies for reaching our prime objective. These strategies are to:

- Modify the Chem-Pelleter in order to increase our market share from 20 to 25 percent in the plastics industries.
- Develop a new mill for the flour industry to recapture at least half of the 40 percent market share lost to competitors.

- Establish a new service center on the West Coast in order to increase market share in that region by around 20 percentage points to match our other regions.

- We believe there will be a spillover effect from this effort into the international markets. Sales generated by these investments will be timed approximately as follows:

CHEM-A-LOT
YEARS 28–30 STRATEGY PLAN
IMPACT OF TACTICS ON BASE PRODUCTS
AND SERVICE SALES

(Dollars in Thousands)

Products and Services	Expected Results	Year			
		27 *(Current)*	28 *(Budget)*	29 *(Estimate)*	30 *(Goal)*
Base products and services sales		$33,000	$38,300	$40,600	$46,000
Chem-Pelleter modification sales	Increase U.S. industry share from 20% to 25%	—	—	500	600[1]
New Chem-Mill sales	Regain 20% of flour industry market	—	—	900	1000[2]
West Coast service center sales	Increase West Coast market share from 5% to 25%	—	—	2,000	2,200[3]
Total sales		$33,000	$38,300	$44,000	$49,800

[1]The total Pelleter market was estimated at $12.0 million in year 27; Chem-A-Lot's share to go from $2.4 million in year 27 to $3.0 million by year 30.
[2]The total flour industry market was estimated at $10.0 million in year 27.
[3]The West Coast market was estimated at $10.8 million in year 27.

With these additions, we can again become a growth company approximating a 15 percent annual average growth rate.

PLANNING WORKSHEET

A summary of the financial highlights expected follows in the form of a flow chart of our income statements and balance sheets for the current year and the three-year planning period.

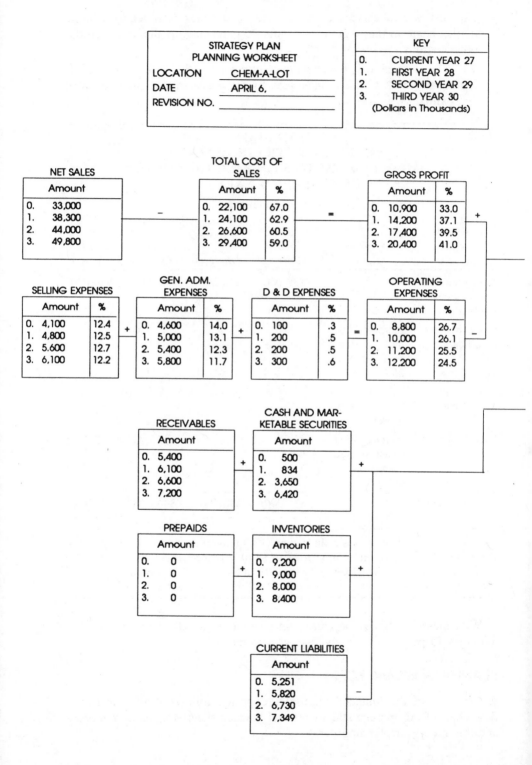

STRATEGY PLAN
PLANNING WORKSHEET

LOCATION   CHEM-A-LOT

DATE   APRIL 6,

REVISION NO. _____

KEY

0.	CURRENT YEAR 27
1.	FIRST YEAR 28
2.	SECOND YEAR 29
3.	THIRD YEAR 30

(Dollars in Thousands)

NET SALES

	Amount
0.	33,000
1.	38,300
2.	44,000
3.	49,800

TOTAL COST OF SALES

	Amount	%
0.	22,100	67.0
1.	24,100	62.9
2.	26,600	60.5
3.	29,400	59.0

GROSS PROFIT

	Amount	%
0.	10,900	33.0
1.	14,200	37.1
2.	17,400	39.5
3.	20,400	41.0

SELLING EXPENSES

	Amount	%
0.	4,100	12.4
1.	4,800	12.5
2.	5,600	12.7
3.	6,100	12.2

GEN. ADM. EXPENSES

	Amount	%
0.	4,600	14.0
1.	5,000	13.1
2.	5,400	12.3
3.	5,800	11.7

D & D EXPENSES

	Amount	%
0.	100	.3
1.	200	.5
2.	200	.5
3.	300	.6

OPERATING EXPENSES

	Amount	%
0.	8,800	26.7
1.	10,000	26.1
2.	11,200	25.5
3.	12,200	24.5

RECEIVABLES

	Amount
0.	5,400
1.	6,100
2.	6,600
3.	7,200

CASH AND MARKETABLE SECURITIES

	Amount
0.	500
1.	834
2.	3,650
3.	6,420

PREPAIDS

	Amount
0.	0
1.	0
2.	0
3.	0

INVENTORIES

	Amount
0.	9,200
1.	9,000
2.	8,000
3.	8,400

CURRENT LIABILITIES

	Amount
0.	5,251
1.	5,820
2.	6,730
3.	7,349

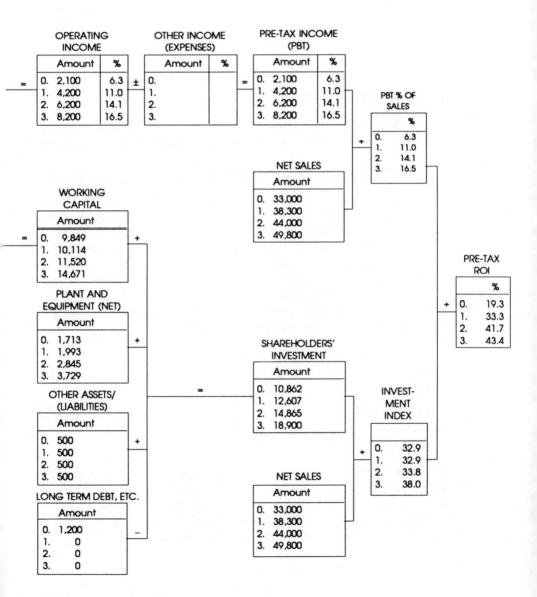

CHAPTER 15

PHASE 2: THE BUSINESS PLAN (THEORY)

WHAT IS A BUSINESS PLAN?

It is a plan containing those tactics of the long-range strategy plan that can be accomplished in two years to move the business toward the prime objective.

WHAT INFORMATION DO YOU NEED FOR A BUSINESS PLAN?

- *Forecasts of base business—the business as it now exists before any new or revised tactics are considered.* For this part of the business, the tactics of previous years have been reduced to routine and do not need to be detailed again. Here we become involved in determining long-term trends, business cycles, seasonal patterns, and irregular events that will affect the base business. The rate-of-change, size, and other charts already encountered are useful for the analysis of base business. Where possible, base business forecasts should include summary as well as detailed numerical forecasts of the following:

  — Human resources.

  — Products.

  — Markets.

  — Manufacturing.

  — Investments.

  — Personnel.

Any knowledge that helps pinpoint threats, opportunities, strengths, and weaknesses as well as problems and subtle relationships should be examined as a basis for improved control, remedial action, or new initiatives. Forecasts and supporting information should be somewhat in-depth for the first 12 months and less detailed for the following 12.

- *Strategic tactics to be accomplished during the next two years in terms of quantifiable revenues and costs that, when added to the base sales and cost forecasts, will result in attaining strategy goals.* The additional impact on the business of new products, new territories, changes in research and development, and changes in capacity should be detailed by activity and time allotted.

HOW DO YOU DETERMINE THE IMPACT OF TACTICS ON THE BUSINESS?

- Unfortunately, the costs of tactics are usually incurred during the first of the business plan years, whereas the benefits may not even start to accrue until the following, or even later, years.

Without careful planning, tactics involving the introduction of a major product could have an adverse effect on existing key growth rates. A special rate-of-change analysis chart can help you predict what will happen to your business under the pressure of implemented tactics. Monitor it so you can take timely corrective action if it appears likely that the tactics will put too much strain on the business. In other words, once you have defined your tactics for the year, this type of chart, together with carefully monitored economic forecasts can provide a kind of early-warning radar.

Here's the way the pattern of rate changes might look for a business not geared to the routine introduction of new products.

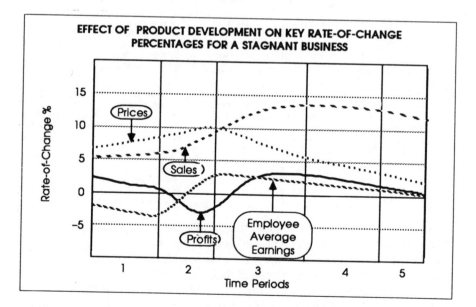

By time period, this chart depicts:

Period 1: A stagnant business tries to increase profits by increasing prices and lowering costs alone.

Period 2: A belated effort to respond to competition by hiring high-salaried experts to update products through the use of new technology drastically affects other key rates.

Period 3: The effort finally pays off—the sales and profit rates increase, prices come down, and average earnings of employees level off.

Period 4: Business starts to stagnate again.

Period 5: Business has failed to maintain growth rates—all are falling. Survival again becomes a critical issue. The stage is now set to repeat the cycle.

Moral: Maintain a steady flow of new products so that enough are in the early high-growth stage to cover the cost of the products that are being developed. The optimum rate of introduction of new products will, of course, vary from industry to industry.

HOW CAN TACTICS GUIDE DAY-TO-DAY ACTIVITIES?

Here's how. Let's go back to that simple strategy plan for a bit.

A SIMPLE STRATEGY PLAN

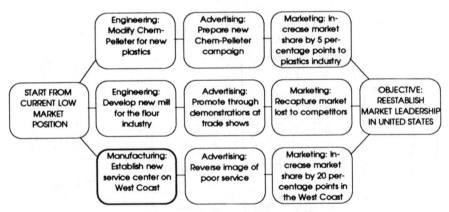

User-friendly personal computer programs are now available to keep track of the time, finances, equipment, and people that are devoted to carrying out tactics. Manually prepared flow charts are equally acceptable and contain identical information. Computer-generated examples follow only because they are less time-consuming to prepare. Here's how they work.

We'll just take one tactic out of a string, the one highlighted in the lower left-hand corner of the Simple Strategy Plan: Establish new service center on West Coast. And we'll focus on one small part of the tactic so you can see how that part becomes an efficient tool for guiding assigned tasks on a day-to-day and even hour-to-hour basis.

ESTABLISH NEW SERVICE CENTER ON WEST COAST

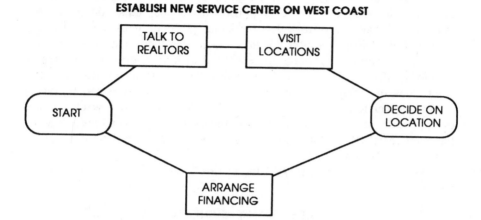

This first portion of a longer chart takes us up to the point at which the team assigned decides upon a suitable site in an appropriate location. Tasks include visiting potential sites for new construction as well as available existing buildings, checking transportation facilities, investigating zoning laws, and comparing possible financial arrangements. Time would have to be allowed for counteroffers before any deal could be made.

After the site decision is made, the next tasks (not charted) would be planning new construction or remodeling of an existing building, furnishing offices, installing equipment, selecting and training the service staff, and so on.

While you are preparing a more detailed chart on your computer, you could enter a lot of information into and around each box. However, this makes the chart rather cluttered, so you might take the option of calling up only selected information for each box. Luckily, most planning programs can produce the following types of supplementary charts and tables:

SERVICE CENTER TIME CHART

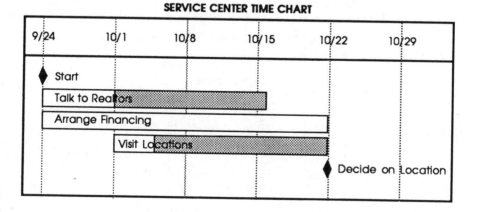

The white section of a given bar indicates how long the associated task will take. It gives the earliest starting and completion dates. The right end of the bar shows the date by which that task must be completed to fit into the schedule; therefore, the grey portion of the bar tells you how much latitude you have in getting that particular piece of work done. The bar labeled Talk to Realtors indicates how much time there is available to visit realtors and compare findings to reach a decision on possible geographic locations. The all-white bar, Arrange Financing, is the critical task that determines the length of time before the location decision can be made. A built-in calendar assures you correct dates for each task—weekends and even holidays are taken into account automatically while you concentrate on the main chart! Black diamonds represent the start or completion of a group of related activities.

This next chart keeps track of the tasks of individuals who visit sites at various locations.

SERVICE CENTER TASK ASSIGNMENT CHART

	9/24	10/1	10/8	10/15	10/22
Tom					
		Talk to Realtors▓▓▓▓▓▓▓▓▓			
Bob					
			Visit Locations▓▓▓▓▓▓▓▓▓		
John					
			Visit Locations▓▓▓▓▓▓▓▓▓		
Jane					
			Visit Locations▓▓▓▓▓▓▓▓▓		
Diane					
		Arrange Financing			

And the following three tables illustrate other types of information that can be automatically prepared for you.

PEOPLE COST

	Name	Cost/Day
1	Tom	$245
2	Bob	138
3	John	126
4	Jane	102
5	Diane	245

TASK EXPENSES AND INCOME

Task Name		Expenses	Income
1	Start	$ 0	$0
2	Talk to Realtors	50	0
3	Arrange Financing	25	0
4	Visit Locations	3000	0
5	Decide on Location	0	0

Since no income has resulted at this stage, zeros are shown in the income column. The cost of doing the string of tactics is accumulated automatically for the time periods involved so that you can call up a cash-flow table and see that $10,664 has been spent up to this point.

CASH-FLOW TABLE

Starting	Costs	Income	Ending	Cumulative
9/24	$2525	0	10/1	–$2,525
10/1	5689	0	10/8	–8,214
10/8	1225	0	10/15	–9,439
10/15	1225	0	10/22	–10,664
10/22	0	0	10/29	–10,664

You can also obtain a summary table for the portion of the strategy covered up to this point.

SUMMARY FOR TACTIC

	Task or Event Name	Days[1]	Earliest Start	Earliest Finish	Latest Start	Latest Finish
1	Start	0	9/24	9/24	9/24	9/24
2	Talk to Realtors	5	9/24	10/1	10/9	10/16
3	Arrange Financing	20	9/24	10/22	9/24	10/22
4	Visit Locations	4	10/1	10/5	10/16	10/22
5	Site Decided	0	10/22	10/22	10/22	10/22

		Task Cost	People Cost	Income	Resource 1	2	3	4	5
1	Start	$ 0	$ 0	0					
2	Talk to Realtors	50	1,225	0	Tom				
3	Arrange Financing	25	4,900	0		Diane			
4	Visit Locations	3,000	1,464	0			Bob	John	Jane
5	Site Decided	0	0	0					

[1]Events, or milestones, such as Start and Site Decided mark the results of activity but take no time themselves. For example, all five people were involved from the start in the location decision and had formal and informal conversations to compare sites until the decision was reached. On day 10/22 they decided by taking a vote—thus the decision itself was made at the point in time when the vote count occurred.

Now imagine a team composed of draftsmen and department heads detailing not only this one tactic but a complete string of tactics as well as the entire, fairly simple strategy plan. Hundreds of hours of labor would be involved. You can see why, before the advent of the personal computer, good planning was quite a burden. It took a long time, and sometimes even good planning got in the way of action.

WHILE YOU'RE PREPARING A BUSINESS PLAN, IS THERE A WAY TO DETERMINE WHEN YOU SHOULD POSTPONE TACTICS TO A LATER YEAR OR ACCELERATE THEM?

- Yes, there is. As a matter of fact, at Chem-A-Lot, Tom wanted to push ahead on a number of strategy strings in addition to the three shown in the simple strategy we have just considered. He found, however, that revenues would not support all of them in the first three-year plan. He was convinced of this partly through the use of a break-even analysis. In the end, a consensus of the staff was reached that Chem-A-Lot just did not have the resources available yet and was not sufficiently recovered to seek outside finances.

- In addition to a break-even analysis, another helpful tool discussed earlier would be a 12/12 pressure analysis comparing the sales of your business with a leading indicator. This technique is particularly handy for picking up forthcoming economic cyclical turning points. It will, for example, permit you to modify base forecasts during the final quarters of the year, before they are used in next year's budget. Of course, it may take some effort to find an appropriate leading indicator, as was explained earlier. Also, neither of these techniques should be relied on as the sole way of determining whether tactics should be postponed.

WHAT ARE THE STEPS REQUIRED TO PREPARE A BUSINESS PLAN?

Step 1: Reconsider the prime objective of the business as defined in the strategy plan to determine if it is still appropriate or needs modification. At this time, also consider how the prime objective might be changed in response to conditions in the years after the current plan ends.

Step 2: Define in more detail all tactics in the first two years of the strategy plan. Have appropriate individuals or teams define each task required as well as review strengths and weaknesses of resources available to perform each task. Determine what resources must be acquired from outside the business.

Step 3: Review the total cost of all tactics required to reach the prime objective.

Step 4: Review all planned activities in terms of anticipated cost and revenue additions to the base business.

Step 5: Divide large sets of tactics into smaller groups more feasible for successive annual business plans. Shift tasks from or to following years as necessary.

Step 6: Add estimated costs and revenues required to reach the prime objective for each annual business planning period, taking into account time lags. Break the first period by quarter or in such detail as is necessary for preparation of the budget.

Step 7: Add estimated revenues and costs on which to base business forecasts.

Step 8: Determine possible effect of the first year's doable tactics on profitability.

Note: Steps 9 and 10 are shown for clarification although they belong to the budget plan phase of the planning cycle.

Step 9: Add the impact of this year's additional tactics on old and new markets, products, and services to base sales forecasts to develop the annual budget.

Step 10: Test the effect of different unit prices and costs, and check figures against the latest economic inputs for reasonableness. Normally, the budget is based on constant budget-year dollars.

CHAPTER 16

PHASE 2: THE BUSINESS PLAN (PRACTICE)

YEAR 27 CONDITIONS CONTINUE TO IMPROVE AT CHEM-A-LOT

By the end of the third quarter, when the business plan was to have been completed for the next year, Chem-A-Lot was well on the road to recovery despite a slight slowdown in sales. Even so, base business sales for the budget could be, and were, forecasted at a higher rate than in the strategy plan.

However, after the forecast was completed, a disturbing fact came to Tom's attention: A study relating Chem-A-Lot sales to a leading indicator showed that, in all probability, year 29 would be a slow year for the U.S. economy and the process industries served by Chem-A-Lot. The base business forecast had to be revised.

Because the information about the prime objective, markets served, and competitors contained in Chapter 14 remains essentially unchanged, it will not be repeated. Here, however, are pertinent excerpts from the business plan for years 28 and 29 as submitted to the board at the end of the third quarter of year 27.

Excerpt: The Strategy Goals Selected

The three strategy plan goals we originally selected are still valid despite the anticipated decline in sales for year 29. We now believe the economic conditions will simply postpone some forecasted sales from year 29 to year 30. Furthermore, we believe the slowdown in year 29 will permit us to concentrate our efforts in the new product and design areas, thus actually enhancing the results of year 30. Our three original strategies in the strategy plan, modified in this business plan for current market conditions are as follows:

- Modify the Chem-Pelleter in order to increase our market share from 20 to 25 percent (now revised to 32 percent) in the plastics industries.

- Develop and sell new mill for the flour industry in order to recapture at least half (now over half) of the 40 percent market share lost to competitors.

- Establish a new sales/service center on the West Coast in order to increase market share from 5 to 25 percent (now revised to 29 percent) in that region to match other regions.

We continue to feel that there will be a spillover effect from this effort into the developing international market.

Every business is affected directly and indirectly by the environment in which it operates. Internal and external conditions must be reviewed as they exist and are expected to persist in the years ahead; Chem-A-Lot is no exception.

Excerpts: The Expected Business Environment

- We are optimistic about the growth prospects within our industry. The market for our products will grow about 10 percent annually in real terms during this planning period.

- U.S. inflation, although a factor, is expected to be in the neighborhood of 6 percent per year. International exchange rates are expected to favor our exports in the next two years. In fact, the U.S. dollar may weaken by 3 percent per year against major European currencies and as much as 5 percent per year versus the Japanese yen.

- Our customers are under pressure to increase the efficiency of their options. Our equipment and service must meet their needs.

- Our major competitors remain substantially the same as last year. Some were or are being acquired by larger, publicly held corporations, and several overseas based firms are increasing their efforts to gain a foothold in the U.S. market. We continue to remain at the high end when our sales prices are compared to those of our competitors. Our principal competitors and estimated market shares by product line are

TOTAL MARKET-YEAR 27

Competitors	Units	Market Share
Conditioners		
Chem-A-Lot	730	30%
Harrison, Inc.	610	25
Johnson Machinery	490	20
George Equipment, Inc.	370	15
Sanalai, Ltd.	125	5
Other	125	5
Total	2,450	100%
Formulators		
Chem-A-Lot	540	20%
Harrison, Inc.	540	20
Johnson Machinery	490	18
Formalonics, Inc.	400	15
Furi, Ltd.	350	13
Other	380	14
Total	2,700	100%
Transporters		
Johnson Machinery	112	35%
Chem-A-Lot	80	25
Convex Co., Ltd.	48	15
Transload, Inc.	32	10
Other	48	15
Total	320	100%

More specific profiles of each of our major competitors are contained in the strategy plan issued earlier this year.

The marketing, sales, manufacturing, design, and development as well as administrative plans must be coordinated as to time and effort with those of every other planning unit if the business plan is to stand a good chance of fulfillment. Chem-A-Lot did indeed have excellent plans in these areas. Let's look at some of them.

Excerpt: The Manufacturing Department Section

Although we may no longer be the lowest-cost producer in our industry, we will regain that position by year 30. Our quality will improve and our production equipment will be modernized on a cost-effective basis.

Our tactics do include the following:

1. Increasing quality control at every production cost center, aided by monthly awareness seminars.

2. Scheduling on- and off-the-job training sessions for all production personnel.

3. Investing approximately $1.8 million during the next two years in state-of-the-art, but well-tested, production equipment and warehouse and storeroom renovation.

4. Holding plant wage and salary pay-rate increases to within 5 percent of present levels per year.

5. Holding vendor material costs to current prices in year 28 and no more than a 5 percent increase (hopefully less) in year 29; having all vendors deliver ordered items on time and meet our quality standards. (Each major vendor will be visited within the next quarter by two members of our management team. The purpose of the visit will be to obtain commitments for quality material at the lowest appropriate prices.)

6. Completing installation of a material requirements planning system next year.

7. Improving inventory turns to 3.0 times per year by the end of year 29.

8. Stepping up on-time shipment of orders to the 90 percent level in year 28 and 95 percent in year 29.

9. The possibility of making subassemblies and other parts ourselves rather than buying them from reputable outside vendors will be studied in detail for 50 percent of our products in year 28 and the remainder in year 29.

Excerpts: Marketing/Sales Section

YEARS 28–30 BUSINESS PLAN
IMPACT OF TACTICS ON BASE PRODUCTS AND
SERVICE SALES REVISED

(Dollars in Thousands)

Products and Services	Expected Results	Year			
		27 (Current)	28 (Budget)	20 (Estimate)	30 (Goal)
Base Products and services sales		$33,900	$39,500	$35,700	$42,000
Chem-Pelleter modification sales	Increase U.S. plastics industry share from 20% to 32%	—	—	400	1,410[1]
New Chem-Mill sales	Regain 20% of flour industry market	—	—	700	2,050[2]
West Coast service center sales	Increase West Coast market share from 5% to 29%	—	—	1,400	2,600[3]
Total Sales		$33,900	$39,500	$38,200	$48,060

[1] The total market was estimated at $12.0 million in year 27, Chem-A-Lot's share to go from $2.4 million in year 27 to $3.8 million by year 30. Business plan increases share 7 percentage points more than strategy plan.
[2] The total flour industry market was estimated at $10.0 million in year 27.
[3] The West Coast market was estimated at $10.8 million in year 27. Business plan increases share 4 percentage points more than strategy plan.

Chem-A-Lot managers prepared detailed programs delineating their strategies for years 28 and 29. Task assignments, task income, costs, personnel required, and time lines clearly stipulated how the strategies would be accomplished, when, and with what results. Reproduced here is just a limited illustration of Chem-A-Lot's approach to increasing Chem-Pelleter's market share.

The Chem-Pelleter modification information forms summarize how investments for research and development are tracked. Such investments are separated from those fixed and variable costs that have an ongoing effect on sales. Once routine production schedules start in year 29 for the modified Chem-Pelleter, ongoing fixed and variable costs will change.

Here's an excerpt from the business plan:

Due to process changes in the plastics industries, the Chem-Pelleter has been in need of a major modification for some time to make it more competitive.

CHEM-PELLETER MODIFICATION
(Summary of Tactics)

IMPACT STATEMENT

Goal: To increase market share by 12 percentage points by year 30, from 20 to 32 percent of the plastics industry, by modifying and repricing the Chem-Pelleter. This will increase total sales by just over $1.8 million in total for years 29 and 30. A secondary goal is to reduce high unit costs of production.

Prime Responsibility: Marketing

Expected Results: Sales of $3.8 million by year 30, up from an estimated $2.4 million in year 27. Revenues expected at the earliest by the third quarter of the second year. Profitability expected to be above average for Chem-A-Lot machines.

Time: Three years

Year	Task	Department Responsible	Task Description	Estimated Quarter Start	Completion
28	1	Sales, market research, product D&D	Determination of Chem-Pelleter modification required by plastics industry	28–1	28–2
	2	Sales, engineering, manufacturing	Chem-Pelleter modification	28–2	29–1
29	3	Sales, pricing, market research	Determination of price	29–1	29–1
	4	Sales, advertising	Ad campaign directed	29–1	29–2
30	5	Sales, manufacturing	Reaching sales forecasts and meeting production schedules	29–2	30–4

The responsibility for task 1 in the summary is outlined here together with estimated costs and completion dates. In addition, actual costs and completion dates will be shown as they become available through our project control system.

CHEM-PELLETER MODIFICATION
DESIGN AND DEVELOPMENT INVESTMENT
(Task 1)

Department Responsible	Task Performed	Estimated Completion		Actual Completion	
		Date	Cost	Date	Cost
Sales	Provide information on customer complaints known to sales engineers and other pertinent facts to those working on the task	1/15/28	$ 500	_____	$____
Market research	Surveys of the plastics industry to determine the extent and nature of the modifications required and the impact on sales of making or not making the modifications	2/30/28	$3,000	_____	$____
Product D&D	Study of typical applications as identified by market research to determine exact needs of the plastics industry	4/15/28	$4,000	_____	$____
			$7,500		$____

A complete program of all tasks is maintained by the president and reported on at monthly management meetings.

Excerpt: The Forecast Revision

Just prior to completing the business plan, a careful analysis of the relationship between Chem-A-Lot sales and the economy was conducted using the 12/12 pressure technique. The findings were verified by our sales engineers and key customers. After that, the base forecast for the strategy plan was revised as follows for the business plan:

SALES, COSTS, AND INCOME BASE BUSINESS
FORECASTS FOR PLAN YEARS 28 THROUGH 30
(Dollars in Thousands)

Year	Earlier Sales Forecasts	Revised Sales Forecasts	Fixed Costs	Variable Costs	Operating Income Amount	%
27	$33,000	$33,900	$ 9,510	$21,690	$2,700	8%
28	38,300	39,500	10,546	24,284	4,670	12
29	40,600	35,700	10,982	21,272	3,446	10
30	46,000	42,000	12,078	25,747	4,175	10

The base business sales forecasts plus new strategies to increase market share are now anticipated to result in the following revisions:

BASE BUSINESS FORECASTS PLUS NEW
STRATEGY INITIATIVES FOR YEARS 28 THROUGH 30
(Dollars in Thousands)

Year	Earlier Sales Forecasts	Revised Sales Forecasts	Fixed Costs	Variable Costs	Operating Income Amount	%
27	$33,000	$33,900	$ 9,510	$21,690	$2,700	8%
28	38,300	39,500	10,546	24,284	4,670	12
29	44,000	38,200	11,321	22,772	4,107	11
30	49,800	48,060	12,417	28,631	7,012	15

We now forecast a cyclical sales decline in our base product lines in year 29 to $35.7 million from the $39.5 million level forecasted for the previous year. Nevertheless, the efforts of our overall strategy plan will start to bear fruit in year 29, adding $2.5 million in sales and, hopefully, another $6.1 million in year 30 due to product line modifications, additions, and the increase in market share from the efforts of our West Coast service center.

Excerpts: Financial Section of Business Plan

SUMMARY OF PROJECTED
FINANCIAL CONDITION

(Dollars in Thousands)

	Year		
	27 *(Current)*	28 *(Budget)*	29 *(Estimate)*
Current Assets	$15,373	$16,076	$15,538
Current Liabilities	5,351	5,962	5,317
Working Capital	10,022	10,114	10,221
Net Property, Plant, and Equipment	1,713	1,993	2,845
Other Assets	500	500	500
Less Long-Term Loans	(1,200)	—	—
Shareholders' Equity	$11,035	$12,607	$13,566
Sales	$33,900	$39,500	$38,200
Operating Income	2,700	4,670	4,107
Capital Expenditures	—	550	1,210
Employees	231	252	247

CHAPTER 17

PHASE 3: BUDGET (THEORY)

WHAT IS A BUDGET?

- It is the best estimate at the time of preparation of the funds received and funds spent during the first year of a long-term plan designed to move the base business through new strategy initiatives toward the established prime objective.
- The budget is also a valuable tool throughout the year. If properly prepared, the underlying documentation and analyses will point out alternative tactics to counterbalance unfavorable trends in sales, costs, profits, and investments.

The budget is not compiled simply to guess next year's operational results and financial condition. Certainly that is one result of the budget process. However, the major benefits of detailed budgeting are derived from using information regarding the interrelationships of unit and dollar sales volumes with expenses and investments in each cost center. It is generally understood that the year's actual results rarely equal those budgeted. What is less understood is why and what to do about it as the days and months pass.

HOW IMPORTANT ARE UNDERLYING BUDGET ASSUMPTIONS?

- A budget based on erroneous or unlikely assumptions is misleading. Columns of numbers that foot and crossfoot to the penny can be a waste of everyone's time unless those numbers are based on realistic assumptions.
- Board members and other users should be apprised of all assumptions so they can question them and react to them. Stating assumptions also makes it somewhat easier for the user to identify those that should have been made and were not.

WHAT ARE SOME OF THE MORE IMPORTANT INFLATION AND PRICE ASSUMPTIONS THAT UNDERPIN SOUND BUDGETS?

- Unit selling-price changes by product line.

- Cost increases or decreases anticipated from vendors of materials, components, utilities, supplies, and maintenance services.

- Expected changes in salaries, wage rates, and related fringe benefits—including social security and health-care and retirement costs.

- Any other expenses and cost revisions.

WHAT ARE SOME OF THE MORE IMPORTANT PERSONNEL ASSUMPTIONS?

- Personnel requirements for the budget year. Most budgets should include departmental summaries for the plant or shop; for research, design, and development; for sales, marketing, and customer service; and for administration.

- In the plant or shop, classification of workers into those who directly produce products and services and those who are an indirect aid to such production.

- Personnel statistics shown by department cost or expense centers.

- Numbers of people and related dollars of payroll.

WHAT ARE SOME OF THE MORE IMPORTANT FORECASTING ASSUMPTIONS?

- *General economic trends and specific trends in the industry.* The old practice of simply estimating a 10 percent increase in dollar sales is not appropriate.

- *Sales by number of units, by piece count, or weight estimated for each product line.* Due to inflation and variances in product pricing, total revenues are not always indicative of profitability or shifts in customer demand.

- *Costs, fixed and variable, by product line.* These allow the budget to be an operating tool if sales vary.

- *Working capital needs.* The major variables will be accounts receivable days outstanding, inventory turns, accounts payable days outstanding, and tax and interest rates.

- *Market share estimates for each product line whenever possible.* Estimates of market share for specific products are often difficult to determine with precision. Yet, those businesses that can ascertain ballpark figures will be in a better position to compete.

- *Sales backlog statistics, when meaningful.*

- *Financing arrangements.* Appropriate financing should be planned and not just allowed to happen. Specific financing methods are not described herein. Each business has a different financial condition, and type of funds and applicable interest rates vary greatly over time.

WHAT ARE SOME OF THE MORE IMPORTANT CAPITAL SPENDING ASSUMPTIONS?

- Capital spending should be planned well in advance of when such assets will be needed. Crisis spending (or unplanned purchases of significant assets) is usually inefficient. It results in "mandatory" purchasing, that is, buying to "keep the doors open." When funds are tight, all known projects or additions should be discussed and compared beforehand so that appropriate assets are purchased rather than those being demanded for immediate funding by departments undergoing an unanticipated crisis.

- A complete budget package should include a summary of the real estate, plant, machinery, equipment, or facility improvements needed to attain budget.

- Leases are often included in a budget as if the related leased assets were purchased. In fact, generally accepted accounting principles require recording certain leases in financial statements as assets and related liabilities when the substance of the lease contract is an installment purchase. In those instances, the use of leased assets dictates the number of years to amortize them against income. The capitalizable amount of such leases is established either by ascertaining the cost of such assets from vendors or appraisers or calculating the present value of all future lease payments for the estimated term of the lease plus the present value of the purchase option price, if any, when the lease term expires.

  (Present values can be determined using readily available formulae, tables in financial textbooks, or computer-generated amounts. That is the easy part. The hard part is to decide on an appropriate interest rate by which to discount those amounts payable in the future to equal amounts as if payable today. Normally, your borrowing rate for similar term loans can suffice, or the lessor can supply today's value.)

HOW DO STRATEGIC PLANS RELATE TO CAPITAL SPENDING?

- Strategic planning and capital spending must go hand-in-hand if the long-term plan is to be accomplished. Mandatory project expenditures and major maintenance programs probably take precedence over spending for cost reductions and growth because they may be necessary to remain in business. Although spending to attain growth sounds conventional and rational, it is also quite difficult to evaluate in advance. Growth via internal expansion can be contrasted and compared to growth via acquisition of other businesses and product lines. Decisions are normally based on expected returns on invested capital computations.

Sounds simple, doesn't it? However, computing a return in advance is subject to the vagaries of economic business cycles, inflation, technological obsolescence, competition, and so on. The key is to keep all requests for capital in perspective, review them at the same time, and evaluate each as they relate to the long-term plan and to each other, given forecasted predictions of the demand for the products and services of the business.

- Estimated returns on capital expenditures should be forecasted. Certain capital items will be necessary to remain at current production and service levels; others will enable expansion. Still others are required to maintain facilities and equipment in good operational order or to achieve manufacturing cost reductions. In some of these situations, a calculation of return on investment (ROI) is not called for. For example, certain expenditures may be required to comply with governmental, environmental, and safety regulations. Mandated expenditures of that type may have a negative short-run ROI for the business as measured by current accounting methods even though such expenditures may be of immense benefit to the business in the long run. It is necessary to replace vital production equipment to keep a production line in operation. On the other hand, most capital expenditures can be equated with anticipated profit returns on those purchases.

SHOULD ACQUISITIONS AND DIVESTITURES PLANS BE BUDGETED?

- Yes. During the process of introspection that naturally occurs in the strategic planning, business planning, and budgeting process, each company routinely examines its products and services to determine whether it should expand into new markets with its current products and services or bring other products and services into its current markets. Yet another alternative would be to contract its current lines in its current markets.

  As a result, the strategy and business plans should normally contain plans for acquiring related or unrelated businesses and product lines for the periods covered. Although details of acquisitions may be sketchy and the probability of successfully concluding acquisitions may be questionable, the possibility deserves periodic—no less than annual—review.

- Another answer to expansion could be to acquire manufacturing and distribution rights rather than purchase an entity to complete certain product lines or entering new markets. Licensing, cross-licensing, and granting manufacturing and distribution rights may be viable alternatives. These are often much less costly than purchasing another business, expending funds for new products and services, or developing new products through basic research and development.

- Each product and service line should be reviewed in depth to determine whether it should be continued, expanded, or curtailed. External factors over which we have little or no control will change the profit and growth potential of each business. These influences include demographics, competition, technology, governmental regulations, and customer demands.

- Divestitures may also be appropriate from time to time. Too often, excessive funds are invested in businesses and products that will not produce investment return objectives or fail to complement other product lines. Divesting a product or business has many important ramifications and should be given serious and ample consideration by every business on an annual basis.

WHAT IS A COMMON FORMAT FOR BUDGETS?

The content of a budget depends on the particular needs of the user. It can vary from year to year and does vary from one company to another. However, the following information is frequently included:

- Balance sheet as of the end of the current year and the budgeted year.
- Income statement for the current and budgeted year.
- Analysis of cash flow.
- Projected departmental expenses compared to the prior year.
- Details of budgeted capital expenditures.
- Basic budgeting assumptions.

CHAPTER 18

PHASE 3: BUDGET (PRACTICE)

THE MANAGEMENT TEAM WORKS DILIGENTLY TO PREPARE THE YEAR 28 BUDGET

Chem-A-Lot's budget represents the first year of a two-year business plan directly related to the strategy plan for years 28, 29, and 30. Rather than include the entire budget package and its many pages of numbers in this chapter, we will examine relevant segments of the president's report to the board of directors. Therefore, excerpts of President Charles B. Fisher's letter follow each budget form.

Part Six of this book reproduces Chem-A-Lot's three-year planning cycle packages—including budget, strategy plan, and business plan—in their entirety.

CHEM-A-LOT
INCOME STATEMENT—ANNUAL
(Dollars in Thousands)

	Current Year 27				Year 28		Following Year	
	Budget		Estimated	Actual	Budget		Forecast	
Sales	$35,000	100.0%	$33,900	100.0%	$39,500	100.0%	$38,200	100.0%
Cost of Sales	22,750	65.0	22,400	66.1	24,530	62.1	24,093	63.1
Gross Profit	12,250	35.0	11,500	33.9	14,970	37.9	14,107	36.9
Selling Expenses	4,200	12.0	4,268	12.6	4,995	12.6	4,865	12.7
General Admin. Expenses	4,450	12.7	4,400	13.0	5,150	13.0	5,000	13.1
Design & Development	145	0.4	132	0.4	155	0.4	135	0.4
Total Expenses	8,795	25.1	8,800	26.0	10,300	26.1	10,000	26.2
Operating Income	3,455	9.9	2,700	7.9	4,670	11.8	4,107	10.7
Sale of Capital Assets	–	–	–	–	–	–	–	–
State Income Taxes	110	0.3	135	0.4	236	0.6	205	0.5
Other	–	–	–	–	–	–	–	–
Total	110	0.3	135	0.4	236	0.6	205	0.5
Profit before Federal Taxes	3,345	9.6	2,565	7.5	4,434	11.2	3,902	10.2
Federal Tax Provision	1,245	3.6	951	2.8	1,508	3.8	1,327	3.5
Net Income	$ 2,100	6.0%	$ 1,614	4.7%	$ 2,926	7.4%	$ 2,575	6.7%
Average Investment	$11,000		$11,000		$11,821		$13,086	
Operating Income ROI	24.6		24.6		39.5		31.4	
After-Tax ROI	14.7%		14.7%		24.8%		19.7%	

CHEM-A-LOT
QUARTERLY INCOME STATEMENT
(Dollars in Thousands)

	1st Quarter	2nd Quarter	3rd Quarter	4th Quarter	Total
Sales	$8,394	$11,292	$10,246	$9,568	$39,500
Cost of Sales	5,558	6,754	6,225	5,993	24,530
Gross Profit	2,836	4,538	4,021	3,575	14,970
Selling Expenses	1,204	1,336	1,206	1,249	4,995
General Admin. Expenses	1,237	1,347	1,281	1,285	5,150
Design & Development	25	35	40	55	155
Total Expenses	2,466	2,718	2,527	2,589	10,300
Operating Income	370	1,820	1,494	986	4,670
Sale of Capital Assets	–	–	–	–	–
State Income Taxes	20	91	76	49	236
Other	–	–	–	–	–
Total	20	91	76	49	236
Profit before Federal Taxes	350	1,729	1,418	937	4,434
Federal Tax Provision	120	588	482	318	1,508
Net Income	$ 230	$ 1,141	$ 936	$ 619	$ 2,926

Excerpts from the President's Letter:
The Income Statement

- *Revenues.* For year 28, we expect $39.5 million in sales revenues, an increase of 16.5 percent over those for the preceding year ($33.9 million) without a price increase. Year 28 would then be the highest sales year ever attained in the company. This real growth is anticipated because of an uptick in the demand cycle related to our particular products. The lack of a price increase is due to our market intelligence which shows that we are still priced 2 to 6 percent over our competition for similar products of similar quality. Product mix is described within the budget package itself, and I will comment on that later in this letter.

- *Operating income.* Operating income should be $4.67 million compared with $2.7 million for the current year, a 73 percent increase. The increase in operating income to a level of 11.8 percent of sales revenues versus 7.9 percent of revenues in year 27 is due mainly to gross profit ratios of 37.9 percent in the budget year compared to 33.9 percent in the year just ending.

- *Net income after taxes.* Net income after taxes should be $2.9 million, or 7.4 percent of sales, versus $1.6 million, or 4.7 percent for year 27. Once again, the main increase in net income is due to a healthy sales increase at higher gross profit levels and, to a lesser extent ($136,000), to a decrease in the net effective federal income tax rate—from slightly over 37 percent last year to 34 percent in the budget year.

- *Return on investment.* On an overall basis for year 28, return on investment (shareholders' net worth) will be 39.5 percent on $11.8 million before state and federal income taxes versus 24.6 percent on $11 million for the year just ending. It will be 24.8 percent after all income taxes versus 14.7 percent for the year just ending.

CHEM-A-LOT
YEAR 28 BUDGET
GROSS PROFIT BY PRODUCT LINE[1]
(Dollars in Thousands)

Product Lines	Quarter 1				Quarter 2			
	Sales		Gross Profit	G.P. %	Sales		Gross Profit	G.P. %
	Amount	Units			Amounts	Units		
Base Business Forecast								
Conditioners[1]								
Kracker	$1,769	20	$ 812	45.9%	$ 3,096	35	$1,684	54.4%
Pelletizer	522	17	78	14.9	645	21	154	23.9
Sifter	239	18	88	36.8	399	30	178	44.6
Dryer	404	17	115	28.5	593	25	237	40.0
Cooler	1,026	65	278	27.1	1,263	80	442	35.0
Washer	214	40	55	25.7	268	50	80	30.0
Total Conditioners	4,174	177	1,426	34.2	6,264	241	2,775	44.3
Total Formulators	2,293	140	603	26.3	2,785	170	869	31.2
Total Transporters	627	20	117	18.7	940	30	202	21.5
Total Machines	7,094	337	2,146	30.3	9,989	441	3,846	38.5
Total Repairs/Parts	1,300	–	690	53.1	1,303	–	692	53.1
New Products, Etc.[2]	–	–	–	–	–	–	–	–
Total	$8,394	337	$2,836	33.8%	$11,292	441	$4,538	40.2%

[1]Only conditioner line is detailed herein for illustrative purposes.　　[2]New product introductions scheduled for years 29 forward.

CHEM-A-LOT
YEAR 28 BUDGET
GROSS PROFIT BY PRODUCT LINE[1]
(Dollars in Thousands)

	Quarter 3				Quarter 4				Total			
	Sales		Gross	G.P.	Sales		Gross	G.P.	Sales		Gross	G.P.
Product Lines	Amount	Units	Profit	%	Amount	Units	Profit	%	Amount	Units	Profit	%
Base Business Forecast												
Conditioners[1]												
Kracker	$ 2,654	30	$1,420	53.5%	$2,034	23	$ 981	48.2%	$ 9,553	108	$ 4,897	51.3%
Pelletizer	583	19	128	22.0	584	19	128	21.9	2,334	76	488	20.9
Sifter	319	24	133	41.6	345	26	147	42.6	1,302	98	546	41.9
Dryer	499	21	188	37.7	451	19	160	35.5	1,947	82	700	36.0
Cooler	1,231	78	430	34.9	1,105	70	376	34.0	4,625	293	1,526	33.0
Washer	252	47	73	28.9	279	52	86	30.8	1,013	189	294	29.0
Total Conditioners	5,538	219	2,372	42.8	4,798	209	1,878	39.1	20,774	846	8,451	40.7
Total Formulators	2,604	159	784	30.1	2,735	167	853	31.2	10,417	636	3,109	29.8
Total Transporters	784	25	165	21.0	721	23	146	20.2	3,072	98	630	20.5
Total Machines	8,926	403	3,321	37.2	8,254	399	2,877	34.9	34,263	1,580	12,190	35.6
Total Repairs/Parts	1,320	–	700	53.0	1,314	–	698	53.1	5,237	–	2,780	53.1
New Products, Etc.[2]	–	–	–	–	–	–	–	–	–	–	–	–
Total	$10,246	403	$4,021	39.2%	$9,568	399	$3,575	37.4%	$39,500	1,580	$14,970	37.9%

[1]Only conditioner line is detailed herein for illustrative purposes. [2]New product introductions scheduled for years 29 forward.

Excerpts from the President's Letter: Gross Profit by Product Line by Quarter

- *Product lines.* We expect no less than 21 percent of our revenues for the year to be shipped in a particular quarter and a high of 29 percent shippable in the second quarter. No discernible patterns yet exist for predicting monthly or quarterly sales patterns precisely, but our backlogs and lead times support the interim estimates. Quarterly results are impacted tremendously by product line mix, as is seen by the varying gross profit margins. In general, our most profitable products are conditioners, which carry 41 percent margins; whereas the transporters, which are fairly old and somewhat inefficient given today's technology, can support only 20 percent margins at the manufacturing cost level.

  Market share estimates by product line have been outlined in the business plan we discussed at the last meeting. No material changes that affect our share estimates have occurred since then.

- *Repairs and parts.* Repairs and parts continue to be excellent in profitability. We plan to contact owners of previously purchased machines as part of a follow-up sales and service program.

CHEM-A-LOT
COST OF SALES SUMMARY BY COST ELEMENT[1]
(Dollars in Thousands)

Product Line	Material[2]			Direct Labor/Fringes[3]			Overhead			Total Manufacturing Costs		
	Budget Amount	Budget % of Sales[4]	Current % of Sales	Budget Amount	Budget % of Sales[4]	Current % of Sales	Budget Amount	Budget % of Sales[4]	Current % of Sales	Budget Amount	Budget % of Sales[4]	Current % of Sales
Conditioners[1]												
Kracker	$2,041	21.4%	21.3%	$ 887	9.3%	9.0%	$ 1,728	18.1%	19.6%	$ 4,656	48.7%	49.3%
Pelletizer	488	20.9	20.8	334	14.3	14.1	1,024	43.9	42.1	1,846	79.1	78.0
Sifter	266	20.4	20.0	133	10.2	9.9	357	27.4	27.2	756	58.1	57.5
Dryer	399	20.5	20.3	177	9.1	8.9	671	34.5	33.1	1,247	64.0	64.0
Cooler	976	21.1	21.0	555	12.0	11.8	1,568	33.9	33.2	3,099	67.0	66.4
Washer	268	26.5	26.1	133	13.1	13.0	318	31.4	31.9	719	71.0	70.8
Total Conditioners	4,438	21.4	22.0	2,219	10.7	11.4	5,666	27.3	27.9	12,323	59.3	61.1
Total Formulators	2,426	23.3	25.5	1,413	13.6	14.2	3,469	33.3	34.9	7,308	70.2	74.4
Total Transporters	789	25.7	27.0	404	13.2	13.9	1,249	40.7	41.0	2,442	79.5	82.8
Total Machines	7,653	22.3	23.1	4,036	11.8	12.3	10,384	30.3	32.9	22,073	64.4	68.5
Total Repairs/Parts	852	16.3	16.9	453	8.7	9.0	1,152	22.0	22.1	2,457	46.9	47.8
Total	$8,505	21.5%	22.6%	$4,489	11.4%	11.9%	$11,536	29.2%	31.4%	$24,530	62.1%	66.1%

[1] Only conditioner line is detailed herein for illustrative purposes.
[2] Raw material and supply costs are not budgeted to increase in real terms over year 27.
[3] Labor and related fringe benefits are budgeted to increase 4.5 percent over year 27.
[4] Percentage of sales relates to sales of respective product lines, not total company sales.

Excerpts from the President's Letter: Manufacturing Cost of Sales by Cost Element

- *Product lines.* Our conditioner line is more profitable than our formulator and transporter lines. Except for the washer line, material costs of conditioners are at a level of about 20 to 21 percent versus 23 to 27 percent of sales revenues for the other lines. We believe our material purchasing practices are close to optimum levels. Our vendors are charging us very competitive prices. Similarly, total direct labor and fringe costs average 11 percent of machine sales revenues in our budget versus 14 percent for formulators and 13 to 14 percent for transporters.

   The pelletizer products do have a labor rate as high as formulators and transporters and also a very high overhead rate that exceeds the overhead rates of formulators (34 percent) and transporters (41 percent), which causes the pelletizer line to show high manufacturing costs relative to the rest of the conditioner products. The conditioner line has an average overhead of 27 percent of sales, but the pelletizer, dryer, cooler, and washer lines are all high-overhead products. An analysis of all overhead expenses with the goal of reducing them to the lowest levels possible while maintaining efficient plant operations is underway. I'll report the results of that study to you in June.

- *Repairs, parts, and service.* Total repairs, parts, and related services continue to be the most profitable aspects of our business, and we plan to push them. However, these things are directly related to products in the field; they will tend to grow rather slowly in real terms and will probably decrease as a percentage of our total revenues if we are able to attain forecasted sales of machines in the coming year.

CHEM-A-LOT
YEAR 28 BUDGET
VARIABLE BUDGET SUMMARY
(Dollars in Thousands)

	85% of Plan		100% of Plan	
	Amount	*Percent*	*Amount*	*Percent*
Sales	$33,575	100.0%	$39,500	100.0%
Variable Costs				
Materials	7,229	21.5	8,505	21.5
Manufacturing	10,545	31.4	12,407	31.4
Design & Development	132	0.4	155	0.4
Selling	1,806	5.4	2,166	5.5
General & Admin.	801	2.4	1,051	2.7
Total Variable	20,513	61.1	24.284	61.5
Contribution Margin	13,062	38.9	15,216	38.5
Fixed Costs				
Manufacturing	3,618	10.8	3,618	9.2
Selling	2,829	8.4	2,829	7.1
General & Admin.	4,099	12.2	4,099	10.4
Design & Development	—	—	—	—
Total Fixed	10,546	31.4	10,546	26.7
Operating Income	$ 2,516	7.5%	$ 4,670	11.8%
Break-Even Point[1]	$27,110	80.7%	$27,392	69.3%

[1]Contribution margin equals fixed costs at the break-even point. Dividing fixed costs by the contribution margin *rate* will give you the break-even point in dollars. There are other methods for determining break-even points. Break-even dollars are sales and are also expressed as a percentage of total sales.
Note: A detailed operating plan has been developed in case budgeted sales do not materialize. These contingency plans trigger at a $36 million sales level, assuming a normal product mix.

Excerpts from the President's Letter: The Variable and Fixed Cost Budget Summary and Break-Even Points

• *Planning for crises*. During the past year, Diane and her staff provided our operations personnel with many analyses of every cost and expense center. These analyses enable us, for the first time, to plan for crises. The single most important crisis Chem-A-Lot might face in year 28 would be a downturn in the demand for its products.

• *Expected break-even*. We expect our break-even point to be $27.4 million of revenues, based on anticipated mix and budgeted sales. Obviously this break-even point, wherein the profit margin contributed by the various product lines equals our fixed costs, will vary, depending on the actual sales mix and the actual sales levels.

- *Major changes needed if revenues drop 15 percent below budgeted $39.5 million*. From our review, we believe major changes will be required in personnel and general spending levels if revenues drop 15 percent below the budgeted $39.5 million. Achieving only 85 percent of plan, or $33.6 million, would take us back to year 27 levels and about 24 percent in revenues above break-even sales of about $27.1 million. The small difference between this break-even and that estimated previously ($27.4 million) is due to a few small changes in variable selling and general and administrative expenses and to smaller design and development expenditures at lower sales levels. This illustrates that some expenses do not vary linearly with revenues.

At the next board meeting, I will discuss the specific actions we will take if such a crisis develops.

CHEM-A-LOT
YEAR 28 BUDGET
CONTRIBUTION MARGIN BY PRODUCT LINE

(Dollars in Thousands)

	Conditioner		Formulator		Transporter		Parts		Total	
Sales	$20,774	100.0%	$10,417	100.0%	$3,072	100%	$5,237	100.0%	$39,500	100.0%
Variable Costs										
Materials	4,438	21.4	2,426	23.3	789	25.7	852	16.3	8,505	21.5
Manufacturing	6,155	29.6	3,802	36.5	1,200	39.1	1,250	23.9	12,407	31.4
Design & Dev.	155	0.7	—	—	—	—	—	—	155	0.4
Selling	1,148	5.5	580	5.6	188	6.1	250	4.8	2,166	5.5
General & Admin.	557	2.7	250	2.4	124	4.0	120	2.3	1,051	2.7
Total Variable	12,453	59.9	7,058	67.8	2,301	74.9	2,472	47.2	24,284	61.5
Contribution Margins	$ 8,321	40.1%	$ 3,359	32.2%	$ 771	25.1%	$2,765	52.8%	$15,216	38.5%
Fixed Costs										
Manufacturing									3,618	9.2
Selling									2,829	7.1
General & Admin.									4,099	10.4
Total Fixed[1]									10,546	26.7
Operating Income									$ 4,670	11.8%

[1]Note: Some businesses may allocate fixed costs to product lines. Chem-A-Lot does not allocate fixed costs to product lines since there are no clear relationships on which to base such allocations in this particular business.

Excerpts from President's Letter: Contribution Margin by Product Line

- *Full absorption manufacturing costs.* The preceding gross profit analysis by product line and the cost of sales summary by cost element display typical full-absorption manufacturing cost relationships to sales. The schedule allocates all associable costs, including selling, general, and administrative expenses, to our three major product lines and parts. We chose not to allocate our fixed or nonvariable costs to the products because clear associations do not exist.

- *Conditioner line most profitable.* As in the other analyses, the conditioner line is our most profitable (40.1 percent contribution toward fixed costs, taxes, and profits). This line has the lowest materials and direct manufacturing costs as a percentage of its sales of all lines except parts. The design and development effort budgeted for year 28 is all for the conditioner line.

  Variable selling, general, and administrative expenses approximate our totals for all lines as a percentage of sales. Commissions, our direct sales force—its expenses, billing, and collection—are some of the expenses included. We are not satisfied with the contribution margins on the conditioner line. They should improve in years 29 and 30 when our redesigned Chem-Pelleter and new Chem-Mill are available. These two products will command a higher margin than an average conditioner line. The West Coast sales office will increase sales and gross profits by spreading fixed manufacturing costs over more volume but will not of itself increase the contribution margins.

- *Formulator and transporter lines show low profit contributions.* The formulator and transporter lines continue as low profit contribution lines and will probably never exceed 38 percent margins for formulators and 32 percent margins for transporters. Technological breakthroughs are not on the horizon, and their markets are mature. We will value engineer these lines to try to reduce materials and certain labor and overhead costs.

- *Parts profits high.* Parts continue to be our highest contributors to profits. We have lost some parts sales to local shops but now have parts and service sales targets and incentives to reach them. Each machine sold in the past eight years has been identified by customer, and each of those customers will be contacted periodically to pursue parts and repair revenues as well as equipment replacement sales.

CHEM-A-LOT
YEAR 28 BUDGET
BALANCE SHEETS—QUARTERLY

(Dollars in Thousands)

			Quarters–Year 28			Forecast
	Last Year	1st	2nd	3rd	4th	Year 29
Current Assets						
Cash and Marketable Securities	$ 500	$ 2,165	$ 687	$ 2,204	$ 691	$ 2,085
Accounts Receivable	5,573	5,350	7,197	6,530	6,300	5,400
Notes Reveivable	—	—	—	—	—	—
Inventory	9,300	6,715	8,606	7,926	9,085	8,053
Total Current Assets	15,373	14,230	16,490	16,660	16,076	15,538
Property, Plant, & Equipment	20,000	20,000	20,000	20,550	20,550	21,760
Less Accumulated Depreciation	(18,287)	(18,354)	(18,421)	(18,488)	(18,557)	(18,915)
Capitalized Leases, Net of Amortization	—	—	—	—	—	—
Net Property, Plant, & Equipment	1,713	1,646	1,579	2,062	1,993	2,845
All Other Assets	500	500	500	500	500	500
Total Assets	$ 17,586	$ 16,376	$ 18,569	$ 19,222	$ 18,569	$ 18,883
Current Liabilities						
Loans Payable	$ 700	$ 700	$ 700	$ 700	$ 700	$ 700
Accounts Payable	3,650	3,190	4,102	3,774	3,694	3,449
Income Taxes Payable	951	183	734	1,183	1,508	1,113
Accrued Expenses, etc.	50	50	50	50	60	55
Total Current Liabilities	5,351	4,123	5,586	5,707	5,962	5,317
Long-Term Loans	1,200	1,200	1,200	1,200	—	—
Other Non-Current Liabilities	—	—	—	—	—	—
Total Liabilities	6,551	5,323	6,786	6,907	5,962	5,317
Shareholders' Equity	11,035	11,053	11,783	12,315	12,607	13,566
Total Liabilities & Shareholders' Equity	$ 17,586	$ 16,376	$ 18,569	$ 19,222	$ 18,569	$ 18,883

Excerpts from the President's Letter: Quarterly Balance Sheets

- *Solid financial position.* We are ending year 27 in a solid financial position, and by the end of year 28 we should be in even better shape. Working capital is now $10,022,000 and will be $10,114,000 by next December 31. We should end the year with nearly $691,000 in cash and marketable securities (up $191,000) with no increase in loans payable ($700,000 level) and having paid the final $1.2 million balance of our long-term loan.

- *Improvement in working capital.* Some of the improvement in working capital (about $216,000) will result from earlier collection of trade accounts receivable. Last year, receivable days outstanding were 60 ($33.9 million revenues ÷ 365 days = $92,876 sales per day in turn divided into receivables of $5.6 million = 60). By aggressively yet professionally pursuing collections, we fully expect days outstanding to drop to 58 ($39.5 million ÷ 365 days = $108,219 sales per day divided into receivables of $6.3 million = 58). Our target will be 55 days in year 29 and 50 to 53 days thereafter.

  Also, our inventories got out of control several years ago, averaging 2.4+ turns, or 152 days of inventory on hand. We will complete a materials requirements planning (MRP) system in year 28 and, helped by increased sales, we have targeted a 2.7 inventory turn as our goal for year's end. This is calculated on an overall inventory basis by dividing cost of goods sold ($24,530,000) by 365 days = $67,205 and then dividing inventories ($9,085,000) by the $67,205 to signify 135 days of inventory on hand at the year end, or 2.7 turns (365 divided by 135). This improvement alone will free up approximately $1,142,000 of cash ($67,205 per day times 17 days less inventory on hand)! By year 29, we will be able to control inventories by production stage and by product line. At that time, we will report inventory turns in more detail. For example, raw material turns, work in process, and finished goods turnover rates will be planned and reported quarterly. We should be able to hit our targets of 3.0 turns in year 29 and 3.5 from then on.

  We intend to pay our vendors in 55 days, much faster than last year. Frankly, we have not treated them kindly for three years and we need their quality materials and cooperation on delivery time.

- *Plant equipment too old.* Our plant equipment on average is too old; we recognize that fact. This budget requests $550,000 for certain machinery and renovations. Over the next three years, we will accelerate our replacement of production equipment.

  In this budget, we request a lathe, a boring mill, and necessary renovations in the storeroom and warehouse. All meet our minimum return on investment hurdle rate.

- *No added borrowings foreseen.* We can finance our needs from budgeted cash flow from operations, so no added borrowings are foreseen. A schedule of outside financing is attached.

- *Shareholder dividends.* Based on expected cash flow (a schedule is attached) we can provide shareholders with about $1.3 million in dividends, as discussed at the last board meeting, and dividends in year 29 of about $1.6 million or so.

CHEM-A-LOT
YEAR 28 BUDGET
OUTSIDE FINANCING

(Dollars in Thousands)

	Current Balance December 31	Budget Year Activity			Budget Year Balance—December 31	Terms
		Date	Payments	Borrowings		
Short-Term Borrowing[1]	$ 700	2/15	$ (350)	$ —	$700	2% over prime, maximum line of credit $1 million
		3/15		350		
		8/15	(350)	—		
		9/15		350		
Current Portion of Long-Term Debt	—				—	
Long-Term Debt	1,200	12/15	(1,200)		—	
	$1,900		$(1,900)	$700	$700	

---

[1] We may pay off the short-term loan in year 28 but list it as outstanding in the event more capital expenditures, working capital, or dividends are required.

CHEM-A-LOT
YEAR 28 BUDGET
STATEMENT OF CASH FLOW

(Dollars in Thousands)

	Quarter 1	Quarter 2	Quarter 3	Quarter 4	Total
Net Income	$ 230	$ 1,141	$ 936	$ 619	$ 2,926
Depreciation and Amortization	67	67	67	70	271
Cash Operating Income	297	1,208	1,003	689	3,197
Additions (Deductions) in Cash Resulting from Changes In					
Accounts Receivable	223	(1,847)	667	230	(727)
Inventories	2,585	(1,891)	680	(1,159)	215
Prepaid Expenses	–	–	–	–	–
Accounts Payable	(460)	912	(328)	–	44
Other Accruals	(768)	551	449	(80)	567
Net Operating Cash Flow	1,877	(1,067)	2,471	335	3,296
Other Receipts (Disbursements)					
Sale of Assets	–	–	–	15	
Capital Expenditures	–	–	(550)	–	(550)
Borrowing (Loan Repayments)	–	–	–	(1,200)	(1,200)
Other—Dividends	(212)	(411)	(404)	(328)	(1,355)
—Miscellaneous	–	–	–	–	–
Total	$1,665	$(1,478)	$1,517	$(1,513)	$ 191
Cash Beginning of Period	$ 500	$ 2,165	$ 687	$ 2,204	$ 500
Cash End of Period	$2,165	$ 687	$2,204	$ 691	$ 691

CHEM-A-LOT
YEAR 28 BUDGET
SELLING EXPENSE
(Dollars in Thousands)

	Previous Year Actual		Current Year Budget		Current Year Estimated Actual		Budget Year	
	Amount	% of Sales	Amount	% of Sales	Amount	% of Sales	Amount	% of Sales
Total Selling Expenses	$2,958	14.3	$4,200	12.0	$4,268	12.6	$4,995	12.6

Expense Items	Estimated Year 27	Budget Year 28	Explanation of Significant Changes
Salaries and Wages	$1,400	$1,825	5% increase in comensation levels, two people added during year for West Coast sales office, one person added in marketing/advertising, and an additional customer service person, plus $230 estimated bonuses based on increased profits
Freight Out	700	790	
Rent	220	220	N/A
Office Expense	530	613	In line with 16.5% budgeted increase in sales
Insurance	88	110	Insurance premiums raised 25%
Conventions & Trade Shows	90	100	
Advertising & Promotional	300	350	In line with budgeted sales increase
Travel & Entertainment	220	257	In line with budgeted sales increase
Maintenance	88	103	Normal items plus $9.2 to redecorate sales offices
Utilities	120	135	
Dues & Subscriptions	30	50	
Depreciation	12	13	N/A
Other	470	429	Increase in commissioned sales ($79) and other miscellaneous expenses less than sales increases
Total	$4,268	$4,995	

Note: Separately list any item equaling 5% or more of total budgeted selling expense; list remaining expenses under caption "Other."

Excerpts from the President's Letter: Selling Expenses

- *Increased sales, adding personnel.* We believe we can obtain the 16.5 percent increase in sales but need four people to accomplish it. They will cover the new West Coast sales service office, marketing/advertising, and customer service. We recently reassigned several of our sales personnel to better target areas and replaced them in their former territories with two excellent representatives who are expected to pull in between $750,000 and $1 million of sales in their first year.

  We expect to pay bonuses of about 10 percent of salaries (overall) under a new incentive plan that provides for incentive levels that are related to gross profit margins on products sold.

- *West Coast sales office leased.* We will continue to lease our West Coast sales office and have just successfully negotiated a three-year extension with no increase. We did agree to redecorate it at our own expense at a cost of $9,200.

- *Total selling expenses down.* We plan to hold total selling expenses to 12.6 percent of revenues, well below last year's 14.3 percent.

CHEM-A-LOT
YEAR 28 BUDGET
GENERAL AND ADMINISTRATIVE EXPENSE

(Dollars in Thousands)

	Previous Year Actual		Current Year Budget		Current Year Estimated Actual		Budget Year	
	Amount	% of Sales	Amount	% of Sales	Amount	% of Sales	Amount	% of Sales
Total G & A Expenses	$3,050	14.7	$4,450	12.7	$4,400	13.0	$5,150	13.0

Expense Items	Estimated Year 27	Budget Year 28	Explanation of Significant Changes
Salaries and Wages	$1,545	$1,285	5% increase in compensation levels, plus $200 bonuses due to increased profits
Office Expense	760	705	Normal inflation increases
Rent	100	100	
Insurance	440	320	50% increase in product liability and casualty insurance ($100) plus increase in all other premiums
Travel & Entertainment	230	220	Normal inflation increases
Professional Fees	650	540	Consultants for new cost and production control system ($30) plus increased legal fees on patent suit ($80)
Utilities	225	200	
Taxes—Non-Income Based	100	100	
Maintenance	424	256	Repair roof and all internal office walls and repaint all offices
Contributions	160	150	
Dues & Subscriptions	50	50	
Director Fees	90	90	N/A
Depreciation	26	24	N/A
Other	350	360	
Total	$5,150	$4,400	

Note: Separately list any item that is 5 percent or more of total budgeted G & A expense; list remaining expenses under caption "Other."

Excerpts from the President's Letter: General and Administrative Expenses

- *No new personnel.* No new personnel are budgeted in the general and administrative expense area. Normal compensation increases, plus bonus on budget attainment, are included.

- *Increased insurance premiums.* The major increase in insurance is due to a 50 percent increase in property and casualty liability premiums. Other businesses in our industrial associations have also received notice from their carriers of very large insurance premium increases, apparently due to an increasingly litigious U.S. scene.

- *Production control system.* A material requirements planning and production control system will be completely installed and operating in the budget year at a cost of $30,000 for consultants.

- *Competitor copies patented Chem-Kraker.* We also plan to sue a competitor who copied our patented Kraker equipment. Patent counsel is confident of our case, and we expect settlement by midyear. No proceeds are recorded in our budget, but our legal counsel fees on this case are estimated to be $80,000.

- *Office repairs.* Finally, long deferred repairs are planned for virtually all of our offices. In future years, normal maintenance levels should approximate $220,000 per year.

CHEM-A-LOT
YEAR 28 BUDGET
DESIGN AND DEVELOPMENT PROJECT
(Dollars in Thousands)

Number	Project Description	Total Cost	Amount to Be Spent in Budget Year	Estimated Completion Date
28-1	Design and produce modified Chem-Pelleter chemical process unit	$ 51	$ 51	June 30, Year 29
28-2	Design and produce new Chem-Mill unit	104	104	October 1, Year 29
	Total for Operating Budget	$155	$155	

CHEM-A-LOT
YEAR 28 BUDGET
DETAIL OF OTHER INCOME (EXPENSE)
(Dollars in Thousands)

	1st Quarter	2nd Quarter	3rd Quarter	4th Quarter	Total
Gain (Loss) on Sale of Capital Assets (Detail)	$–	$–	$–	$–	$ –
State Tax (Expense)	20	91	76	49	236
Other Income (Expense)(Detail)	–	–	–	–	–
Total Other Income	$20	$91	$76	$49	$236

CHEM-A-LOT
BUDGET
FEDERAL/FOREIGN INCOME TAX PROVISION
(Dollars in Thousands)

	Rate		Quarter 1 Taxable Income	Quarter 1 Tax Liability	Quarter 2 Taxable Income	Quarter 2 Tax Liability	Quarter 3 Taxable Income	Quarter 3 Tax Liability	Quarter 4 Taxable Income	Quarter 4 Tax Liability	Total
Profit before Taxes			$350		$1,729		$1,418		$937		$4,434
Add (Deduct) Reconciling Items			—		—		—		—		—
Non-Deductible Expenses			—		—		—		—		—
			$350		$1,729		$1,418		$937		$4,434
Taxable Income Calculation:											
Ordinary Income	34%	×	$350	= $120	$1,729	= $588	$1,418	= $482	$937	= $318	$1,508
Capital Gain	%	×	—	—	—	—	—	—	—	—	—
Foreign	%	×	—	—	—	—	—	—	—	—	—
Other (specify)	%	×	—	—	—	—	—	—	—	—	—
			$350	$120	$1,729	$588	$1,418	$482	$937	$318	$1,508
Less: Investment Tax Credit on											
Qualified Property 10%				(0)		(0)		(0)		(0)	(0)
Other Credits				(0)		(0)		(0)		(0)	(0)
Foreign Tax Credit				(0)		(0)		(0)		(0)	(0)
Total Provision for Income Taxes				$120		$588		$482		$318	$1,508

237

CHEM-A-LOT
YEAR 28
CAPITAL EXPENDITURES REPORT SUMMARY
(Dollars in Thousands)

Classification	Carryover from Prior Year(s)	Current Year	Total	Expenditures by Quarter				Total Expenditures	Carryforward to Future Year(s)
				First	Second	Third	Fourth		
N—New Item for Capacity	$0	$0	$0	$0	$0	$ 0	$0	$ 0	$0
E—Environmental									
R—Replacement				0	0	550	0	550	0
O—Other									
Total	$0	$0	$0	$0	$0	$550	$0	$550	$0
Investment Tax Credit	$0	$0	$0	$0	$0	$ 0	$0	$ 0	$0

Budget Item	Description	Classification	Total Budget Year	Future Years	Expected DCF[1] Return
28-1	Computer-controlled lathe	R	215	0	18%
28-2	Boring mill	R	275	0	22
28-3	Additions and renovations in storeroom and warehouse	R	60	0	15

[1]Discounted cash flow.

CHEM-A-LOT
YEAR 28
CAPITAL EXPENDITURE BUDGET
CARRYOVER FROM PRIOR YEAR(S)
(Dollars in Thousands)

Item #	Description	Classification	Total Authorization Approved	Amount Spent before Budget Year	Authorized Amount Remaining	Amount to Be Spent in Budget Year	Amount to Be Spent in Future Year(s)
				NONE			
	Total		$	$	$	$	$

CHEM-A-LOT
YEAR 28
BUDGET ASSUMPTIONS

Accounts Receivable Days Outstanding	58 days
Inventory Turns	2.7 times
Accounts Payable Days Outstanding	55 days
Sales Price Change	0%
Raw Material and Supply Cost Inflation	0%
Wage, Salary, and Benefits Increase	4.5%
Bank Average Prime Loan Rate	8%
State Income Tax Rate	5%
Federal Income Tax Rate	34%
Sales Backlog—Beginning of Year	$9.4 million
—End of Year	$8.1 million

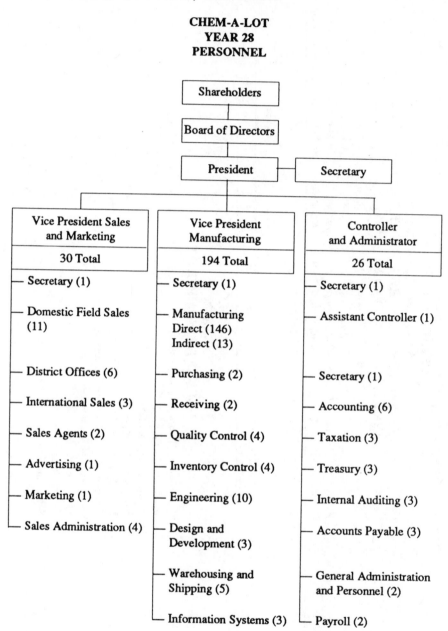

**CHEM-A-LOT
YEAR 28
PERSONNEL**

Note: Total number of employees is 252; they are designated above in parenthesis for departments with more than one person.

PART FOUR

SUCCESS: THE FRUITS
OF PLANNING

CHAPTER 19

HOW SWEET, SUCCESS

If all good people were clever,
And all clever people were good,
The world would be nicer than ever
We thought that it possibly could.

But somehow, 'tis seldom or never
That the two hit it off as they should;
For the good are so harsh to the clever,
The clever, so rude to the good!

Elizabeth Wordsworth

AND THE YEARS PASSED SWIFTLY

A few days before the end of year 30, a "Well Done!" bash was scheduled to celebrate the success of the first three-year comprehensive plan. Everyone at Chem-A-Lot and their spouses were invited; well-earned holiday bonuses had been distributed earlier. The year-end figures were certain to show that actual sales and profits had exceeded plan. Charlie called a brief staff meeting on the morning before the party.

Charlie: I called this meeting to tell you how deeply I appreciate your co-operation during the last few years. Your efforts have helped keep Chem-A-Lot on course during some rough economic weather.

Diane: Charlie, a lot of the credit goes to all the employees. There's a new sense of cooperation here at Chem-A-Lot that goes beyond just the margin staff. And, Charlie, a lot of credit for that goes to you!

Charlie: Thank you, Diane. I'd say the pat on the back belongs to you and all our people for your willingness to give new ideas a fair try. Frankly, at times I sometimes wondered if we were on the right track. Here's an update of one of those rate-of-change charts that contributed so much to our understanding of the critical growth relationships here at Chem-A-Lot.

243

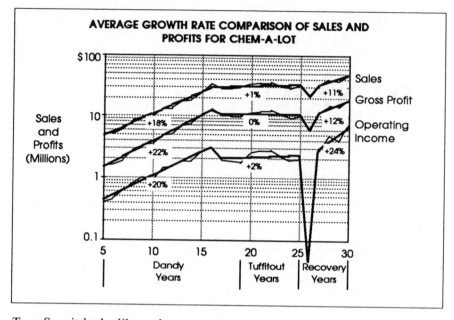

AVERAGE GROWTH RATE COMPARISON OF SALES AND PROFITS FOR CHEM-A-LOT

Tom: Say, it looks like we've got a chance to equal the golden Dandy years at Chem-A-Lot.

Charlie (smiling at Tom): Given your latest marketing plans here and abroad, Tom, and the renewed spirit of cooperation and competition here at Chem-A-Lot, we might just have that chance!

I would like to remind all of you to make it a point to find some special words of encouragement, tailored to each of your people, to say at the party this evening. I know you normally do this sort of thing, but in the glow of the moment, it's so easy to overlook the feelings of others. Tom, with your department's plans and our current resources, if we can keep morale high, we'll have more than a good chance to match that early record.

The chart Charlie used on this morning was shortly available to all staff members at their desk consoles through a decentralized department-controlled computer network. Information from each department's working computer programs was coordinated by a team made up of the department heads and chaired by Diane. It was then put on the network to give Chem-A-Lot a responsive, yet integrated management information system.

Before leaving the plant that afternoon, Charlie executed the computer commands that permitted him once again to compare a summary of actual figures with the original plans the staff had so painstakingly worked out during the year after the big loss. He grinned but tempered his jubilation with the knowledge that fate had a way of dealing out unexpected heavy blows.

	28		29		30		3-Year Totals	
Year	Plan	Actual	Plan	Actual	Plan	Actual	Plan	Actual
Sales	$39.5	$39.5	$38.2	$37.9	$48.1	$48.4	**$125.8**	**$125.8**
Gross Profit	15.0	14.7	14.1	13.8	17.8	18.5	**46.9**	**47.0**
Operat. Income	4.7	4.8	4.1	3.9	7.0	7.4	**15.8**	**16.1**

CHEM-A-LOT THREE-YEAR PLAN
(Millions of Dollars)

After the disaster of year 26, efforts were begun to improve old products, to create innovative new products, to provide quicker repair services, to introduce new production methods, to reduce costly inventories, to coordinate efforts with suppliers, and to further enhance product value through an average reduction in prices. These efforts were coordinated in a strategic plan designed to move toward a shared vision of the future, namely *to reestablish Chem-A-Lot as a leading producer of quality conditioner, formulator, and transporter equipment for the process industries in the world.*

Chem-A-Lot was beginning to move toward a more cooperative internal corporate culture and a more competitive posture worldwide. These initial efforts made the company profitable again in year 27. Year 28 brought further progress. But the next year, 29, while profitable, was a bit of a disappointment. However, in year 30, everything had come up roses—bonuses for everyone! Charlie felt that Chem-A-Lot's long range strategic plans, so meticulously and enthusiastically worked out with the cooperation of everyone, had really made the difference.

Charlie executed another command on his computer to display the following sales fan:

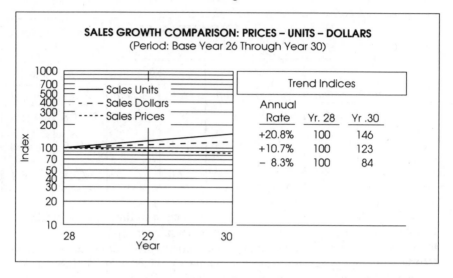

SALES GROWTH COMPARISON: PRICES – UNITS – DOLLARS
(Period: Base Year 26 Through Year 30)

From the growth indicated by the average rates-of-change it had seemed obvious to the staff in the morning meeting that customers were currently much happier with the value of Chem-A-Lot products and services. Charlie had also realized that since unit counts were now rising faster than sales dollars, further office cuts would not be necessary. In fact, it might be feasible to increase prices, if necessary, to cover additional costs for product and customer service development. He knew, however, that the period since the new strategic plans had kicked in was too short to be certain that year 30 was not an aberration.

Charlie (talking to himself half aloud): It's a good record . . . not a great one . . . but a sound one. Those numbers and trends sure make this New Year a happy one for us all. (*Then he mused*) Chem-A-Lot's on a steady course now because we *do* have a hung watch and we *do* know which way is up!

Charlie was reminiscing about a training flight he had made in a two-seater Taylorcraft many years before. The flight path had gone through a dark prairie squall line. As he entered the storm clouds, the instructor had taken out his pocket watch and hung it by its chain above the windshield. *You see, the puzzled student who asked "Why?" had been a much younger Charlie Fisher.*

COULD YOU LEAD AS WELL AS CHARLIE?

Yes, you could! To understand fully how Chem-A-Lot's turnaround was accomplished would take five books, not one. However, the techniques and tactics explored in the foregoing chapters provide sufficient detail to allow you to compare your own approaches with those described.

Success did *not* result from pure luck, magic, or fleeting management fads. Chem-A-Lot managers worked at their situation. They spent countless hours analyzing competitor personnel, products, strategies, and "fire power." They carefully determined customer needs and market conditions; at the same time, they developed methods to make such tasks simpler in the future. They made every effort to reduce unnecessary paperwork by storing information in their accessible computer system. Above all, they inspired and cooperated with everyone who worked at Chem-A-Lot. They had learned two lessons: Cooperating did not necessarily mean becoming easy pushovers for anyone who came along, and competing did not necessarily mean stepping on anyone on the way up.

In the following chapter, we'll talk about how best to wield the levers of power. We hope that, as a result of reading it and the story of Chem-A-Lot, life will become a bit more pleasant for you!

CHAPTER 20

HOW TO WIELD THE LEVERS OF POWER

Nothing discloses character like the use of power.

*There is no real reforming power in fear and pun-
ishment. Men cannot be tortured into greatness, into
goodness. In the atmosphere of kindness the seed of
virtue bursts into bud and flower.*

Robert G. Ingersoll

SO YOU ASPIRE TO BECOME A SEASONED LEADER AND MANAGER LIKE CHARLIE!

Here's how Charlie did it. He either had or developed:

- The Individual Motive Force (IMF) to push toward a clear vision of how he wanted Chem-A-Lot to serve all its stakeholders in the future— owners, managers, workers, customers, and public alike.
- The ability to communicate his vision to stakeholders in such a manner that they too visualized just how their effort would lead to a share in the results achieved from the fulfillment of his vision.
- The foresight to push for a truly cooperative planning procedure that involved more than stiff bottom-up and top-down communication—in this cooperative environment, each individual's motive force combined to create a powerful Organizational Motive Force (OMF).
- Firm command and full responsibility for keeping Chem-A-Lot on course.

Charlie's approach is simple to describe but difficult to do well. As CEO, Charlie knew that the buck indeed stopped at his desk! He knew he had to

248

know how all parts of the business functioned, and he was wise enough not to be distracted by the temptation to continue performing the tasks he had liked best when he was in charge of operations. He delegated those tasks to others so he could find the time to acquire more knowledge about other areas of the business.

CHARLIE KNEW HE NEEDED THE LEVER OF PEOPLE POWER

Charlie had heard it said before, and he really believed that he couldn't change Chem-A-Lot by himself. He had to create a lever. The creation of that lever depended on his ability to coordinate, integrate, and inspire the activities of all workers and to win the support of all stakeholders. He instinctively knew that how much people power he would have available to him depended upon how well he meshed with the people who were to perform all the tasks necessary to reaching his vision.

More and more, in his years as a department head, Charlie had come to conceive of his role as that of a coach rather than that of a performer—a role that now called for him to help develop the star quality of all the performers at Chem-A-Lot. To do so effectively, he knew that he had to repress his own urge to be the star performer himself.

Insecure managers tend either to make all the decisions themselves, delegating little, or they adopt consensus thinking. They feel others cannot be trusted to do the job right. This distrust, which breeds distrust in return, is frequently based on nothing more than the need to be the star performer. Such on-stage performers often break, or tire as Jim Dandy did, from carrying too many monkeys on their backs that should have been entrusted to competent, Charlie-type subordinates. Managers like Dandy really do not know how to use the lever of management well, even though they may run a successful business for years.

Poor managers do assign tasks to others but delegate very little decision-making responsibility. These managers do have leverage because their efforts are multiplied by the number of workers supervised. The level of accomplishment, however, is usually quite low because the creative juices of individual workers are not tapped.

Top managers delegate the responsibility for results to carefully selected and trained people. Such managers get maximum leverage because they tap the creative talents of workers, who are given the freedom to find innovative solutions in an environment of cooperation. Under these circumstances, total efforts will be more than the sum of the efforts of each individual.

SO WHERE DO YOU START?

When you look at a company like Chem-A-Lot, or your own, you'll find tasks being performed by many individuals with varying degrees of expertise and organization.

You know, as Charlie knew, how often objectives and strategies that are meant to help end up confusing workers. You also know how some CEOs like Tuffitout, who are not really aware of what's happening, become disliked and how the future business that arises out of confused relationships declines and falls. In addition, you know how a traditional, static organization chart—composed of status boxes connected by lines of vassalage—doesn't really help much. Traditional organization charts are often an illusory cover for the dynamics of the real business world beneath.

Enough! For now, let's look at leadership from the viewpoint of a competent CEO like Charlie.

DYNAMIC LEADERSHIP

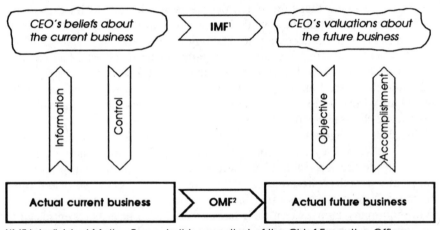

[1]IMF is Individual Motive Force. In this case, that of the Chief Executive Officer.
[2]OMF is the total Organizational Motive Force that the Cheif Executive Officer is able to muster among all the employees of the company.

LET'S TAKE THIS CHART APART AND LOOK AT THE PARTS

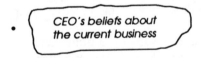

A CEO may have extensive knowledge of certain departments in a business, such as production. At Chem-A-Lot, production was Charlie's bag. In other areas, such as marketing, Charlie's beliefs were at first hazy representations of reality. But Charlie knew it was up to him to gain accurate knowledge about each department in which he was deficient, even though he also knew he would seldom be called upon to perform the functions of those departments directly.

Charlie also knew that his beliefs had to change constantly because they only partially represented the dynamic underlying reality at Chem-A-Lot.

Therefore, as the CEO, Charlie constantly and consciously sought new information to update his beliefs.

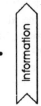

Accounting data is but one of the information streams that flows to managers. Company departments structured to do something about information tend to be organized around six major information streams. These streams flow from:

1. The customers who use your products.
2. The competitors who produce like or similar products.
3. The suppliers who provide the raw materials or ideas for your products or organization.
4. The internal operations of your company.
5. The general public, which has positive, negative, or no impressions of your company.
6. Other national and international organizations that have an impact on your company, for example, taxing authorities, tariff setting authorities, and regulatory bodies.

Real control, Charlie knew, is much more subtle than is implied by the traditional organization chart. It involves the creation of a working environment that permits that other hidden hand, cooperation, to operate effectively.

Information and control are the two ends of a measurement, analysis, and reporting system, the effectiveness of which depends on the extent of cooperation for appropriate action.

Through her work, Diane had demonstrated to Charlie that reports for supervisors highlighting deviations from norms should not be buried in reams of computer runs. Even workers performing production or staff-support activities should be trained to understand and use simple statistical control techniques.

Unfortunately, traditional financial statements, accounting-period ratios, and arithmetic charts, as we saw in the Jack Tuffitout years, are also insufficient guides to businesses moving on space-age trajectories. So you'll also want to consider rate-of-change measurements, which go beyond the traditional custodial function of accounting. Charlie, of course, was wise enough to listen to Diane about how personal computers could provide quick instrument readings to tell him which way was up.

- **Actual current business**

A smart executive knows that no instrument readings and no amount of information can fully represent the real business. During his long years at Chem-A-Lot, Charlie had gained an intuitive sense of conditions by being alert to people relationships inside and outside the business.

The belief that a good manager can manage anything is, at best, a partial truth. Even a brilliant manager must take the time to learn the nuances of the business to be managed as well as those of its industry. When the chips were down, the Chem-A-Lot board of directors made a wise choice in selecting Charlie. The directors, in their desperation, might have opted for another fast-track manager.

Unfortunately, many fast-track managers—those who are adept at juggling books and people to make a quick profit, to skyrocket a reputation, and then to move on—can't hope to develop the sixth sense required to make appropriate decisions for the long-term success of a business. For would-be fast-track manager Jack Tuffitout, this approach proved harmful to both himself and Chem-A-Lot. The world economic conditions in which Chem-A-Lot was operating were changing rapidly. Simultaneously, competitors were increasingly attacking Chem-A-Lot's specific markets with new, innovative products and lower prices.

Because many prestigious business schools have, in the past, produced an abundance of fast-track managers who often behaved like hit-and-run drivers, the United States is paying dearly in business lost to other nations.

- *CEO's valuations about the future business*

With Charlie's developing knowledge of Chem-A-Lot, he naturally evaluated alternative visions about how the company could survive and serve all stakeholders in the future as well as what would happen if the current course was continued. He considered the feasibility of reaching each vision, taking into account current and acquirable resources and the likely prevailing local and world economic conditions.

He knew through hard-won experience that visions based solely on an assessment of current reality as represented by accounting numbers — be they accurate or inaccurate — are but a mirage on the horizon of possibility.

To reach his vision of the future, Charlie selected the following **prime objective:**

To reestablish Chem-A-Lot as a leading producer of quality conditioner, formulator, and transporter equipment for the process industries in the world.

This prime objective was an attainable future business condition rooted in customer needs that he knew Chem-A-Lot either had or could develop the resources to meet. Furthermore, this objective was acceptable to the old-timers who had served the company well and the young newcomers who had read books like *In Search of Excellence*.[1]

To avoid confusion among the ranks, Charlie did not select an accounting objective, such as:

Our company will maximize both annual profits and annual sales growth.

The logic of such an objective would have been faulty because the size of profit versus sales is often a trade-off. For example, you can buy high sales with too low prices and wind up showing a loss on your income statement. Like a single airplane, a single business cannot be scheduled to arrive at two different air terminals at the same time.

Charlie knew that it was necessary to mark the boundaries of a business clearly. Boundary delineation becomes even more important when the CEO finds himself in charge of more than one business. An objective that is suitable for one business might not be for another. Indistinct boundaries between objectives tend to confuse pilots and crew. Like an airport landing field, the objective should be well-lighted for all to see.

---

[1]Thomas J. Peters and Robert H. Waterman, Jr., *In Search of Excellence* (New York: Warner Books by arrangement with Harper & Row, Publishers, Inc., 1982).

Ideally, objectives should be so well-founded that they can remain rock firm for many years. Like airports, objectives are expensive to move.

Coordinated subsidiary objectives for various functions—such as sales, purchasing and manufacturing—will also emerge from evaluation of the six streams of information.

In addition, a corporate objective may be established if there are several separate businesses under one ownership. A corporate objective is a single objective that coordinates the different objectives of several businesses.

This can be tricky. It's like the coordinated flight of the Navy's Blue Angels, except that each jet would be a very different model!

- IMF

Charlie took action to channel his own motive force as well as that of all his co-workers so that the business did indeed move toward the future envisioned. Change normally starts with a vision; it energizes movement through three stages: the long-range strategy plan, the business plan, and the annual budget.

Living business systems have different life spans and varying degrees of complexity that are largely determined by intentional tactics or unforeseen events. Growth, stagnation, or decline can result from either.

Strategies may be tailored to cover a wide spectrum of possibilities. A few generic types are market penetration, market development, product development, product acquisition, improved customer service, opportunity exploitation, conglomeration, and integration (backward, forward, or horizontally with other companies) as well as unplanned strategies.

To help in supplying information for strategy formulation, research groups are often formed. Departments for market research and development, product research and development, and operations research and development are typical examples. Care must be exercised to ensure that departmental jargon does not become a barrier to communication, which would defeat the purpose for which such departments are created.

Based upon the several-years-long strategy plan, detailed annual business plans and budgets are prepared.

- OMF

Charlie knew his vision for Chem-A-Lot's future would have to be so enticing and so realistic that it could be shared by all stakeholders. The vision would have to become the driving force behind any strategy devised. OMF would develop when all felt a real responsibility for carrying out the long-range strategy to reach the envisioned objective and share in its fruits. That is the ultimate test of leadership, whether for good or for evil. A good example of OMF developed among stakeholders: Most Americans were proud and supportive stakeholders in our space program at the time Neil Armstrong said, "One small step for man; one giant leap for mankind."

Any selected product, production, marketing, or financial strategy designed to reach an objective must be broken down into strings of tactics to be performed by individuals or teams in order to harness the OMF developed.

Often military nomenclature—such as "targets," "tactics," "task force," "missions," "strategy," "superior combat power," and "campaign"—is used to describe marketing, although the analogy is far from exact. On the international competitive scene, killing people is not the prime objective. Even those who are genuinely fearful of other nations and have reason to be are now trying to develop shield technologies as opposed to killing technologies. Hopefully, most businesses in the evolving international community will improve the lot of their international customers and their own workers, thus enhancing the chances for peace.

The world business economy is not a zero-sum game in which someone always loses when someone else wins. When economies become truly dynamic, individuals from declining businesses that are operating under the aegis of the hidden hands of cooperation and competition will be challenged to form better, new alternatives.

Product development, unlike marketing, is often described in terms like "projects," "tasks," "critical paths," and "project milestones." A project may be thought of as the development of items for use in carrying out a marketing strategy. Strategy, with embedded tactics, guides individuals or teams in the day-to-day effort put forth to reach the prime objective.

Tactics are planned, spontaneous, or emergency actions that yield a desired result along a path leading to the objective. Of course, workers can waste time on actions unrelated to the business.

Final estimates of annual revenues, costs, and net assets associated with those tactics and tasks to be undertaken during a year represent the new growth portion of the business plan and budget. They are similar to the anticipated annual growth rings in the trunk of a tree. The complete annual budget includes the maintenance of base business plus an estimate of the annual resources (people and balance sheet items) needed to reach the sales targets and project milestones (income statement and cash-flow statement items) for new initiatives.

A number of highly successful businesses plan for crises. These companies prepare plans and budgets that cut in if interim results fall significantly below or above plans.

Separate forecasts of sales revenues and costs should be made for each base business. Potential planning-engendered revenues and costs can then be added to or subtracted from these amounts to obtain final total budget figures for the year.

Timing is also important. Planning efforts should be timed to the rhythm of each business calendar or fiscal year. Normally, the review of objectives and strategies for future years takes place by the end of the first quarter of each year. Cooperative task and competitive tactic development takes place during the second and third quarters of the current year. The budget, funded for action, should be available by the beginning of the new year.

The information system must be able to provide reliable progress reports along the way toward the vision that you and all members of your business, hopefully, share. In addition to the charts and tables already used to tell the story of Chem-A-Lot, there are many other techniques available, like PERT—Program Evaluation Review Technique—or CPS—Critical Path Scheduling—or simple bubble charts to start with.

At Chem-A-Lot, Diane chose an excellent project program that incorporated these techniques for personal computers. With the program she selected, managers didn't have to have people spend long hours at a drafting board drawing complicated charts or figuring out the complex interrelationships between tasks. It was a very simple, time-conserving matter on the personal computer network at Chem-A-Lot. Planning no longer delayed real action; it sped up competent action.

•   **Actual future business**

When a prime objective like Charlie's has been reached, everyone has cause for celebration. However, it is important to realize that all the people in a business have also reached a real danger point if each individual now decides to rest on his or her laurels or tires of the effort, as Jim Dandy did. The need for new visions of future products and services for the customers will never end as long as humanity exists.

WARNING! ALWAYS REMEMBER YOUR PLANNING TARGET IS THE CONSUMER

Don't get so lost in the details of planning that you lose sight of one very important fact: When you plan, your fundamental purpose is to focus your efforts on that moving target—the consumer. With new personal computer techniques, you can simplify much of the stultifying paperwork that accompanied the traditional planning function.

Many years ago, Alben Barkley, then Vice-President of the United States, told a story about making a campaign speech in which he was listing and extolling all the actions he had taken in the past on behalf of his constituents. He was rudely interrupted by a loud voice from the rear of the auditorium that asked, "But Alben, what have you done for me lately?"

Remember that consumers, your prospective customers, perpetually look for ways to improve their lives. Consumers become your customers when they cast dollar votes for your products or services. The consumers' current evaluation of your products, not *your* evaluation, is crucial to the survival of your business. The beauty of this system is its wonderful flexibility and the multiplicity of products it generates.

Every minority can cast dollar votes for products to fill their special needs. That's very unlike the political arena, where the majority's wishes normally prevail. Ultimately, the more international and domestic competition and cooperation there is and the less governmental economic interference there is—except for enforcement of the rules of fair competition, cooperation, and safety (both personal and environmental)—the better off all minorities around the world will become.

Only consumers, through a free market, can justly reward each business for its products and services according to their value judgments through the mechanism of price. The more innovative businesses are often rewarded with revenues much larger than their total costs of current production. However, the reaping of high profits cannot be the sole reason for business planning because that leads to unrealistic pricing, consumer avoidance, increasing competition, and finally market share erosion.

Profits must be plowed back into new or old businesses in innovative ways. Such a policy permits you to anticipate the creative destruction of products no longer in demand and the replacement of these products with new or improved ones to better serve the customer. Because we in the United States did not anticipate the decline of the smokestack industries, millions of workers are paying the price through unemployment. The continuing search for excellence, when successful, permits your business not only to survive but thrive.

GOOD RULES FOR BUSINESS LEADERS

- *Define your business prime objective.* It should be a statement of purpose that can be adhered to for many years. It should be a clear guide to action. It should represent potential worth to all stakeholders. Furthermore, the prime objective should be attainable through an appropriate long-range strategy.

- *Know your markets.* Search for your own and your competitors' marketing strengths and weaknesses from the viewpoint of customers. Your product is not fully produced until it is used. Your customer is really a part of your production line.

- *Adopt a policy of excellence.* An unending search for excellence that will inspire and harness the individual motive force of each participant in the production process by example and direct effort should be mounted. This policy should even influence your suppliers of raw materials and services. A search for excellence reduces costs.

- *Know your costs.* Sales volume without adequate profit is deadly, but the usual knee-jerk reaction, raising product prices, will not always produce profits. A focus on short-term profit undermines product quality and, in turn, customer demand. Do analyze significant costs and expenses and compare them with those of your competitors.

- *Know your prices.* The price tag on your products or on the materials you purchase for the production of your products is not a sufficient measure of value. Buying on price alone can result in all sorts of costly production problems due to inferior quality.

- *Cooperate with suppliers.* Help them help you. It often works best to develop relationships based on trust with a few quality suppliers. If your supplier is equally committed to excellence, you may then be able to work toward cost savings for both through *just-in-time* inventory practices.

- *Train supervisors to lead.* Authoritative bosses who control by fear should be replaced or retrained. They must become supervisors who help people to improve their work habits after having determined, through good process control data, which people need help. Supervisors should operate under the premise that the production system controlled by management is much more often at fault than are the workers. Workers should be encouraged to help supervisors solve production problems.

- *Replace worker-performance with system-performance measurements.* With few exceptions, the bulk of workers perform most of the time within appropriate upper and lower limits set on process control charts. Fluctuations within those limits should be considered due to the production system—beyond the control of the workers. Faulty equipment and defective materials that come into a department because of faulty upstream production processes are often the cause of wide fluctuations. Worker penalties resulting from such fluctuations are deeply resented— they are inherently unfair and should be eliminated.

- *Establish training programs.* Too often workers become disgusted because they have been trained by co-workers who were not properly trained themselves. You should understand the need for and cost of rigid rules for poorly trained workers as well as the cost of and time required for good training. A finely honed and enthusiastic work force can't be put in place overnight.

- *Develop a flexible production system.* Competence leads to respect and mutual trust between workers and management. Then the authority to act can be entrusted to workers at the site of the action.

- *Promote teamwork.* A concerted effort should be made to remove barriers between departments. Teams made up of well-trained people from several departments can often solve a production problem quickly. But these teams will do a good job only if the members feel that it is safe to speak freely. Fear can destroy a company. That's one reason why Japanese firms often provide lifetime employment.

- *Discourage jargon.* Make every effort to develop language that can be used universally in your business. Most of the time plain, simple English will express ideas more clearly than professional jargon.

- *Eliminate quantity quotas and narrow slogans.* Misplaced emphasis can cause workers to meet quantity quotas at the expense of quality. In all activities, never sacrifice excellence to a single value stressed in a slogan.

- *Surprise competitors.* Strike in a place and at a time when your competitors are not prepared. However, realize that they will respond in kind with improvements of their own. Recognize that letting people know that they have a real stake in your continuing cooperative search for excellence is the best assurance of business security.

- *Develop competitive momentum through acquisition.* At the appropriate time and place, an acquisition may be considered. However, acquiring is no substitute for cleaning up one's own act. Great care must be exercised in selecting an acquisition since ignoring differences between too very unlike business cultures can do severe injury to both.

- *Go on the offensive.* The top management team, by its example, must eliminate fear and make a long-term commitment to developing a climate of cooperation. It must take the initiative, both internally and externally, for laying the plans required to reach a better future for all stakeholders. The CEO, the supervisors, the production workers, or groups of other stakeholders cannot create a healthy business culture just by acting alone.

HOW TO APPLY THE CHEM-A-LOT EXPERIENCE

PART FIVE

THE EVALUATION OF BUSINESS PERFORMANCE

Explains exactly how the diagnostic tools and management concepts were applied to define the Chem-A-Lot system of problems

CHAPTER 21

GETTING STARTED

THE WILL TO USE APPROPRIATE MANAGEMENT TOOLS EFFECTIVELY

Doing a situation analysis has no value in itself! A laudable short-term objective is to find and correct problems, but what is the ultimate objective?

At Chem-A-Lot, the stakeholder shared prime objective embodied a vision: *to reestablish Chem-A-Lot as a leading producer of quality conditioner, formulator, and transporter equipment for the process industries in the world.* The prime objective provided the motive force for constructive change.

THE COORDINATED USE OF MANAGEMENT TOOLS

This section of the Strategic Planning Workbook demonstrates how to select and use appropriate management tools for the task at hand. Through the years, the practical tools described have been tested in both large and small businesses.

The Chem-A-Lot composite case history highlights the coordinated use of a set of analytical tools that are indispensable in uncovering and correcting problems. These tools make improved modes of planning for the future possible.

Rolling business plans (described on page 177) developed during cycles of analysis, planning, and control are the most cost effective because they make it unnecessary to start afresh each year.

THE SITUATION ANALYSIS

To determine if managerial beliefs and decisions are based upon sufficient information is critically important. This is done through a situation analysis.

These are some fundamental questions asked in a situation analysis: Is the information accurate and sufficient? Is there an overload of superfluous information? Is the information analyzed properly? Are the analytical tools used capable of identifying systems of problems? Are problems addressed promptly? Is control properly exercised?

It may help to visualize a situation analysis as follows:

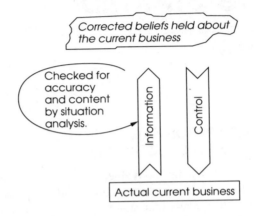

RESPONSIBILITY OF THE BOARD

Chem-A-Lot's Board had the duty of overseeing the company's financial performance on behalf of the stockholders. Perhaps not by chance, the word oversight has two meanings: One is "watchful care," and the other is "failure to notice or think of something."

For Chem-A-Lot's Board, oversight slipped from watchful care to failure to take rumors of customer, employee, and vendor discontent seriously enough. Eventually, after a huge loss of business to competitors, the Board exercised its duty to oversee. Consultants were hired, and the cause—a number of interactive problems—was uncovered.

The financial pain caused by a system of interactive problems can be a great motivator. Fear of continued financial pain will often cause top decision makers to recognize the need for a situation analysis as well as to back it, fund it, and see to its completion.

THE PROJECT MANAGER'S ROLE

If either a consultant or an in-house executive were assigned the responsibility of evaluating the performance of a business or of solving certain specific operating problems, the first task would be to get a handle on the company's culture. Root causes of operating problems lie in the evolving relationships between individuals and groups. It would be not only shortsighted but also of little value to go looking for someone to blame. As at Chem-A-Lot, the person whose well-intentioned actions gave rise to a system of underlying problems may have long since departed the company.

What the project manager needs is the wholehearted support of either a concerned CEO or the Board. In addition, the project manager must be known as a fair and trustworthy person with whom *everybody* from janitor to the CEO can talk safely. This may prove to be a difficult hurdle for an in-house project manager because of long-standing friendships, generation gaps, professional turf battles, or other reasons. Any project manager must take *everybody* seriously including young employees and those new to their jobs as well as old timers. The former often have fresh ideas, and the latter may give important insights into company history.

BASE BUSINESS DEFINITION

Initially, define the business(es) conducted. If there is more than one, it will be necessary to distinguish them carefully. To confuse two or more businesses with one another can destroy the validity of the situation analysis. Objectives and the strategies for reaching them nearly always differ for different businesses.

MAINTAIN SECURE RECORDS

Maintain secure records with adequate backup. Keep a running dated list of pertinent discussion notes. It's surprising how memory can play tricks on a person over time and how statements taken out of context can be misconstrued if good records are not kept.

Also generate additional topic files as needed. Topics important enough to require a separate file often turn out to be symptoms of problems. In topic files, assemble copies of germane items from the dated running list and other sources that may be needed to help trace interactive problems. Such record keeping is simple with the quick copying capability of computer word processing programs.

Computer project monitoring programs can also assist the project manager. The diskette accompanying this book illustrates a proven approach for organizing interview and data records.

LET THE PICTURE EMERGE

Be slow in drawing conclusions; let the picture emerge gradually. Later, the emerging picture can be corroborated by details from accounting and personnel records.

The contents of your files will become the flesh and muscle around accountings' skeleton depiction of your company—a situation analysis, analogous to an X-ray image.

HELPFUL RULES OF CONDUCT FOR A PROJECT MANAGER

It is, of course, easier to conduct a situation analysis if a healthy, cooperative business culture exists. Occasionally, a business culture may have deteriorated to the point that the project manager must use extreme care. In either case the following rules of conduct are worth heeding:

- Be forthright with people about the reasons for the situation analysis. Stress the positives: for example, that the analysis can lead to improved performance in the future through better strategies which will in turn benefit all stakeholders.

- Assure everyone you contact that you are searching for interrelated problems that can involve many people unwittingly. A search for scapegoats defeats the purpose by narrowing the focus to a small part of what may prove to be a system of problems.

- State honestly why you are asking specific questions.

- Take a firm position that you will take no sides in, and will not be part of, a personal or group vendetta.

- Provide positive assurance that information about any hidden messes uncovered will be made available to all as a basis for self-improvement as well as for overall improvement of company performance.

- Assure individuals held hostage by hidden systems of problems that they will be invited to contribute toward the elimination of those harmful systems.

- Promise that you will never quote people by name without their written permission. No one should ever feel that they might be singled out for censure. That would be a sure way to encourage people to conceal pertinent information.

CHAPTER 22

WHAT TO LOOK FOR

TOPICS LIKELY TO ARISE

Memory jogging references to the Chem-A-Lot composite case history are provided here for your convienience. The Management Tool Kit (Section 2, Part 7) also provides a compilation of diagnostic tools and useful management concepts. Topics likely to arise include the following:

- *Declining profitability.* Often, one of the first indicators of an ailing buisness is declining profits. However, if short-term profits are maintained at the expense of the long-term future of a business then those profits simply mask hidden problems.

- *Communication barriers, misunderstandings, and even vendettas.* What is the nature of the problems existing between departments, between managers and workers, between the company and suppliers, and between the company, its customers, and its competitors?

  In the past, separate accounting journals were necessary in large firms both for efficient record keeping and for control of manufacturing, sales, purchasing, personnel, and other functions. Individuals within departments often developed departmental viewpoints that were detrimental to the overall goal of the business.

  Today information technologies are dissolving both departmental and hierarchical barriers. Flexible organizations of cooperating teams of individuals in which each person is competent in several skills are evolving as layers of unnecessary intermediate management are eliminated. Furthermore, companies are adopting cooperative rather than adversarial relationships with suppliers and even joint R&D ventures with competitors that may cross national boundaries.

- *Ineffecient production and poor service.* Poor work environments are often the result of stodgy management, isolated departments, and obsolete equipment. Decreased expenditures on equipment and increased employee termination rates are often symptoms.

- *Customer awareness.* How are specific customers and groups of customers treated? Are they treated with respect regardless of their current importance to the business?

269

- *"Quick fix" syndrome.* Have there been multiple incompatible problem fixes that have started or aggravated existing messes?

- *"I know best" syndrome.* Have pet solutions been imposed by managers instead of obviously better solutions known to employees directly involved with the problems?

  The opening chapters of the Chem-A-Lot story, *"The Need to Survive"* and the *"The New Broom,"* demonstrate that the "quick fix" and "I know best" syndromes are really the two faces of a single syndrome.

- *Exodus of competent people.* What are the real reasons for workers leaving the company as opposed to the reasons given by the workers or their supervisors? Is high turnover of employees the norm?

  Start with personnel records. Sometimes it can be very helpful to talk to ex-employees, who no longer have any reason to fear the loss of their jobs. Exit interviews may prove helpful, but objectivity is usually lost during an emotional termination.

- *Noncommunicative workers.* How open are the lines of communication? Why do workers depend on the grapevine for information? Why do subordinates keep their lips zipped in the presence of superiors?

  You'll develop a sixth sense about the lack of free information flow in authoritarian cultures.

- *Compensation fairness.* Is compensation considered unfair by executives or others? Is the feeling severe enough to reduce morale or increase turnover?

  Executive compensation should be compared honestly against that paid by competitors worldwide. With a rapidly developing world economy, new books on executive compensation are being published. For example, *In Search of Excess* by Graef S. Crystal, is worth reading.[1] Be alert for other fairness issues.

- *Conflict resolution methods.* How are conflicts being resolved? You may wish to review page 36, *"Conflict Resolution: Negotiating Conflicts in the Struggle for the Future."*

- *Reactivist, inactivist, preactivist, interactivist managers.* How many of these types does your company have? Do managers tend to be of the same type? If so, why? How do managers relate to the individuals they supervise? For definitions see Chapter 3 of this book.

- *Authoritarian and "fast track" managers.* Do your managers delegate authority effectively? Do they give the impression of being unconcerned about the long-term best interests of company or of the individuals supervised?

  Examples: Authoritarian CEO Jim Dandy failed to delegate appropriately, and "fast track" CEO Jack Tuffitout was self-serving to the detriment of the interests of company stakeholders.

---

[1]Graef S. Crystal, *In Search of Excess* (New York: W. W. Norton & Company, 1991).

- *Competition/cooperation imbalance.* Are relationships between people open or of the "protect your rear" variety? Do workers have the knowledge and authority to stop production if defective parts are being produced? Will fear of losing their jobs prevent workers from taking appropriate action?

   Competition and cooperation are but two sides of a coin. For business success they are equally important.

- *Motivation levels.* How much training and retraining of workers does the company do? Is the company meeting the aspirations of its people? Do workers and managers feel they have a long-term stake in the success of the company? Are workers given training in a number of jobs so they can substitute for one another as necessary in a team environment? In other words, has the glow and the promise of a better future remained strong or faded?

- *Leadership capablilities.* Is your CEO an inspiring or a lackluster leader? Does the CEO have good or poor management skills?

   You may wish to review "*Good Rules for Business Leaders*" in Chapter 20. It contains a collection of leadership ideas developed over many years.

- *Plans for the future.* Do plans really act as everyday guides, or are they just tomes that simply gather dust on a shelf?

- *Research and Development (R&D), Design and Development (D&D).* Is research funding sufficient to protect the product base? Are products continuously being upgraded to meet competition? Just how is R&D viewed by your company?

   The company's attitude toward R&D and D&D is important; it may underlie more general attitudes that give rise to messes. For example, some corporations regularly invest in small companies that have developed new products through R&D, then skimp on further research and finally divest them when the products no longer produce adequate profits. Such a policy can play havoc with morale and produce poor operating results. Other companies concentrate on design improvements for existing products (D&D). These companies may become vulnerable to the innovations of competitors.

   On the other hand, some products are milked as "cash cows" to support other, more promising products. If understood by stakeholders concerned, this may be just the right thing to do . . . or it might not be.

- *Cash flow crunches.* How often do they occur? Why?

- *"Creative" accounting.* Do you suspect some accounting records are deliberately or unintentionally designed to obscure problems? It happens.

   Sometimes old-fashioned departmental accounting practices and production rules can cause problems. Other times deliberate practices may touch on fraud. If you suspect this might be the case, don't go it alone. Obtain help from the chief financial officer or another independent in-house officer or from a professional auditing firm. There have been instances when honest persons, unable to obtain support, have felt and were justified in becoming whistle blowers.

DATA SOURCES

As the project manager's collection of information grows, it becomes necessary to scan current accounting and other records for pertinent data. Often studying original sales orders and employee terminations pays huge dividends. Note the location of applicable records in topic files. They can be used to corroborate or refute the accounts of witnesses to events that led to turning points.

If a thorough, unbiased job is done, one is often amazed at the depth of concern expressed by workers for others as well as themselves. Some may even bring forth records squirreled away at home or in their desks — discarded records that they felt were important to the future of the company or copies of records saved to defend themselves should the need ever arise.

To understand the part control records play, examine:

- *Total sales and profit records.* Data going back 10 or more years will be required in order to search for critical turning points.

- *U.S. and global industry records kept.* Such data is needed to check the significance of turning points.

- *Year-end financial statements.* Is the current year compared only with the previous year? At least five years should be compared on income statements. Simply presuming that past records are known can be dangerous.

  Has a real effort been made to make financial statements useful management tools?

  Detailed financial statements for at least five years — or from the last turning point — will be needed to identify significant trends.

- *Annual sales records including unit counts and unit prices.* How far back do accurate company records go? How complete are they for dollar sales, unit sales, and prices for product lines and individual products? Are there breakdowns by type of customer and by geographic region? Are there records of sales lost? Is the market share for each geographic area known so that it is possible to determine current sales performance?

  Data for at least five years or from the last verified turning point will be required in this case also.

- *Vendor purchase records.* Analysis of major raw material component costs is essential to determining why material product costs were what they were. Sales price changes should be related to both raw material and labor cost changes.

- *Production and service cost records.* It is important to establish the relationship between total sales and total costs. Complete cost records, including manufacturing and SG&A (sales, general, and administrative) costs, are desirable.

When total sales and costs converge, it is often because competitors have found ways to reduce their costs on comparable products, which permits them to reduce prices. To meet the competition, the company is then forced to reduce prices or suffer a loss in profits and market share. To recover market position as well as profitability, the company must eventually reduce costs and prices or hold prices while differentiating products from those of competitors.

One of the major reasons for the recent loss of U.S. market postition is the very high cost of warehousing manufacturing inventories, which are excessive because of competition from Japan. Efforts are now being made to counter the Just-In-Time inventory policies of Japanese businesses. An easy-to-understand book on a method for reducing inventory cost is *The Race* by Eliyahu M. Goldratt and Robert E. Fox.[2]

- *Types of tables and graphs.* How useful are they? Are they merely for "show and tell" at Board meetings? Are they made to misrepresent the true situation? Yes, politics do exist within a business. How do company records compare with the inadequate records kept by Jim Dandy and Jack Tuffitout as CEOs in the opening chapters of the story of Chem-A-Lot?

- *Paperwork.* Do workers face loads of unnecessary paperwork? How much of it do you think is wasted effort?

If paperwork has gotten out of hand, it may prove cost effective to trace the flow of information and evaluate the forms used. The flow of paperwork through several departments may no longer serve a useful purpose yet can be amazingly difficult to stop even in a small company.

PITFALLS TO BE AVOIDED

Through interviews, evidence of interrelated problems as well as "quick fixes" may have turned up. For this reason, the project manager may be tempted to jump to an unwarranted conclusion. It would be tragic to fix something that's not broken. Alternately, why fix only part of what is broken?

All that has been done at this stage is that a kind of "medical history" of the company has been taken. The hard work is yet to come—the determination of the precise diagnosis and the remedial steps required to cure what ails the current business. Later, in the planning stages, long-term strategy with embedded short-term tactics will be considered.

---

[2]Eliyahu M. Goldratt and Robert E. Fox, *The Race* (Croton-on-Hudson, New York: North River Press, 1986).

CHAPTER 23

TOOLS REQUIRED TO DO A SITUATION ANALYSIS

FUNDAMENTAL MEASUREMENTS

Analytical tools are used to count or compare things. Counts were originally made by marks on a tally, numbers on a card, or units of length on a ruler. Comparisons were made by observing counts directly or by calculating abstract count ratios or percentages. From these basic counts and comparisons more sophisticated accounting records and statistical comparisons have evolved. In business today, rate-of-change and size measurements are fundamental measuring methods.

Tools that measure rate-of-change are analogous to speedometers in cars. The average percentage change per year is like the average speed traveled. Tools that measure size, on the other hand, are like the odometer, which measures total distance traveled.

To date, rate-of-change charts have been used only rarely in business. Until they are used more frequently, valuable knowledge will be lost, and the value of such charts will not be fully appreciated.

RATE-OF-CHANGE CHARTS

Differences in rate of change—between sales, gross profits, and operating profits, for example—can be compared directly just as easily as the speeds of several large or small cars. Rates are displayed as the slopes of lines on rate-of-change, semi-log charts. These charts can highlight not only slight rate differences but major turning points in change rates. They are also versatile enough to make estimation of absolute dollar amounts possible.

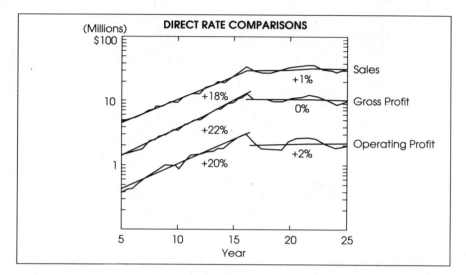

Indexed rates of change also lend themselves readily to comparisons on semi-log fan charts. Checking the fan shown below is comparable to checking dial indicator positions on three separate speedometers at once:

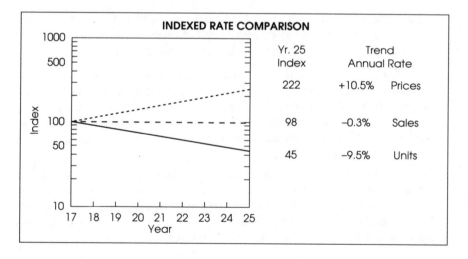

For convenience, these comparison charts are referred to as fan charts, or simply fans.

SIZE CHARTS

One must be careful to limit the traditional size (arithmetic) charts like the one shown below to size comparisons. The size trend lines are particularly deceptive since rates of change along them are not constant. The reason will be explained in detail later.

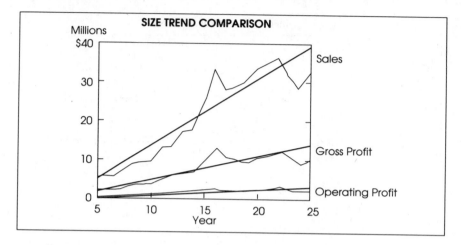

The project manager must have the skill to determine if analytical tools have been used properly. This chapter, therefore, will describe in more detail how to use these tools.

PERCENTAGE TOOL

The percentage tool (%) is powerful but often misapplied. It is basic. It compares relative sizes. Its use to compare rates of change will be demonstrated later. Keep the following in your collection of information:

- *Financial statements and observations about company performance that you derive from them.* Always list document locations if you have not copied them for your files. Do financial statements cover more than the current and one previous year? Changes can be spotted more easily on tables with data from five or more years. Trends can be calculated from consistent patterns of change.

- *Observations on how well percentages on financial statements enhance information content.* The two simple income statements below illustrate how percentages can be used to make two relative size comparisons: (1) comparisons of accounts within each of two years and (2) comparisons of identical accounts from one year to the next.

ACCOUNT COMPARISON WITHIN INCOME STATEMENTS
(Dollars in Thousands)

	Year 17		Year 18	
Sales	$28,000	100.0%	$28,100	100.0%
Cost of Goods Sold	17,900	63.9	18,300	65.1
Gross Profit	$10,100	36.1	$ 9,800	34.9
Operating Expenses:				
Operating and Selling	4,099	14.6	4,000	14.2
General and Administrative	4,100	14.6	4,000	14.2
Total Operating Expenses	8,199	29.3	8,000	28.5
Pre-Tax Income	$ 1,901	6.8%	$ 1,800	6.4%

ACCOUNT COMPARISON BETWEEN INCOME STATEMENTS
(Dollars in Thousands)

	Year 18	Year 19	Change
Sales	$28,100	$30,000	+ 6.8%
Cost of Goods Sold	18,300	20,400	+11.5
Gross Profit	9,800	9,600	−2.0
Operating Expenses:			
Selling	4,000	3,950	
General and Administrative	4,000	3,950	
Total Operating Expenses	8,000	7,900	−1.3
Pre-Tax Income	1,800	1,700	−5.6
Income Taxes	808	763	
Net Income	$ 992	$ 937	−5.5%

For good measure, observe the more elaborate application of these two uses in the following income statements.

COMPARISON OF INCOME STATEMENTS
(Dollars in Thousands)

	Year 21	Year 22	Year 23	Year 24	Year 25
Sales	$35,000	$36,200	$30,500	$28,600	$32,000
Cost of Goods Sold	23,100	23,900	20,100	19,400	21,800
Gross Profit (G.P.)	11,900	12,300	10,400	9,200	10,200
% G.P. of Sales	34.0	34.0	34.1	32.2	31.9
% G.P. of Year 21 G.P.	100.0	103.4	87.4	77.3	85.7
Operating Expenses:					
Operating and Selling	4,600	4,775	4,071	3,650	4,100
General and Administrative	4,600	4,775	4,129	3,650	4,100
Total Operating Expenses (O.E.)	9,200	9,550	8,200	7,300	8,200
% O.E. of Sales	26.3	26.4	26.9	25.5	25.6
% O.E. of Year 21 O.E.	100.0	103.8	89.1	79.3	89.1
Pre-Tax Income (P.T.I.)	2,700	2,750	2,200	1,900	2,000
% P.T.I. of Sales	7.7	7.6	7.2	6.6	6.3
% P.T.I. of Year 21 P.T.I.	100.0	101.9	81.5	70.4	74.1
Income Taxes	1,212	1,234	988	853	898
Net Income (N.I.)	$ 1,488	$ 1,516	$ 1,212	$ 1,047	$ 1,102
% N.I. of Sales	4.3	4.2	4.0	3.7	3.4
% N.I. Year 21 N.I.	100.0	101.9	81.5	70.4	74.1

PERCENTAGE CHANGES FROM YEAR 21
(Dollars in Thousands)

	Year 21	Year 22	Year 23	Year 24	Year 25
Sales	$35,000	+$1,200	−$4,500	−$6,400	−$3,000
% Change from Year 21	100.0	+ 3.4	− 12.9	− 18.3	− 8.6
Gross Profit	11,900	+ 400	− 1,500	− 2,700	− 1,700
% Change from Year 21	100.0	+ 3.4	− 12.6	− 22.7	− 14.3
Operating Expenses	9,200	+ 350	− 1,000	− 1,900	− 1,000
% Change from Year 21	100.0	+ 3.8	− 10.9	− 20.7	− 10.9
Pre-Tax Income	$ 2,700	+$ 50	−$ 50	−$ 800	−$ 700
% Change from Year 21	100.0	+ 1.9	− 18.5	− 29.6	− 25.9

WHY RATE CHARTS ARE INCREASING IN IMPORTANCE RELATIVE TO SIZE CHARTS

Until recently an individual's social position, strength, possessions, and control of information loomed large in our world view. The populace generally admired elite groups, stone buildings, brute force, mass production, and authoritarian personalities. Loyalty paid off. Things seemed solid. Very little changed in a lifetime. Size dominated thinking.

As the millennium nears its end, cooperative relationships, speed, flexibility, shared experiences, product variety, broad access to information, fads, fleeting fame, multiple careers, aerospace travel, and miniaturization are moving to the forefront. People are increasingly into exercise, bicycling, diets, holistic medicine, environmental concerns, VCRs, RVs, desktop computers, modems, faxes, car phones, computerized bulletin boards, you name it. The rate-of-change is accelerating. Blind loyalty appears unjustified. Institutions crumble. Huge changes occur in a lifetime or less. Problems mount everywhere. Relations between and among people, businesses, and nations increasingly dominate thinking. A new emphasis on cooperation in a wide variety of forms will take place. Cooperation and competition will be recognized as two sides of a coin.

In this challenging environment, rate-of-change measurement will take its place beside traditional size measurement. Both size and rate charts are easy to create with desktop computers.

HOW TO USE SIZE CHARTS

Size charts come in several forms: bar, column, line, area, pie, scatter, and combinations of these types. They are particularly useful for what can be called "cross-section analysis" of account sizes for a given year or for sales by geographic region.

Layered strata of products (sales geology) displayed on a size chart can reveal the changing mix of product lines in either units or dollars. Sometimes the changes in the mix can explain turning points.

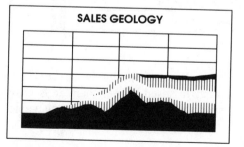

Size comparison graphs in bar form are useful for task assignment charts. Such charts clearly compare the length of the time periods required for each of a particular set of tasks.

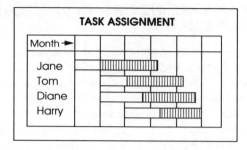

Pie charts are excellent for comparing market shares of competitors by sales territory as well as for other comparisons involving single time periods.

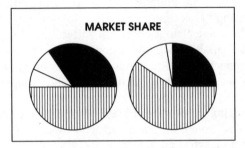

A combination size chart in breakeven and columnar form can be used to compare several projected profitability levels of sales clearly.

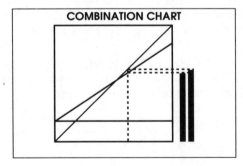

Arithmetic size charts like the one below show size changes effectively; however, they are often misused. From them it is easy to infer incorrect growth estimates, especially between or among disparate data series.

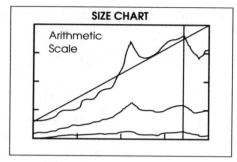

Remember how Board Chairman, Reginald Jones, added a trend line to sales on an updated Jim Dandy size chart in an attempt to get at the truth about CEO Tuffitout's performance. Jones did not view year 16 as a major turning point but rather as an aberration in the continued growth in sales up through year 22. He didn't even bother to calculate trends for gross profit and operating profit, which were less variable than sales.

Also remember how Tuffitout lopped off the earlier portion of this chart, which showed the high growth of the Jim Dandy years, in order to make his own mediocre performance less obvious.

When experimenting with size charts, be sure to include among them a chart comparing sales volumes and profits over the years for conversion to a rate chart.

HOW TO USE RATE CHARTS

Convert the size chart showing sales volumes and profits for your business to a rate chart. This can be done instantly with a desktop computer. Here is what chart conversion showed in the case of Chem-A-Lot: (1) The growth rate trends of sales, gross profits, and operating profits became parallel, and (2) the deviations of actual data from trends were reversed. Profits, as gut feeling suggested, showed more volatility than sales on the rate chart.

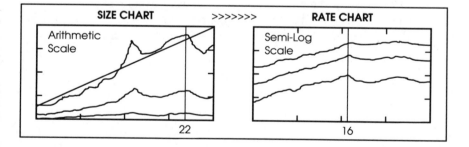

Suddenly it became clear that the true turning point was year 16, not year 22. Jones had unwittingly concentrated his attention on Tuffitout's current problems rather than on the hidden system of long-term problems.

So, when you have converted your chart, look for pronounced turning points in each data series. Also look for any pronounced convergence or divergence between pairs of data series. Recall how the convergence of sales and costs finally resulted in Chem-A-Lot's disastrous year 26.

TURNING POINTS AND RATE TREND LINES

The next step is to add trend lines to the sales and profit rate chart. Statistically fitted, straight-line rate trends provide a clearer representation of the changes in a data series. If you spotted turning points, have your computer calculate separate trend lines for the periods before and after each turning point as shown here.

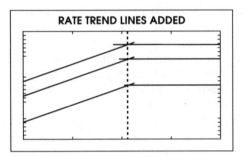

In a charting program such as Microsoft Excel®, the computer uses a regression formula to do the job. You need be no more concerned about how the regression formula works than you are about how the engine in your car works. It is more important to understand what the regression formula tells you about the business than to understand the details of its operation.

If, out of curiosity, you want to see just how tedious calculating trends can be with a hand-held calculator, do some simple examples from a statistics textbook. Then you'll fully appreciate the amazing speed with which the same work can be done on a desktop computer.

Trend lines on arithmetic charts are obviously a poor choice for determining rate-of-change relationships. To demonstrate why, we will use the Chem-A-Lot sales data for years 5 through 16, the first turning point.

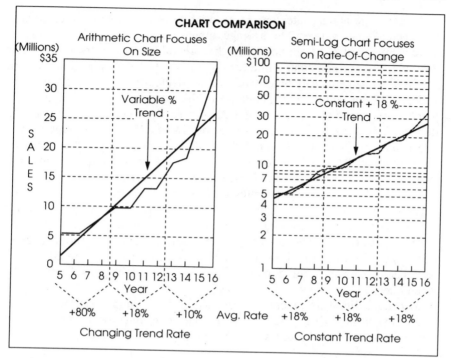

It is easier to compare numerical data in tables to data positions on charts when the charts are large and have grid lines rather than scale tick marks. Data tables for the charts just compared follow:

DATA COMPARISON

	Accounting Record (Dollars rounded)		Arithmetic Values (Above left chart)		Semi-Log Values (Above right chart)	
Year	Actual Sales	Ave. Annual Rate	Size Trend	Ave. Annual Rate	R-O-C Trend	Ave. Annual Rate
5	5.1		1.4		4.6	
6	5.0	+18%	3.6	+80%	5.4	+18%
7	6.0		5.8		6.4	
8	8.3		8.1		7.5	
9	9.4		10.3		8.9	
10	9.6	+12%	12.5	+18%	10.5	+18%
11	12.9		14.7		12.5	
12	13.3		17.0		14.7	
13	17.3		19.2		17.4	
14	18.4	+25%	21.4	+10%	20.6	+18%
15	24.4		23.6		24.4	
16	33.8		25.9		28.8	

Note: The accounting figures in millions have been rounded. The computer program generates trend values accurate to many decimal places.

The average annual rates on the accounting record table were calculated from actual sales values. The average annual rates on the arithmetic values table were calculated from endpoints that are values on size trend lines. For example, the average annual rate for the endpoints 1.4 in year 5 and 8.1 in year 8 is 80 percent. Any other two values selected from the table will yield widely different annual rates, ranging in this case from a very high +157 percent for years 5 to 6 to a low of +9.7 percent for years to 15 to 16. Using the year 5 and year 16 size trend values of 1.4 and 25.9, the average annual rate comes out at +30 percent. Which of these rates would you consider representative? This lack of consistency is the reason it is nearly impossible to infer representative rates of change from size charts.

Finally, the average annual rates on the semi-log values table were calculated from values on the rate-of-change trend line. For example, using 4.6 in year 1 and 7.5 in year 8, the average annual rate is +18 percent. Furthermore, any two rate-of-change values selected from the rate-of-change trend line will yield the same average annual rate. (Because trend figures have been rounded by the computer, rates will deviate slightly from +18% when checked on a hand calculator.)

Size trend lines are practically useless for determining relationships between two or more data series. Normal volatility of data for most businesses further reduces their usefulness for this purpose.

RATE-OF-CHANGE FORMULA

This is the formula used to calculate average annual rates of change between any two points:

Formula

$$\text{Rate} = \sqrt[n]{\frac{\text{Final Year}}{\text{Start Year}}} - 1$$

where n = final year minus start year.

Sales Example

Let:

Final Year(16) = $28,800,000

Start Year(5) =   4,600,000

$$\text{Rate} = \sqrt[11]{\frac{28,800,000}{4,600,000}} - 1 = +.18, \text{ or } + 18\%$$

In words: To find the average annual rate, divide the final year amount by the start year amount and take the nth root (n equals the number of the final year minus the number of the start year). The nth root in this case is 1.18 from which 1 (equivalent to 100% for the start year) is subtracted. Thus +18% represents the positive average rate of growth from the start or base year.

Observation: The average annual rate-of-change is constant for any two years that occur between major turning points on a semi-log rate trend. During periods between such turning points, companies—like many living organisms—normally grow or decline at a more-or-less constant annual rate. Turning points mark changes in conditions that may have remained stable for many years. They may be due to any of numerous possible causes, for instance, the accumulated weight of slow but long-term changes, shifts in business culture, critical management decisions, and pressure from competing products.

There have, of course, been companies in which management was so erratic that there were no periods of relatively normal growth. These situations must not be confused with a situation like Chem-A-Lot, which has volatile markets for its high-cost durable equipment.

While semi-log charts are appropriate tools for comparing rates of change over time, they are not appropriate for making cross-section comparisons such as the market share held in several sales territories at a given time. Consider log-log scatter charts for the latter purpose. They are powerful business tools, and they have many of the advantages of semi-log charts.

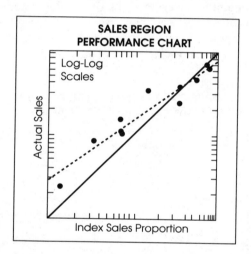

This log-log chart as used at Chem-A-Lot indicated that the market shares held in all of the smaller sales territories were greater than in the larger sales territories. The higher the plot points were above the diagonal black line the better the sales performance. For details see Chapter 8, "How to Use a Broad Market Index to Determine Market Shares."[1]

---

[1]To learn more about the results of using this fair measure of sales territory performance, see Karsten Hellebust, "Case History: Bindicator Finds a Fair measure for Sales Territory Performance," *Sales and Marketing Management,* Vol. 135, No. 7 (November 11, 1985): 45–46.

After some experience, a project manager will find that even the selection of the proper tool, just like the proficient use of a tool, is a learned skill. Improper tools and improperly used tools lead to wrong decisions. Unless an individual knows what he or she is doing, using a computer simply speeds up the arrival at a wrong conclusion!

THE POINT AT WHICH TO START A DETAILED PRODUCT ANALYSIS

Has evidence of systems of interrelated problems been found? Does the evidence seem linked to suspicious converging, diverging, or flattening growth rates or to turning points in total sales and total costs? Is the reason known? If not, perhaps it would be good to dig deeper.

The project manager's work may prove difficult if records are incomplete or shoddily kept. In such cases, recorded interview notes made earlier in the situation analysis project may come in handy. They can help in locating hither to forgotten sources of information.

Having found a turning point, the project manager must determine if it is important. At this point it is wise to check the turning point against trends in the company's industry or the economy. If the turning point simply matches an external turning point, it may not be significant. Recall the compelling proof that the turning point at Chem-A-Lot was significant:

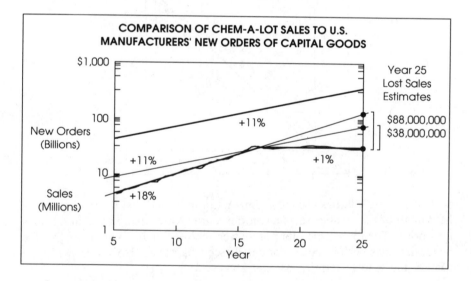

Over the years after the turning point, the total of sales lost to Chem-A-Lot amounted to many times the estimated loss for year 25 alone! Obviously, there were also profound effects on all the stakeholders, capital expenditures, cash flow, and, yes, literally everything about the company.

What if the turning point does not correspond to a change in the general economy? It is just possible that the U.S. industry in which the company operates is suffering from a system of problems unique to it. The same industry in other countries may have avoided or corrected problems. Consider, for example, the U.S. auto industry, which has been playing catch-up to foreign competitors for some time. It also may be that products are becoming obsolete, as when the slide rule was replaced by the hand-held calculator. If obsolescence occurs gradually, there may be no sharp turning point.

Declining profitability may be related to costs. If so, look for points at which the rates for total sales and total costs start to converge. Treat events as starting points for detailed analyses. Recall the convergence of sales and costs that finally led to Chem-A-Lot's disastrous year 26:

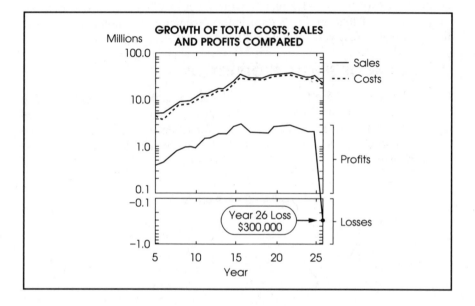

Also recall how gradually converging sales and distribution costs for Chem-A-Lot products led a New England distributor to decide to promote other products.

If there is no clear turning point, arbitrarily select a point at least five years prior to the present. The reason for going back so far is the decreasing relative importance of endpoint deviations from trend as the number of years is increased. In simple terms, including more years will produce a more representative trend line.

Up till now we have been concerned with long-term major changes. Calculation of long-term sales and cost trends is intended to eliminate the confusion caused by annual or monthly fluctuations in these areas. Short-term sales fluctuations and forecasts are handled separately by such techniques as sales pressure analysis using leading, lagging, and coincident indicators.

WORK AT BEDROCK

Start a situation analysis at the product level within each line. Sometimes, even the mix of different sizes of a product must be examined for patterns of change. For now, products with constant size mixes will be considered.

For a selected product, gather data on unit sales, sales prices, and dollar sales of the last five or more years.

Unit counts will be the bedrock of the work. Sales dollars alone won't do. Price changes cause identical dollar amounts to measure different amounts of production. When actual prices are compared directly to unit sales for a specific product, there is no need to make a further adjustment for inflation. It will, however, be necessary to keep track of how changing currency exchange rates affect the unit prices in foreign countries. Incidentally, by keeping track of units and prices for a product in this manner, one makes a measurement of that product's contribution to national inflationary or deflationary forces. Yes, your pricing policies do have an impact on inflation.

DERIVATION OF SINGLE-PRODUCT INDEXES

In the Chem-A-Lot case history, Chem-Kraker was the product selected first for a detailed analysis. It was the only product with a good track record after the year 16 turning point. Unit sales for Chem-Kraker were so volatile that this product provided a good test of the efficacy of analytical tools. Chem-Kraker data is shown and charted below.

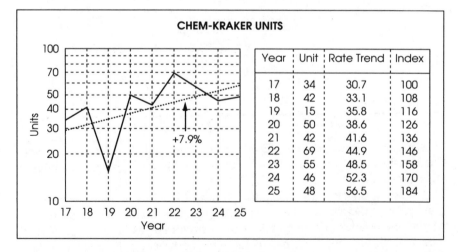

CHEM-KRAKER UNITS

Year	Unit	Rate Trend	Index
17	34	30.7	100
18	42	33.1	108
19	15	35.8	116
20	50	38.6	126
21	42	41.6	136
22	69	44.9	146
23	55	48.5	158
24	46	52.3	170
25	48	56.5	184

The average annual rate-of-change in unit count was +7.9 percent. For comparison, consider the endpoints of 34 units for year 17 and 48 units for year 25. When the calculation is based on these endpoints, the average annual rate-of-change decreases to a nonrepresentative +4.4 percent. Why?

Year 17 is selected as the base year, and its average annual rate of 30.7 units is set equivalent to 100 percent to create the basis for an indexed rate trend. This index can be compared directly to other indices computed in the same way. Later this indexing procedure will be illustrated in detail in the section on Index Calculation (page 298).

Take any set of two numbers from either of the last two columns of the table and apply the rate-of-change formula previously described. The result will be close to the +7.9 percent per year average rate-of-change. (Deviations will be due to rounding.)

The change in unit counts and the change in price level together determine dollar sales. Therefore, it is important to maintain records in which correct prices are coupled with unit counts through the years. If such records are not available, it may be necessary to recreate them from original invoices or make appropriate guesstimates. It is a chore, but it has been done with good results.

Prices for the Chem-Kraker are shown below. The average annual increase for the trend line is +22.9 percent. For actual prices it is +23.5 percent— only a 0.6 percent difference.

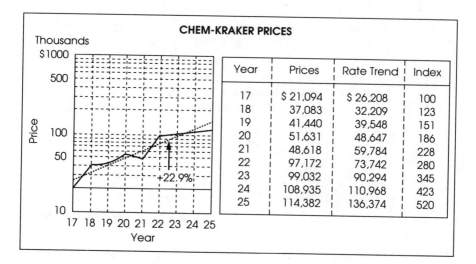

CHEM-KRAKER PRICES

Year	Prices	Rate Trend	Index
17	$ 21,094	$ 26,208	100
18	37,083	32,209	123
19	41,440	39,548	151
20	51,631	48,647	186
21	48,618	59,784	228
22	97,172	73,742	280
23	99,032	90,294	345
24	108,935	110,968	423
25	114,382	136,374	520

In this instance, because prices do not fluctuate as widely as units, the use of raw data endpoints to calculate the annual average growth rate does not distort the growth rate as much as it did for unit counts. Both of the raw data endpoints happen to be about the same relative distance below the trend line, which also helps.

On the other hand, for the Chem-Kraker unit counts, the year 17 raw data endpoint was above the trend line, and the year 25 raw data endpoint was below the trend line. This results in an unrepresentative +4.4 percent growth rate, which is considerably lower than the trend rate of +7.9 percent.

In the next chart, the average rate-of-change in sales shows an average annual increase of +32.8 percent in the trend line and 29.2 percent in the actual accounting sales figures.

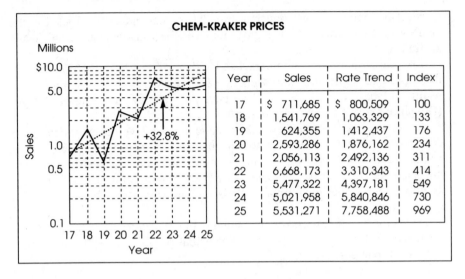

CHEM-KRAKER PRICES

Year	Sales	Rate Trend	Index
17	$ 711,685	$ 800,509	100
18	1,541,769	1,063,329	133
19	624,355	1,412,437	176
20	2,593,286	1,876,162	234
21	2,056,113	2,492,136	311
22	6,668,173	3,310,343	414
23	5,477,322	4,397,181	549
24	5,021,958	5,840,846	730
25	5,531,271	7,758,488	969

Finally, the indexed average rates of change for Chem-Kraker unit counts, prices, and sales are combined on the following comparison fan.

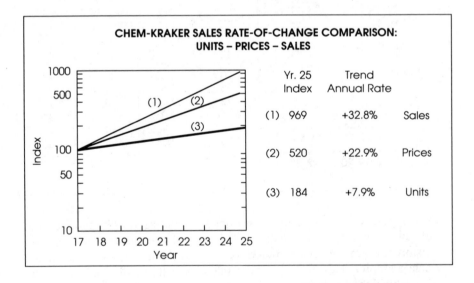

CHEM-KRAKER SALES RATE-OF-CHANGE COMPARISON: UNITS – PRICES – SALES

	Yr. 25 Index	Trend Annual Rate	
(1)	969	+32.8%	Sales
(2)	520	+22.9%	Prices
(3)	184	+7.9%	Units

Why did Chem-Kraker sales grow faster than prices and units? Is this situation likely to continue? To render a judgment on the latter question, you will have to study the three growth charts just prior to this one, in which original unit, price, and sales data for each year are plotted. Before doing that, let's take a look at another product, Chem-Lift. With the exception of Chem-Kraker, all the other Chem-A-Lot products have fan patterns similar to this one, but this is one of the worst.

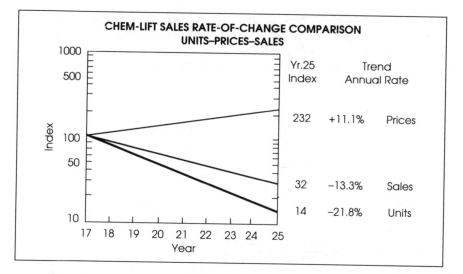

Why did dollar sales and units fall sharply while prices increased? There may be reasons other than just the rapid rise in prices. Documents and observations collected in the situation analysis might provide clues in a similar situation.

At the current rate of decline, how may years will it be before no Chem-Lifts are sold? Extend the trend line and estimate. Was it almost too late to do something for this product? Should it simply be deleted from the line? Maybe. Before reaching that conclusion, market intelligence related to future demand at various price levels and profitability based on costs at those demand levels should be considered. In addition, simple product changes that would increase product acceptance might be discovered.

Now let's go back to the questions: Why did Chem-Kraker sales grow faster than prices and units? Is this situation likely to continue? Management may have established high prices intentionally to increase profit margin percentages while accepting a limited life for the product. Or, they might not have had any rational plan.

During the last three years, Chem-Kraker original sales data showed a decline. Was this symptomatic? Was Chem-Kraker, like all the other Chem-A-Lot products, also reaching a downward turning point even though sales overall fluctuated widely? The fan below, which covers that short period was created to help find out. (This was done even though a five-year period is normally recommended.)

Compare this fan's pattern to the Chem-Lift pattern. What do you think is happening? Of course, a four-year period isn't long enough to form the basis for a definite conclusion, but the negative slopes of both sales dollars and sales units does look ominous for the future of Chem-Kraker. At least the sales trend for Chem-Kraker units for three years is decelerating at a lesser rate then the eight year rate for Chem-Lift (−11.9 percent versus −21.8 percent). Note that for the eight-year period, Chem-Kraker prices increased at double the rate of Chem-Lift prices (+11.1 percent as opposed to +22.9 percent). Obviously, prices on Chem-Kraker were raised in an attempt to improve overall profitability. The increase of only +6.0 percent in Chem-Kraker prices during the last three years of the period may account for the lower rate of decline in sales for those years.

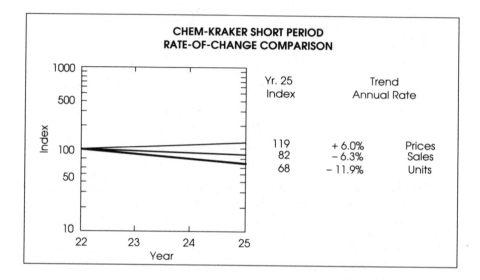

Every Chem-A-Lot product as well as every time period will have different fan patterns for units, prices, and sales growth. The comparison fan is a powerful tool if used judiciously.

After studying this example, take sales data for all the products in a product line and prepare a series of arithmetical, size-oriented charts. Because of the familiarity of size charts, it will be simple to do. These size charts will provide a rough idea of the degree of sales volatility in the product line.

Next, have your computer change these arithmetical charts to semi-log, rate-of-change charts. Also have your computer prepare trends for both types of charts. These two steps take but moments since the computer eliminates the drudge work. Many in business freeze when they have to deal with anything statistically complicated, but it need not be this way. Treat the insides of the computer like the engine of your car. You don't really have to understand what goes on under the hood to drive. As you perform the steps study the changes made in the charts.

Finally, take each rate-of-change trend line and set the first year equal to 100 as an index base to create an indexed growth line. This line can be transferred to a fan as previously illustrated. The slopes of the lines now provide a true comparison of rates of change at a glance.

Caution: Don't make the mistake of calculating rate trend lines and plotting them on a size (arithmetic) chart or vice versa. If you do, it will not be possible to make the rate-of-change comparison.

INDEX CALCULATION

Some chart programs will not permit index calculation. In such cases, indices can be calculated on a computer spreadsheet and transferred to the chart program to be plotted. Here's how the unit count index for Chem-Kraker was prepared:

UNIT COUNT INDEX CALCULATION									
Year	17 Base	18	19	20	21	22	23	24	25
Chem-Kraker units	34	42	15	50	42	69	55	46	48
Rate trend data*	30.7	33.1	35.7	38.6	41.6	44.9	48.5	52.4	56.4
Divide through by base 30.7									
Multiply through by 100									
Unit count index*	100	108	116	126	136	146	158	171	184
*Figures rounded									

The unit count data on the table, when graphed at each step, appears as follows:

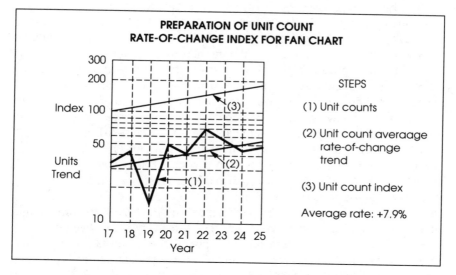

PREPARATION OF UNIT COUNT RATE-OF-CHANGE INDEX FOR FAN CHART

STEPS

(1) Unit counts

(2) Unit count averaage rate-of-change trend

(3) Unit count index

Average rate: +7.9%

Rates of change are equivalent to the slopes of their representative lines. In this instance, the slopes of the lines in steps 2 and 3 are equivalent. Both have an average annual rate of change of +7.9 percent.

Try various combinations of data series of fans, for example, units, sales, prices, wages, costs, profits, and so on. Or try data series of just one type such as product counts. It's possible to review dozens of combinations quickly. Some may prove highly significant, others not. Fans are versatile, cost effective search tools!

Surprises may be found in totally unexpected areas of the company. Chapter 5, "Unit Sales Versus Dollar Sales: A Surprising Analysis," and Chapter 6, "Individual Product Sales Tale: Order In Chaos," describe what was found at Chem-A-Lot.

Findings at Chem-A-Lot happened to point directly to a "quick fix" price decision taken years before by a well-liked CEO, Jim Dandy. His pricing decisions caused a number of interconnected sales and people problems. These problems were further aggravated by Dandy himself as well as by his fast-track successor, Jack Tuffitout, who also suffered from the "I know best" syndrome. Unfortunately, because of the latter's personality, he was unjustly blamed for the entire mess by fellow workers.

So far, the tools have been used to show how to analyze separate products. All the bits of data and pieces of information on the company culture, like the pieces of a jigsaw puzzle, must now be assembled to provide a sound foundation on which to build a successful strategy for the future.

HOW TO PREPARE SUMMARY FAN CHARTS FOR PRODUCTS

Start with the product count data in rate index form. Assemble a comparison fan of all the company's products similar to the chart "Average Annual Growth by Product," page 68. To provide a single growth line representing all company products or all the products in separate product lines requires some number crunching, but this can be done easily, even on a desktop computer.

Sales figures for a product are determined by price and number of units sold. Whether a price is high or low means nothing unless customers find the price acceptable and buy the product. However, unit counts of high-priced products sold do need to be given more weight in a summary growth index.

The three following tables demonstrate how the price weights for the summary fan for all products were calculated for Chem-A-Lot.

The first table which follows, "Calculations for Unit Price Weights," lists the average price for each major type of product. The average price depends upon the size mix as well as price changes. In this instance, the average annual price for Chem-Driers sold in year 18 was $35,550, and the very next year the average jumped to $59,369. What happened? In year 19, the mix of units contained a number of very large and, therefore, very high-priced driers.

For most products, the size mix remains relatively constant from year to year. This first table does take both mix and price change into consideration. For those products that display a definite size mix trend over the years it may be necessary to break unit and price data out at the size level. The procedure for combining the different sizes to create a representative price trend line is identical to that at the product level.

The second table, "Actual Unit Counts to Be Multiplied by Price Weights," lists actual product counts by product type without regard to size.

The third table, "Unit Counts Multiplied by Price Weights to Produce Weighted Unit Index," demonstrates how the data from the two previous tables are combined to provide a weighted unit index.

CALCULATIONS FOR UNIT PRICE WEIGHTS
(Repair parts excluded)

Year	Chem-Alizer	Chem-Blender	Chem-Washer	Chem-Sifter	Chem-Kraker	Chem-Drier	Chem-Flasher	Chem-Cooler	Chem-Mixer	Chem-Veyor	Chem-Pelleter	Chem-Lift
17	6,220		4,698	9,851	21,093	15,436	15,328	14,041	13,223	49,499	24,160	5,902
18	8,809		5,705	10,603	37,083	35,550	17,869	15,161	15,168	56,759	30,748	5,351
19	13,049		6,742	12,944	41,440	59,369	20,494	22,887	18,702	81,149	37,932	7,917
20	9,873	13,800	6,502	21,203	51,631	25,840	20,464	20,238	20,424	78,321	26,032	6,770
21	10,455	11,992	7,328	14,274	48,618	27,532	21,324	24,736	20,286	96,064	32,818	7,312
22	13,266	12,000	6,281	21,079	97,172	26,343	26,596	24,670	24,656	92,858	44,285	12,830
23	13,862	12,493	6,372	16,222	99,032	30,677	36,224	19,779	24,067	95,662	40,102	10,388
24	14,971	13,118	7,009	16,871	108,935	33,438	37,001	20,768	25,271	105,228	42,107	11,427
25	15,720	13,773	7,359	17,715	114,382	120,374	38,851	21,806	26,535	110,489	44,212	11,998
Total of Prices ($)	106,225	77,167	57,996	140,762	619,386	374,559	234,151	184,086	188,332	766,029	322,396	79,895
Divided by Years Manufactured	9	6[1]	9	9	9	9	9	9	9	9	9	9
Average Price/Year ($)	11,803	12,863	6,444	15,640	68,821	41,618	26,017	20,454	20,926	85,114	35,822	8,877
Divided by Total Average Price ($)	354,399[2]	354,399	354,399	354,399	354,399	354,399	354,399	354,399	354,399	354,399	354,399	354,399
Price Wts.	3.3	3.6	1.8	4.4	19.4	11.7	7.3	5.8	5.9	24.0	10.1	2.5

[1] All products have been marketed for nine years with the exception of Chem-Blender. Only when the number of years marketed varies from product to product is it necessary to divide each product by the years marketed to obtain appropriate weights.
[2] Total of the average prices for all the products in the row of figures immediately above.

Next, the unit counts are multiplied by the price weights.

ACTUAL UNIT COUNTS TO BE MULTIPLIED BY THE PRICE WEIGHTS

	Price Weight	Year 17	18	19	20	21	22	23	24	25
Chem-Alizer	3.3	215	151	129	170	148	179	75	57	58
Chem-Blender	3.6				25	38	26	15	12	13
Chem-Washer	1.8	283	157	200	151	116	111	166	135	132
Chem-Sifter	4.4	84	83	67	31	37	116	60	57	55
Chem-Kraker	19.4	34	42	15	50	42	69	55	46	48
Chem-Drier	11.7	42	39	51	19	63	63	30	28	26
Chem-Flasher	7.3	232	208	196	264	349	238	111	89	88
Chem-Cooler	5.8	312	232	165	270	254	153	201	177	147
Chem-Mixer	5.9	291	166	169	163	122	111	101	89	92
Chem-Veyor	24.0	84	88	68	69	42	26	20	18	18
Chem-Pelleter	10.1	135	92	35	75	58	26	70	57	58
Chem-Lift	2.5	194	264	204	232	153	69	45	35	61
	100.0[1]									

[1]Price weights actually add to 99.8 because of computer rounding. If rounded to one more place, weights would have added to 99.99. In its calculations, the computer uses the complete unrounded numbers, making the tables very accurate.

UNIT COUNTS MULTIPLIED BY PRICE WEIGHTS TO PRODUCE WEIGHTED UNIT INDEX

	Year 17	18	19	20	21	22	23	24	25
Chem-Alizer	716	503	430	566	493	596	250	190	193
Chem-Blender	0	0	0	91	138	94	54	44	47
Chem-Washer	515	285	364	275	211	202	302	245	240
Chem-Sifter	371	366	296	137	163	512	265	252	243
Chem-Kraker	660	816	291	971	816	1,340	1,068	893	932
Chem-Drier	493	458	599	223	740	740	352	329	305
Chem-Flasher	1,703	1,527	1,439	1,938	2,562	1,747	814	653	646
Chem-Cooler	1,801	1,339	952	1,558	1,466	883	1,160	1,022	848
Chem-Mixer	1,718	980	998	962	720	655	596	526	543
Chem-Veyor	2,017	2,113	1,633	1,657	1,009	624	480	432	432
Chem-Pelleter	1,365	930	354	758	586	263	708	576	586
Chem-Lift	486	661	511	581	383	172	112	87	152
Price: W. × Units	11,845	9,979	7,866	9,718	9,287	7,829	6,163	5,249	5,169
Division by Base	11,845	11,845	11,845	11,845	11,845	11,845	11,845	11,845	11,845
Weight Unit Index	10	84	66	82	78	66	52	44	44

Finally, the weighted unit index (bottom line of the preceding table) is transferred to a charting program with which the computer calculates and plots the average rate for all products. The average annual rate trend is then base adjusted so a fan can be made. To make this adjustment, divide all the numbers in column (2) by the first number in the column (98). The adjusted rate index for each appears in column (3).

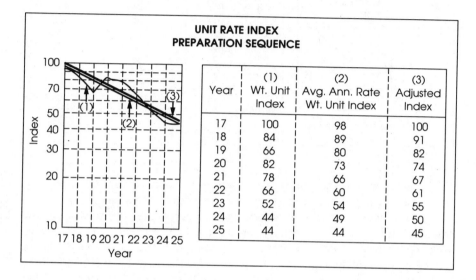

UNIT RATE INDEX
PREPARATION SEQUENCE

Year	(1) Wt. Unit Index	(2) Avg. Ann. Rate Wt. Unit Index	(3) Adjusted Index
17	100	98	100
18	84	89	91
19	66	80	82
20	82	73	74
21	78	66	67
22	66	60	61
23	52	54	55
24	44	49	50
25	44	44	45

To calculate the average rate-of-change, in this instance a decline of 9.5 percent for units, apply the rate formula to the endpoints for the whole period in the last column (100 and 45).

Next, the summary price index is produced in the same manner as the summary unit growth index. The average rate-of-change, an increase in this instance, is 10.5 percent.

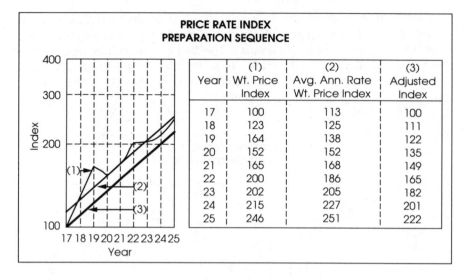

PRICE RATE INDEX
PREPARATION SEQUENCE

Year	(1) Wt. Price Index	(2) Avg. Ann. Rate Wt. Price Index	(3) Adjusted Index
17	100	113	100
18	123	125	111
19	164	138	122
20	152	152	135
21	165	168	149
22	200	186	165
23	202	205	182
24	215	227	201
25	246	251	222

To summarize: The initial weighted unit count index numbers and weighted price index numbers in the preceding tables and charts were given to average out and summarize the effect of the fluctuations in the original unit counts and prices for all products. Then a representative annual rate trend for these initial index numbers was calculated. These numbers, in turn, had to be adjusted to reflect a base of 100 to facilitate easy comparison of slopes when transferred to fans. The slopes of the representative lines being compared are, of course, equivalent to their rates of change.

The calculation of the sales rate-of-change index below, which shows an annual average decrease of .03 percent, is simpler. Each sales figure already represents prices times units, so further weighting is unnecessary. The sales and rate-of-change figures are, therefore, calculated directly from the total sales figures by the computer, which automatically rounds them. Next, the first dollar figures in the column (2), $27.2, is divided into all the dollar figures in column (2) to obtain the rate index in column (3).

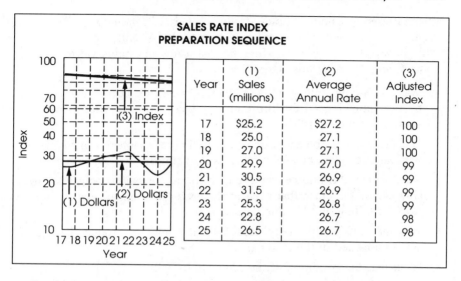

SALES RATE INDEX
PREPARATION SEQUENCE

Year	(1) Sales (millions)	(2) Average Annual Rate	(3) Adjusted Index
17	$25.2	$27.2	100
18	25.0	27.1	100
19	27.0	27.1	100
20	29.9	27.0	99
21	30.5	26.9	99
22	31.5	26.9	99
23	25.3	26.8	99
24	22.8	26.7	98
25	26.5	26.7	98

Graphed together, the three indices revealed the long-term relationship between units, prices, and sales at Chem-A-Lot.[2]

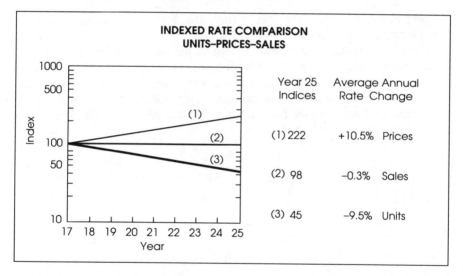

INDEXED RATE COMPARISON
UNITS–PRICES–SALES

	Year 25 Indices	Average Annual Rate Change	
(1)	222	+10.5%	Prices
(2)	98	−0.3%	Sales
(3)	45	−9.5%	Units

This fan, together with the turning point in sales in year 17, seems to indicate that there was one sole reason for the millions of dollars in lost

---

[2]Variations of rate-of-change charts and comparison fans for single and multiple products were developed and tested for practicality over a long period by Karsten Hellebust, first while at the C. A. Norgren Company in Colorado and next at Dorr-Oliver Incorporated in Connecticut. The present form of the rate-of-change fans grew out of a continuing effort to create practical marketing information systems for Norgren in the U.S. and Dorr-Oliver worldwide. Recently, as an economic consultant Hellebust has applied these techniques to marketing research projects for firms in a number of different industries.

sales suffered by Chem-A-Lot: *customers, obviously, thought prices were too high.* Is this the whole answer? Not necessarily. A skilled project manager will go beyond the obvious. Here are just a few questions yet to be raised about Chem-A-Lot at this stage:

- Was the pricing strategy initiated by the first CEO, Dandy, and continued by the following CEO, Tuffitout, the sole cause of all Chem-A-Lot's subsequent problems?

- What role did customer service play? In this case, notes from an interview with an outspoken business owner were helpful.

- Was worker and middle management morale a major contributor to the slow down and crash that occurred? Recall the strained relationships between Tuffitout and his middle managers.

- Was the situation partially caused by a failure in product innovation? What happened in the R&D area?

- What was the condition of the production facilities?

AFTER THE NUMBER CRUNCHING

Project managers were cautioned earlier: Be slow to draw conclusions; let the picture emerge slowly.

Once the hard numerical data is analyzed, the situation depicted may seem clear, but this can be deceptive. It's time to sift through those bits and pieces of information in the project files to see what events shaped the numerical picture. Only after that is done can the correct picture fully emerge. Only then can solid foundations for the future be laid based on sound strategies and correct operating procedures.

PART SIX

THE PLANS THAT TURNED CHEM-A-LOT AROUND

A strategy plan package, a business plan package, and a budget package are presented, complete and ready for submittal to the Chem-A-Lot board of directors. The packages show you how both numerical and descriptive information should be organized for ease of understanding.

CHAPTER 24

PREPARING PLANS FOR PROFITABLE ACTION

Once hidden problems are found, it's time to correct them and assemble any additional information needed to prepare functional plans for the future.

Ultimately, the success of a company depends upon the stakeholders' shared vision of their future and the degree to which each stakeholder participated in its development.

Earlier contacts with people, together with records kept, will help in developing a plan for the future, but they are not enough. The Board, representing shareholders, must be fully supportive. If the problems uncovered are extensive enough and the associated monetary pain severe enough, this should be no problem. The directors will be interested and will support the strategy plans and related tactics adopted by management.

Normally, the role of the CEO now comes to the fore. It is important that both this individual and the Board understand the situation analysis, believe it, and desire action based upon it. This is a critical juncture that will test the mettle of the situation analyst as well as the CEO.

The project manager must provide the professional support required as the CEO seeks to guide the business toward an improved vision of the future. In doing so, the CEO must lead efforts to achieve the following:

- *Develop a prime objective (perhaps by revising an old one) that makes sense to all stakeholders—one that stakeholders can support with enthusiasm.* Full information should be provided to all regardless of how interested they are. Leaving a participant out of the loop before a change is introduced is asking for real trouble.

- *Inspire others by example to cross departmental barriers to work directly with each other on an ad hoc basis to develop and coordinate plans.* Sending instructions down an old-fashioned heirarchy is no longer good enough. Communications technology has moved beyond that.

303

- *Review sources of marketing information.* With the ongoing information revolution, new sources are being developed so fast that it's difficult to keep up. Through computer modems, employees can tap into large public library information networks or the databases of private suppliers. This reality must be considered.

- *Investigate existing as well as other possible channels of distribution, and simultaneously investigate sales performance.* One of the basic underpinnings for this effort is a fair analysis of market penetration by sales territory. You already have the tools necessary for such an analysis at hand—a log-log scatter chart. Like the semi-log chart, it is used far too seldom.

- *Cause stakeholders to never forget that each customer judges the features of a product in relation to competitors' products.* In the long run, no amount of sales promotion will suffice against a competitor who continually introduces product innovations of value to the customer. American executives are currently learning this lesson anew from European and Asian competitors.

SHORT-TERM SALES FORECASTING

To supplement the long-term trends discussed, it now becomes important to review the short-term forecasting methods needed to fine-tune strategies. A variety of such techniques are described in Chapter 8.

Executives are generally familiar with forecasting problems. However, it should be noted that the need for longer-term forecasts can be minimized by just-in-time, or similar, inventory control policies.

If we operate with high inventory relative to our competitors, it means that our production lead time is longer than the valid forecast horizon of the industry. The length of the valid horizon will be dictated by our low-inventory competitors. As a result, the high-inventory company's production plans are based on pure guesses and not on reliable forecasts.[1]

MANUFACTURING PLANS

Strategic plans for marketing pave the way for plans in other parts of the company, such as manufacturing.

Determine how the manufacturing plan will be prepared and what it will cover. Work closely with sales to integrate it with the marketing strategy. One helpful tool is the breakeven chart, which was used at Chem-A-Lot.

Other important considerations are the return on investment and the relationship of people to costs.

---

[1]Eliyahu M. Goldratt and Robert E. Fox, *The Race* (Croton-on-Hudson, NY: North River Press, Inc., 1986). See chapter 30, "Low Inventory—The Key to More Accurate Forecasts."

PEOPLE ARE NOT ROBOTS

In all planning, remember that men and women are not robots to be ordered about or chess pawns to be sacrificed at will.

When the foundations for a cooperative corporate culture begin to get under way, individual talents will be just beginning to be unleashed. It's a time of surprises. Just recall the recent explosion of energy in eastern Europe and the former USSR. Seemingly lethargic people wanted to improve their living conditions. They swept away the hidden messes of Communist leadership that were revealed to them through *glasnost*. Centralized bureaucratic planning failed on a grand scale! People affected by plans need and want to be involved in their own destiny in turn giving rise to suppressed and new problems.

Vast numbers of people in formerly Communist countries were virtually trained to be dependent upon centralized authority over the years. This has also happened in many of our large bureaucratic corporations. With a renewed emphasis on cooperative cultures, it is time for a better understanding of motivation. In a balanced cooperative/competitive environment, people become more optimistic. A catharsis often occurs: Individuals rid themselves of their feelings of helplessness. In doing so, they become more successful.[2]

Freedom of information is a powerful tool for revival. Don't let the awe of status or the tyranny of an ideology erode cooperation in your business. Unleash the talents of people.

Explain the following to everyone:

- *Their participation in the planning cycle is essential to them*. It's a way for them to help improve their own working conditions, to have a stake in the success of the company, and to improve their own and co-workers' careers.

- *Their suggestions for how to improve and implement strategy plans, business plans, and budgets will be considered in the internal market for ideas along with those of other stakeholders.*

PLANNING TOOLS

There are an increased number of user-friendly computer tools available for planning.

- *Project-monitoring programs keep track of the multitide of actions that must be coordinated to complete a plan*. The power of such tools has been illustrated in Chapter 15. Such programs, coupled with word processing and filing programs, really take most of the drudgery out of planning.

- *Computer spreadsheet and charting programs make the processing of accounting data easy*. The various accounting formats and mathematical

---

[2]Martin E. P. Seligman, Ph. D., *Learned Optimism* (New York: Alfred A. Knopf, 1991).

operations used in the Chem-A-Lot planning cycle can be produced quickly with such programs.

SUMMARY

Long-term strategy planning is best founded on a detailed analysis of the current business situation. This analysis should include every significant function and area. The object is to set the course for the future based on a careful evaluation of the internal relationships of stakeholders and the external relationships with customers and suppliers. Long-term success cannot be taken for granted. Good participatory planning is the key.

Finally, it may be wise to consider how the people participating in the preparation of plans are likely to react to the success or failure of those plans. Stakeholders' reactions to success will itself likely become a critical turning point!

CHAPTER 25

CHEM-A-LOT STRATEGY PLAN PACKAGE: YEARS 28–30

SECTION A—EXECUTIVE SUMMARY

Our strategy objective for years 28 through 30 is:

Reestablish Chem-A-Lot as a leading producer of quality conditioner, formulator, and transporter equipment for the process industries in the world.

The Economy for Our Products

1. Inflation for each of the next three years is forecasted to be 6 percent for those experts we interviewed, including our trade association.

   Our annual inflation rates are predicted to be 5 percent for raw material costs and 4 to 6 percent for salaries and wages.

   Foreign-exchange rates should work in our favor. The U.S. dollar should weaken over the next three years by 12 (European currencies) to 15 percent (Japanese yen).

2. Our future selling price assumptions need refinement and will be covered in the business plan in some depth. For now, we assume no price change in year 28 and 3 percent increases in years 29 and 30.

3. Chem-A-Lot sales should increase significantly in years 28 through 30. At present, we see real growth in units of over 10 percent and between 14 and 15 percent annualized growth with inflation in prices.

We checked our sales forecasts with our major customers, our trade association, and U.S. Department of Commerce published statistics.

Market Share

1. Our markets are not mature; real growth will continue. However, we have lost measurable market share in all lines. We will regain our share.

Our market share targets for year 30 are:

	Now	*End Year 30*
Conditioners	30%	34%
Formulators	20	23
Transporters	25	27

2. To attain the increase in market shares, we will invest in our facilities, upgrade quality, open a West Coast sales services center, redesign the Chem-Pelleter, design and sell a new Chem-Mill for the flour industry, and invest in more advertising.

Competition

1. Competitors are accelerating their attack on our markets and customers. We have the same competitors as in the past, plus the threat of competition from several overseas companies that are making footholds in the United States.
2. We tend to be priced higher than our main competitors.
3. Our competitors have not yet become product innovators in our specific market niches, but a few are now capable of doing so.

People

1. We have competent and experienced personnel in all departments, but many of the engineers who developed our original machines have since retired or left. We need to strengthen our capabilities in research and engineering.
2. More team input will be used to boost morale and keep everyone involved with attaining our objective.

Facilities

1. We will invest approximately $3.1 million in our facilities—including equipment, warehouse, and the sales/service center on the West Cost.
2. We intend to be *the* low-cost producer by year 30.
3. Zero-defect and training programs will be instituted for direct and indirect personnel.

Financial

1. The business plan will contain more detailed and refined forecasts of operating results.
2. At this time, the following financial achievements should accompany attaining our objective:

| | (Dollars in Millions) Year | | | |
	28	29	30	Total
Sales	$38.3	$44.0	$49.8	$132.1
Operating Income	4.2	6.2	8.2	18.6
Percentage	11.0%	14.1%	16.5%	14.1%

3. Cash generated will be about $12.8 million. Shareholders' return on their investment, which ranges from $12.6 million in year 28 to $18.9 million in year 30, should average 39 percent at the operating income level.

SECTION B—INTRODUCTION TO YEARS 28–30 STRATEGY PLAN AND LONG-RANGE VISION

Chem-A-Lot will be 30 years young at the end of this strategy plan. Times, markets, and people have changed during those 30 years. Yet, a brief look back will help support our plan for future survival and growth.

This plan has been developed with the active participation of many employees. The Chem-A-Lot management team endorses the plan, and we view this document as an integral part of a business plan and budget that will be developed after all revisions to the company's strategy plan are completed. We do not see the strategy plan, business plan, and budget as separate projects; rather, they will be interwoven and interdependent and will result in an active and continuous operating road map.

The Past

1. Sales in units have been declining for 10 years except for Chem-Kraker, and even that line shows some signs of faltering. This serious situation has arisen for two reasons: First, we were always a price leader, but our erratic pricing policies pushed us beyond reasonable customer limits. Second, we lost our leadership position as a product innovator and *the* service company. Our technology has aged as we have.

2. Competitors, domestic and foreign, sensed our lack of a valid control plan and priced their products accordingly. Fortunately, the competition has not yet focused very much on new products, although we have lost market share. Their quality and service have improved; ours have not. Our dollar sales have been virtually flat on average since year 16, but our trade association and the federal government report on manufacturers' new orders have grown about 11 percent per year in that same period.

3. As we evolved from a young company with under $10 million in sales in year 5 and $18 million in year 10 to our current size, the need for soundly based planning and execution became more necessary. More team effort was and still is also required. One person can only do so many things well. Our customers want improved products and prices commensurate with service and quality. We have not performed well or consistently in these categories. Our products have aged as we have. Both need revitalizing with renewed effort and real commitment to the principles of operations that once distinguished us from the pack.

Our Vision

1. The industry in general and our products in particular should grow at least 10 percent annually in real terms (constant dollars or units) for the next three years. This growth rate is supported by U.S. Department of Commerce and our own trade association statistics. We do not expect each year to equal the three-year average, but the three-year annual average should come close. Our business is cyclical and not predictable to the month, quarter, or year. Shifts in customer purchasing plans impact us tremendously.

2. The expected growth rates for our products will continue to attract competition from producers here and abroad.

   In addition, a number of mergers and acquisitions have occurred within our industry, and one or two more might take place in the next three years. We believe the purchase of some of our smaller competitors by two large conglomerates poses a threat, but certainly not a deathblow, to Chem-A-Lot. On the one hand, the extra and substantial "firepower" now available to these formerly undercapitalized firms could allow them more flexibility in pricing and product development. On the other hand, the track record of several of the conglomerates shows them to be already fully leveraged (high debt compared to shareholders' equity) and lacking in real knowledge about our industry. We are prepared to meet our competition squarely, and by adhering to our strategy plans, we will recover lost market share.

Some competitors will try to be full-line producers to attract customers. We continue to believe specialization in a narrow line of products is better. We aim to be number one in our main product niches.

3. Our optimism for growth within our industry and for our own product lines is based in part on available projections or orders obtained from the U.S. Department of Commerce and supported by our trade industry reports and projections received from a number of our customers. We no longer intend for our sales to grow at the 1% rate shown on the following chart.

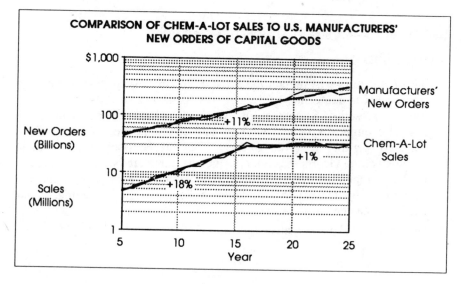

COMPARISON OF CHEM-A-LOT SALES TO U.S. MANUFACTURERS' NEW ORDERS OF CAPITAL GOODS

4. Our customers will demand more energy-efficient and productive equipment. Also, because downtime will be critical, service capabilities will be an important issue.

5. Inflation in the United States as measured by the gross national product deflator is predicted to be 6 percent in years 28, 29, and 30. Nonetheless, we project manufacturing labor rate increases of 4 to 6 percent and similar salary increases in the selling and general and administrative expense categories. Raw material and supply costs are assumed to rise 5 percent per year.

6. According to the experts, U.S. currency-exchange rates will decline over the next three years by 12 percent in terms of the European Economic Community and by 15 percent compared to the Japanese yen. These changes should make our products more competitive overseas.

Our Role

1. Chem-A-Lot will have total sales in the range of $132 million for the next three-year period.

2. Operating income will be between 11 and 16 percent of sales ($18.6 million total for the three-year plan period).

3. Cash generated will be $12.8 million, of which about $3.1 million will be reinvested in facilities and equipment. The remainder will be available for future periods and dividends.

4. One major product modification will be completed and marketed.

5. One new product for the flour process market will be introduced.

6. A major market (West Coast) will be penetrated, and lost market share will be recaptured.

SECTION C—COMPETITIVE ENVIRONMENT

Market Share

1. Our competitors will remain the same as before, except that one or two more overseas companies will enter—as Sanalai, Ltd. did—via acquisition of a present U.S. competitor. Also, one or two domestic companies may be acquired by larger, publicly held conglomerates. We have three major competitors in North America. They are Harrison, Inc., Johnson Machinery, and George Equipment, Inc. All three are based in this country. The competitors moving in from other countries are not an immediate threat, but will present a formidable challenge to the marketing of our machines outside North America.

2. An overview of market share follows:

TOTAL MARKET—YEAR 27

	Units	Market Share
Conditioners		
Chem-A-Lot	730	30%
Harrison, Inc.	610	25
Johnson Machinery	490	20
George Equipment, Inc.	370	15
Sanalai, Ltd.	125	5
Other	125	5
Total	2,450	100%
Formulators		
Chem-A-Lot	540	20%
Harrison, Inc.	540	20
Johnson Machinery	490	18
Formalonics, Inc.	400	15
Furi, Ltd.	350	13
Other	380	14
Total	2,700	100%
Transporters		
Johnson Machinery	112	35%
Chem-A-Lot	80	25
Convex Co., Ltd.	48	15
Transload, Inc.	32	10
Other	48	15
Total	320	100%

COMPETITIVE PROFILE OF GEORGE EQUIPMENT, INC.

Background: An independent company that was founded 1965 in Los Angeles, California. None of the founders currently works for the company. Professional managers were first employed in 1979. Sales efforts have been concentrated on the West Coast of the United States and in Mexico. In recent years, the company has moved into markets east of the Rocky Mountains. It appears to have competent as well as innovative engineering and management staffs. Growth appears to have been steady. According to Dun & Bradstreet and 10K reports, it has no financial problems at this time. Employs 25 people.

Competitive Products	Sales (MM$)	Market Share	Manufacturing Facilities	Distribution Strengths	Perceived Strategy
Pelleter	$3.3	45%	Newly expanded plant Los Angeles, Cal. 30,000 sq. ft.	Warehouses in Mexico and Denver. Uses only sales agents, no direct sales force.	High quality, excellent engineering, and good services. Prices are competitive. Now appears to be acquiring complimentary products and courting our major customers with a broad line.
Sifter	0.9	35%			
Washer	0.8	—			
Cooler	0.4	—			
Other	0.1	—			
Total	$5.5				

Note: All sales figures are based on the estimates of sales engineers by region. We do not yet have worldwide estimates. Confidence level for accuracy of data above is high.

COMPETITIVE PROFILE OF HARRISON, INC.

Background: Family-owned since founded in 1947 in Milwaukee, Wisconsin. Managed by sons of founders except for president, who assumed CEO responsibilities five years ago. Have broadest line of competitive products, covering conditioners and formulators. Growth seems higher than ours in both product lines. No reliable financial data are available. Employs 100 people.

Competitive Products	Sales (MM$)	Market Share	Manufacturing Facilities	Distribution Strengths	Perceived Strategy
Conditioners	$14.0	25%	40,000 sq. ft. in Milwaukee, Wis. and 35,000 sq. ft. in Philadelphia, Pa.	Excellent direct sales force in U.S.	Average quality, emphasis on sales by lower prices (5%) and 74-day payment terms.
Formulators	8.5	20%			
Transporters	—	—			
Noncompetitive Products	2.5	—			
Total	$25.0				

COMPETITIVE PROFILE OF JOHNSON MACHINERY

Background: Founded in 1952 by two entrepreneurs who sold business last year to Amidic Co., Inc., a publicly held conglomerate with consolidated sales of $250 million, net income of $14 million, borrowings of $40 million, and shareholders' equity of $44 million. Employs about 85 people in Johnson business.

Competitive Products	Sales (MM$)	Market Share	Manufacturing Facilities	Distribution Strengths	Perceived Strategy
Conditioners	$11.0	20%	80,000 sq. ft. in Atlanta, Ga., including head-quarters of 15,000 sq. ft.	Direct sales force in major markets and sales agents elsewhere.	Excellent transporter and conditioner designs, high quality, and 5–10% under our prices. Service good for conditioners and acceptable for other lines. Lacked working capital in past; may now be in position to expand if new parent finances them.
Formulators	7.7	18%			
Transporters	3.5	35%			
Noncompetitive Products	4.0	—			
Total	$26.2				

Note: Each significant competitor should be included. Only three were used herein as examples.

SECTION D—OUR POSITION: STRENGTHS AND WEAKNESSES

The attainment of our long-term strategy plan objective will be affected by our ability to maintain our strengths in the marketplace and eliminate, or at least reduce, the potential impact of our weaknesses as perceived by our customers. We see our present position as follows:

Strong Areas

1. Experienced managers with broad-based industry knowledge equal to or better than competitors.
2. Experienced and technically sound employees in plant and offices.
3. Recognition and acceptance as leader in our niches.
4. Detailed knowledge of customers' application needs and their recognition of our capabilities.
5. Freedom from dependence on small number of customers.
6. Established customers and adequate inside sales force and strong representatives and distributors in most markets.
7. Fairly extensive product lines in special niches.
8. Personnel and facility capacity to easily produce and sell 60 percent more unit volume than year 27.

Weak Areas

1. Lost momentum in marketplace because of too-frequently changed directions in pricing, delivery, and service (customers question the sincerity and consistency of our approach to serving their needs).
2. Mature products in most lines.
3. Long delays in product redesigns and development that allow competitors to take some market share.
4. Aging production equipment and inefficient warehouse facilities.
5. Products in a number of product lines that are overpriced.
6. Poor coverage of sales and service in West Coast region.
7. Lack of needed or appropriate systems in manufacturing, accounting, and reporting areas such as material requirements planning and production control.

SECTION E—ALTERNATIVE STRATEGIES

Alternative strategies, ranging from diversifying the business to selling it, were seriously studied before the recommended plan was selected.

Diversify

1. Many companies in business cover more than one industry. Some firms may desire to have complementary operations from a marketing or production standpoint. Others seek countercyclical operations to balance cash flow generation, usage, working capital demands, and so on. Still others find no main focus of attention. Some are successful; others are not.

2. We want to be a significant factor in each of our individual product niches. We seek a large market share in small markets.

   As a result, we reject further diversification because it will dilute our managerial attention and probably be less profitable from a return-on-investment viewpoint.

Sell

1. Chem-A-Lot was sold eight years ago. At that time, we had $30 million in sales and a $1.7 million operating income, and we were floundering. We expect $33 million in sales and $2.1 million at the operating income level for year 27. That is not much of an improvement; it is negative growth when adjusted for inflation.

   If our horizon looked as bleak today as then, we would sell the business.

2. Our outlook is different today. Industry experts are optimistic, and we are now poised to grow faster than industry projections by regaining some lost market share and investing more heavily in our facilities and product development.

3. Although eventual sale of the company should always be considered a viable alternative, the coming three-year period is not the proper time. We will increase the inherent fair market value of our business materially in the immediate years to come.

Harvest

1. Harvesting, or turning the company into a "cash cow," is a strategy that calls for minimizing reinvestment in the company facilities, people, and products. Selling prices would remain at high levels. We would live off our reputation for quality products and service while "milking," or stripping, every dollar from the operation.

2. In the short term (one to two years), considerable cash could be generated by continuing our previous policies of cutting back on all but truly mandatory spending. We could again stop orders for new equipment in the plant, defer maintenance, stop advertising, and even raise product sale prices. This strategy might work for two more years but would again result in loss of market share and an eventual steep decline in the value of the business.

3. We do not recommend harvesting the business during the three-year strategy period. Some products within our three lines may qualify for a harvesting strategy. We will study those; but in the main, harvesting is not the answer.

Grow

1. Growth is not our objective. Our prime objective is to reestablish Chem-A-Lot as a leading producer of quality conditioner, formulator, and transporter equipment for the process industries in the world. Attaining that objective will result in maximizing the long-term returns on our shareholders' investment. Our forecast for the next three years shows a healthy environment for our products and fairly high customer demand each year. Profitable growth will be one result of achieving our objective.

2. Our objective is subdivided into first- and second-priority types of goals:

Priority 1: Turning the base business around through a combination of moves such as improved pricing practices, needed but overdue product modifications, and development of new markets for old machines.

Since these goals have required a minimum of funding, they are already well under way.

Priority 2: Developing entirely new products to sell to existing and new markets.

This strategy is recommended and is reviewed in detail in the next section.

SECTION F—STRATEGY PLAN

Our three-year strategy includes growth: first, because the demand for our products should increase, and second, because we fully plan to stop the erosion in our market share. In fact, we will regain share. Shareholders will see above-average returns on their investment each year.

Strategy Objective

Reestablish Chem-A-Lot as a leading producer of quality conditioner, formulator, and transporter equipment for the process industries in the world.

The foregoing prime objective can be achieved within the next three years by implementing the series of coordinated tactics outlined here. Each tactic is individually important and all should be treated as building blocks which, when placed one on top of the other, will reach the objective. However, to be really effective, the tactics must be related to and reflect the basic culture or character of the company.

Chem-A-Lot's Character/Culture

1. Customer driven (market orientation), but supported by quality engineered products and serviced by technically superior individuals.
2. Team oriented—all employees.
3. Company name and reputation precede any individual.
4. Long-term view.
5. Introspective, but not numbers driven.
6. Seeks high market share niche products.
7. Price leader, not follower.
8. Minimum gross profit hurdle target rate of 35 percent of sales.
9. Avoids commodity products and seeks those with high value added.

Marketing/Sales

Our serviced markets are not yet mature and will not become so during this three-year period. Our old customers and potential new customers do not appear to face unusual or insurmountable competition for their products. Substantial optimism abounds in their circles.

Our lost market share in North America in virtually every product line must be regained, and we must reestablish ourselves as the leader in our market niches. We fully intend to stay and compete successfully and profitably in the conditioner, formulator, and transporter product lines.

1. We have developed a plan for the next three years, primarily for the United States, to concentrate on three strategies on the way toward our prime objective. These strategies are to:

   - Modify the Chem-Pelleter in order to increase our market share from 20 to 25 percent in the plastics industries.
   - Develop a new mill for the flour industry in order to recapture at least half of the 40 percent market share lost to competitors.
   - Establish a new service center on the West Coast in order to increase market share in that region by around 20 percentage points to match our other regions.

   We believe there will be a spillover effect from this effort into the international markets. Sales generated by these investments will be timed approximately as follows:

STRATEGY PLAN
IMPACT OF TACTICS ON BASE PRODUCTS AND SERVICES SALES
(Dollars in Thousands)

			Year		
		27	28	29	30
Products and Services	*Expected Results*	*(Current)*	*(Budget)*	*(Estimate)*	*(Goal)*
Base Products and Services					
Sales		$33,000	$38,300	$40,600	$46,000
Chem-Pelleter Modification Sales	Increase share of U.S. plastics industry from 20% to 25%	—	—	500	600[1]
New Chem-Mill Sales	Regain 20% of flour industry market	—	—	900	1,000[2]
West Coast Service Center Sales	Increase West Coast market share from 5% to 25%	—	—	2,000	2,200[3]
Total Sales		$33,000	$38,300	$44,000	$49,800

[1]The total Pelleter market was estimated at $12.0 million in year 27; Chem-A-Lot's share to go from $2.4 million in year 27 to $3.0 million by year 30.

[2]The total flour industry market was estimated at $10.0 million in year 27.

[3]The West Coast market was estimated at $10.8 million in year 27.

With these additions, we can again become a growth company reaching approximately a 15 percent annual average growth rate.

2. Pricing recommendations by product line will be contained in the business plan and annual budget. Some unit prices might conceivably be reduced. All will be based on rational competitive pricing. For the purposes of this strategy plan, we held prices in year 28 and raised them 3 percent in the following two years.

3. More time will be spent becoming better acquainted with our competitors. We believe we know their strategies, but will second guess them again and again and analyze their competitive strengths and weaknesses. We will use lost orders, customer surveys, and other data to educate ourselves about every market niche.

4. Our new sales targets are based on market intelligence rather than last year's sales. We want and will obtain our share of each region's available sales.

5. Each of our three product lines will be supervised by a product manager— a champion who has an engineering degree and no less than seven years' experience with those products.

6. Our upcoming business plan will contain an action program to pursue parts and repairs revenues. We want to maintain good communications with all of our customers so we are called first when parts and repairs are needed.

Manufacturing

Although we may not be today, Chem-A-Lot will be the low-cost producer by year 30. We will upgrade quality in production and in repairs and service. An injection of capital will be needed to accomplish this. Our business plan will contain more specific tactics, but a general program follows:

1. A zero-defect manufacturing system will be instituted.

2. Personnel, in both direct and overhead positions, will be trained on and off the job in areas such as manufacturing efficiency, purchasing, and inventory control programs.

3. Production equipment replacement will be accelerated. We had virtually ceased investing in new production equipment in recent years. Our current needs are for replacement items. We do not need to increase capacity. On the other hand, some renovations and expansion will be needed in our warehouse and storeroom.

4. All major vendors will be asked for price concessions.

Design and Development

In the last 10 years, we have not innovated in our markets. All our current sales are from products introduced over 10 years ago. Yes, we have redesigned and improved some; however, not one product was totally reengineered, and none was a brand new item. We must change some of our products as well as our image.

With comparatively small expenditures during the next three years, we can redesign Chem-Pelleter to make it produce high-quality products much more efficiently, and we can also complete development of a new flour mill. Our business plan, which will be prepared later this year, will include more specific tactics, costs, and anticipated rewards.

The Chem-Pelleter has been in need of a major modification for some time to make it more competitive because of process changes in the plastic industries.

A summary of this project follows: The Chem-Pelleter modification proposal includes an impact statement covering the Chem-Pelleter sales expected, the department responsible for the project, task descriptions, estimated costs, and a rough schedule for completion by quarter.

Chem-Pelleter Modification
Impact Statement

Goal: To increase market share by five percentage points by year 30 (from 20 to 25 percent of the plastics industry) by modifying and repricing Chem-Pelleter. A secondary goal is to reduce high unit costs of production.

Prime Responsibility: Marketing.

Estimated Cost: $55,000.

Expected Results: Sales of $3.0 million by year 30, up from an estimated $2.4 million in year 27. Revenues are expected at the earliest by the third quarter of the second year. Profitability is expected to be above average for Chem-A-Lot machines.

Time: Three years.

Several major processing companies in the flour industry have switched to a competitor's equipment. Based on a prototype now being developed in our laboratory, we believe we can produce a mill with the latest technology that is capable of producing flour of designated qualities in large quantities at 25 percent less cost per ton than any competitor's equipment.

Since many of the talented engineers who developed our original machines are no longer here, we must recreate this capability—no mean task. In addition, we can only work on a few new prototype machines at a time.

Administration

1. We are adequately staffed to handle all anticipated workloads for this three-year planning period.

2. A material requirements planning and production control system will be completely installed in year 28.

3. Certain previously deferred office repairs need to be accomplished soon.

SECTION G—FINANCIAL HIGHLIGHTS

1. Because of the price level change, our forecast is primarily based on the sales for each machine since the first of the year, plus customer plans reported by our sales engineers in the field.

We believe the rapid recovery rate experienced during the first three months of the year will slow down next year. For the balance of this year, we believe sales will continue to grow, but at a reduced rate. This information has resulted in a sales forecast that has been used to prepare a rough forecast of profit levels for years 28 through 30, using the fixed and variable cost data now becoming available. We needed to make these preliminary cost and profit forecasts in order to evaluate how rapidly we could push our second-priority goals of developing new products for existing and new markets.

In the next few months, as work proceeds on the business plan, and later on the budget, we believe these forecasts will need revision. For now they are conservative; hopefully, they will have to be revised upward.

2. Forecasts of our base business sales, costs and operating income, and the additional revenues and profits resulting from proposed strategy initiatives follow:

STRATEGY PLAN
SALES, COSTS, AND PROFITS BASE BUSINESS FORECAST
FOR PLAN YEARS 28 THROUGH 30
(Dollars in Thousands)

Year	Sales	Fixed Costs	Variable Costs	Operating Income
27	$33,000	$ 9,800	$21,100	$2,100
28	38,300	10,000	23,800	4,500
29	40,600	10,700	24,800	5,100
30	46,000	11,400	27,600	7,000

To this base forecast we anticipate additional sales, costs, and profits from our planned strategy initiatives as follows:

BASE BUSINESS FORECAST PLUS STRATEGY INITIATIVES FOR PLAN YEARS 28 THROUGH 30

(Dollars in Thousands)

Year	Sales	Fixed Costs	Variable Costs	Operating Income Amount	Operating Income % of Sales
27	$33,000	$ 9,800	$21,100	$2,100	6%
28	38,300	10,100	24,000	4,200	11
29	44,000	10,900	26,900	6,200	14
30	49,800	11,700	29,900	8,200	16

3. Returns on shareholders' investments (ROI) will be detailed in the business plan and budget. At this time, given the assumptions included in this strategy plan, the ROI ballpark ranges, and cashflow after taxes, working capital and plant and equipment needs in thousands of dollars will approximate those in the following table:

(Dollars in Thousands)

Year	Shareholder's Investment	Operating Income	Pre-Tax ROI
27	$10,862	$2,100	19.3%
28	12,607	4,200	33.3
29	14,865	6,200	41.7
30	18,900	8,200	43.4

4. Cash generated during the planning period of three years will approximate $12.8 million. We expect to invest about $3.1 million in capital expenditures.

5. Balance sheet and income statement highlights for the planning period are shown in flow-chart format on the schedule on pages 326 and 327.

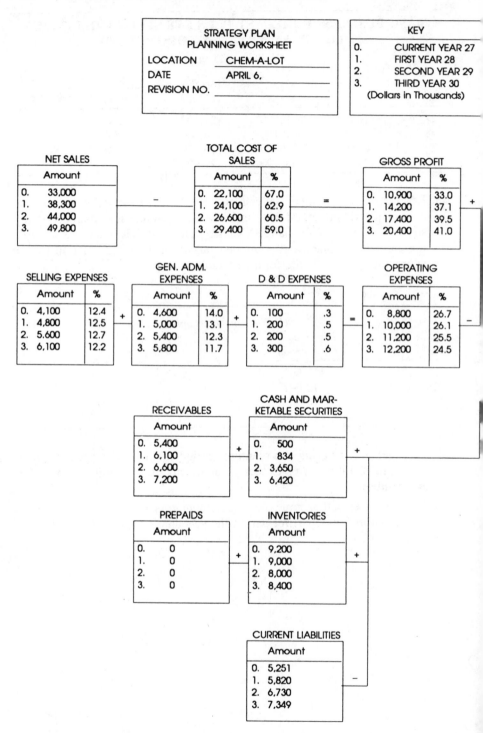

STRATEGY PLAN
PLANNING WORKSHEET

LOCATION   CHEM-A-LOT
DATE   APRIL 6,
REVISION NO.

KEY	
0.	CURRENT YEAR 27
1.	FIRST YEAR 28
2.	SECOND YEAR 29
3.	THIRD YEAR 30
(Dollars in Thousands)	

NET SALES

	Amount
0.	33,000
1.	38,300
2.	44,000
3.	49,800

−

TOTAL COST OF SALES

	Amount	%
0.	22,100	67.0
1.	24,100	62.9
2.	26,600	60.5
3.	29,400	59.0

=

GROSS PROFIT

	Amount	%
0.	10,900	33.0
1.	14,200	37.1
2.	17,400	39.5
3.	20,400	41.0

+

SELLING EXPENSES

	Amount	%
0.	4,100	12.4
1.	4,800	12.5
2.	5,600	12.7
3.	6,100	12.2

+

GEN. ADM. EXPENSES

	Amount	%
0.	4,600	14.0
1.	5,000	13.1
2.	5,400	12.3
3.	5,800	11.7

+

D & D EXPENSES

	Amount	%
0.	100	.3
1.	200	.5
2.	200	.5
3.	300	.6

=

OPERATING EXPENSES

	Amount	%
0.	8,800	26.7
1.	10,000	26.1
2.	11,200	25.5
3.	12,200	24.5

−

RECEIVABLES

	Amount
0.	5,400
1.	6,100
2.	6,600
3.	7,200

+

CASH AND MAR-KETABLE SECURITIES

	Amount
0.	500
1.	834
2.	3,650
3.	6,420

+

PREPAIDS

	Amount
0.	0
1.	0
2.	0
3.	0

+

INVENTORIES

	Amount
0.	9,200
1.	9,000
2.	8,000
3.	8,400

+

CURRENT LIABILITIES

	Amount
0.	5,251
1.	5,820
2.	6,730
3.	7,349

−

SUBMIITTED BY

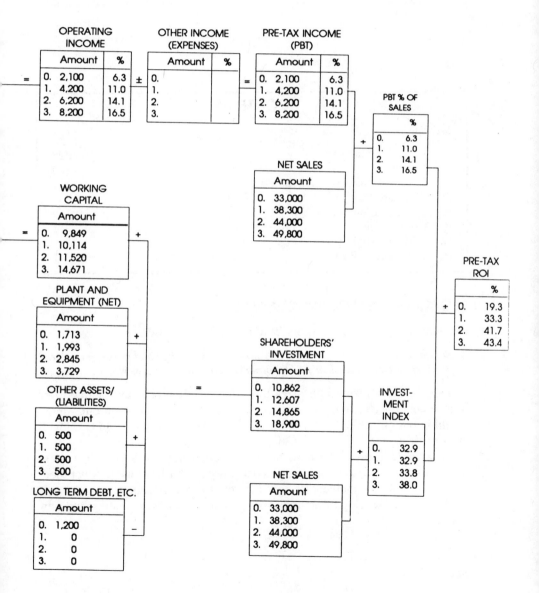

CHAPTER 26

CHEM-A-LOT BUSINESS PLAN PACKAGE: YEARS 28–29

<table>
<tr><td colspan="2" align="center">**CONTENTS**</td></tr>
<tr><td>*Section*</td><td>*Page*</td></tr>
<tr><td>A.   Executive Summary</td><td>328</td></tr>
<tr><td>B.   Objective</td><td>330</td></tr>
<tr><td>C.   Expected Business Environment</td><td>331</td></tr>
<tr><td>D.   Strategies</td><td>333</td></tr>
<tr><td>E.   Human Resources</td><td>339</td></tr>
<tr><td>F.   Critical Issues</td><td>341</td></tr>
<tr><td>G.   Financial Highlights</td><td>342</td></tr>
<tr><td>H.   Contingency Plan</td><td>347</td></tr>
</table>

SECTION A—EXECUTIVE SUMMARY

Our strategy objective for years 28 through 30 is as follows:

Reestablish Chem-A-Lot as a leading producer of quality conditioner, formulator, and transporter equipment for the process industries in the world.

This business plan emphasizes the principal strategies and tactics to be implemented—mainly in the next two years—to put us well on our way to attaining our objective by the end of year 30. We have established two levels of priorities:

Priority 1: Turning the base business around through a combination of moves such as improved pricing practices, needed but overdue product modifications, and development of new markets for old machines.

Priority 2: Developing entirely new products to sell to existing and new markets.

Business Environment

Growth prospects for our products are good. Real growth measured in units should approximate 10 percent per year. A slight slowdown is now predicted in year 29, compared to the growth projected in the strategy plan. Year 30 should be excellent. Normally, inflation estimated at 6 percent per year would allow product price increases. However, we intend to hold the line on prices in year 28 (we reduced them this year) and increase prices 3 percent in year 29.

Strategies

We will stop the market share erosion and regain our position by:

1. Modifying the Chem-Pelleter.
2. Developing and selling a new mill for the flour industry (Chem-Mill).
3. Establishing a new sales service center on the West Coast.

Our sales distribution system will remain in place, and commission rates will be the same. Salaries, wages, and related fringe benefits will increase 4 to 6 percent each year. Raw materials and other outside purchases are projected to increase 5 percent per year.

Impact of Strategies

Pursuit of the strategies will not increase sales in year 28 but will add noticeably to revenues in succeeding years. Briefly, we expect these benefits:

(Dollars in Thousands)

	Year		
	28	29	30
Base Sales	$39,500	$35,700	$42,000
Chem-Pelleter Modification (increase market share to 32%)	—	400	1,410
New Chem-Mill	—	700	2,050
West Coast Office	—	1,400	2,600
Total Sales	$39,500	$38,200	$48,060

We lost our position as the low-cost and best-quality producer but will regain it by year 30. This will be accomplished by:

1. Investing $1.8 million in new production equipment and facilities.
2. Keeping wage and salary increases to 5 percent per year at maximum.
3. Containing vendor material and supply prices at present levels in year 28 and at a 5 percent increase in year 29.
4. Completing the material requirements planning and scheduling system and improving inventory turns.

5. Other program tactics to train our people and make everyone cost conscious, more efficient, and more responsive to customer demands and needs.

Resources Required

Other than the capital needed for manufacturing and warehousing ($1.8 million), we will add a total of 15 to 21 people during the next two years. Their functions will be:

Manufacturing — Indirect	2
— Direct	9 to 15
Marketing/Sales	4
General and Administration	0
Total New Employees	15 to 21

Financial Highlights

	(Dollars in Thousands) Years			
	28		29	
	Income	*%*	*Income*	*%*
Sales	$39,500	100.0%	$38,200	100.0%
Gross Profit	14,970	37.9	14,107	36.9
Operating Income	4,670	11.8	4,107	10.8
Net Income	2,926	7.4	2,575	6.7

No additional debt will be required to fund this business plan.

Contingency Plan

Our operating break-even point will be about $27 million in sales. If sales drop 15 percent below those shown in this business plan, we will reduce costs, cut wage and salary levels, terminate some employees, and defer some capital expenditures.

We will not stop the design and development program. We can defer some expenditures, but our future growth depends on investing now.

SECTION B—OBJECTIVE

Our industry and our company are in a profound period of change. Business cycles are accelerating and also becoming much less predictable. Competition continues to be strong from our traditional U.S. competitors, and overseas competitors are increasing their share here as well.

We must become more responsive to customer needs through better service and better products (innovations). Our customers need more efficient, top-quality equipment to equal or exceed products sold by their competitors.

Our recommended basic approach to our markets continues to follow the strategy plan objective:

Reestablish Chem-A-Lot as a leading producer of quality conditioner, formulator, and transporter equipment for the process industries in the world.

Our objective is subdivided into first- and second-priority types of goals:

Priority 1: Turning the base business around through a combination of moves such as improved pricing practices, needed but overdue product modifications, and development of new markets for old machines.

Priority 2: Developing entirely new products to sell to existing and new markets.

SECTION C—EXPECTED BUSINESS ENVIRONMENT

Our strategy plan included sales forecasts that now differ from our best current projections of sales. Our customers and a leading indicator point to a real slowdown in year 29. Although a major recovery is anticipated in year 30, we will not reach the heights we previously predicted ($48.1 million compared to $49.8 million in our strategy plan).

	(Dollars in Thousands)	
Year	*Strategy Plan*	*Business Plan*
27	$33,000	$33,900
28	38,300	39,500
29	44,000	38,200
30	49,800	48,060

Business Environment—External

1. We are optimistic about the growth prospects within our industry. The market for our products will grow about 10 percent annually in real terms during this planning period.

2. U.S. inflation, although a factor, is expected to be in the neighborhood of 6 percent per year. International exchange rates are expected to favor our exports in the next two years. In fact, the U.S. dollar may weaken by 3 percent per year against major European currencies and as much as 5 percent per year versus the Japanese yen.

3. Our customers are under pressure to increase the efficiency of their operations. Our equipment and service must meet their needs.

4. Our major competitors remain substantially the same as last year. Some were or are being acquired by larger, publicly held corporations, and

several overseas based firms are increasing their efforts to gain a foothold in the U.S. market. We continue to remain at the high end when our sales prices are compared to those of our competitors. Our principal competitors and estimated market shares by product line are:

TOTAL MARKET—YEAR 27

	Units	Market Share
Conditioners		
Chem-A-Lot	730	30%
Harrison, Inc.	610	25
Johnson Machinery	490	20
George Equipment, Inc.	370	15
Sanalai, Ltd.	125	5
Other	125	5
Total	2,450	100%
Formulators		
Chem-A-Lot	540	20%
Harrison, Inc.	540	20
Johnson Machinery	490	18
Formalonics, Inc.	400	15
Furi, Ltd.	350	13
Other	380	14
Total	2,700	100%
Transporters		
Johnson Machinery	112	35%
Chem-A-Lot	80	25
Convex Co., Ltd.	48	15
Transload, Inc.	32	10
Other	48	15
Total	320	100%

More specific profiles of each of our major competitors are contained in the strategy plan issued earlier this year.

Business Environment—Internal

The following are the more substantive assumptions in our business plan:

1. No change will be made in our selling prices in year 28 and a 3 percent increase will be implemented in year 29. We have reduced unit prices in this current year 27 to halt market share erosion.

2. Chem-A-Lot's commission structure will remain as is.

3. No changes will be made in our sales distribution system: in-house sales force in the United States and sales representatives overseas.

4. Salaries, wages, and benefits, in aggregate, will increase 4 to 6 percent in year 28 and at the same rate thereafter.

5. Raw material, supply, and purchased services will increase 5 percent per year.

Our employees are generally well motived and capable. A healthy attitude exists at all levels concerning each individual's role in contributing to this formal planning process.

Our strengths and weaknesses are set forth in the strategy plan that was prepared and issued earlier this year. No real changes in our posture have occurred since that time.

SECTION D—STRATEGIES

The three strategy plan goals we originally selected are still valid despite the anticipated decline in sales for year 29. We now believe economic conditions will simply postpone some forecasted sales from year 29 to year 30. Furthermore, we believe the slowdown in year 29 will permit us to concentrate our efforts in the new product and design areas, thus actually enhancing the results of year 30. Our three original strategies in the strategy plan, modified in this business plan for current market conditions, are as follows:

1. Modify the Chem-Pelleter in order to increase our market share from 20 to 25 percent (now revised to 32 percent) in the plastics industries.

2. Develop and sell a new mill for the flour industry in order to recapture at least half (now over half) of the 40 percent market share lost to competitors.

3. Establish a new sales/service center on the West Coast in order to increase market share from 5 to 25 percent (now revised to 29 percent) in that region to match other regions.

We continue to feel that there will be a spillover effect from this effort into the developing international market.

More specific plans for each of our functional areas follow.

Marketing/Sales

Our objective is to regain market share by pursuing the three strategies listed at the beginning of this section. Sales will reap benefits from the investment of time and money fairly rapidly, and this will result in a fast payback. The forecasted sales listed here are less than those estimated in the strategy plan for years 28 through 30 by about $6.3 million because of a perceived softness in demand in years 29 and 30.

BUSINESS PLAN IMPACT OF TACTICS ON BASE PRODUCTS AND SERVICES SALES
(Dollars in Thousands)

Products and Services	Expected Results	Year 27 (Current)	28 (Budget)	29 (Estimate)	30 (Goal)
Base Products and Service Sale		$33,900	$39,500	$35,700	$42,000
Chem-Pelleter Modification Sales	Increase U.S. plastics industry share from 20% to 32%	—	—	400	1,410[1]
New Chem-Mill Sales	Regain 20% of flour industry market	—	—	700	2,050[2]
West Coast Service Center Sales	Increase West Coast market share from 5% to 29%	—	—	1,400	2,600[3]
Total Sales		$33,900	$39,500	$38,200	$48,060

[1] The total market was estimated at $12.0 million in year 27; Chem-A-Lot's share is to go from $2.4 million in year 27 to $3.8 million by year 30. Business plan increases share 7 percentage points more than strategy plan.
[2] The total flour industry market was estimated at $10.0 million in year 27.
[3] The West Coast market was estimated at $10.8 million in year 27. Business plan increases share 4 percentage points over strategy plan.

Our marketing/sales tactics for the coming two years are as follows:

1. North America has been divided into nine regions that, except for the Canadian and Mexican territories, will continue to be covered by direct factory sales engineers. The rest of the world will be covered by independent distributors or our sales representatives, as in the past. In general, our distribution system is in place and is good. We will add three or four distributors and representatives overseas to capitalize on a projected weak dollar. International sales are expected to increase 11 percent in year 28 and 15 percent in year 29.

2. Parts and service sales are included within the sales categories of our equipment at present. We will analyze such revenues and establish goals by product line and by territory. We expect to reduce the amount of spare and repair parts sold by our competitors to our customers. We will accomplish this by paying special incentives based on profit margins and by offering "repair kits" with new machines at attractive prices.

3. We will continue our traditional approach to advertising, but our agency will produce special promotional materials on the new Chem-Mill line and redesigned Chem-Pelleter line at no added cost. We will reduce the number of trade journal ads and increase direct mailings and telemarketing. A limited in-house advertising program with a one-time cost will begin next year to make our expenditures more cost effective. Our goal is to develop 150 to 200 more customer leads in year 28 and beyond for our current products and the innovations planned.

4. Videocassette training aids are being developed to assist our sales force (internal and external) in getting our message across to customers here and abroad. Also, these tapes will be helpful in training new personnel. Five training sessions are scheduled for year 28. More are planned for the following year.

5. We will continue the year 26 program of having potential customers visit our testing laboratory and other facilities when possible.

6. Statistics and graphs will be used to chart the ratio of lost orders versus requests for quotes.

7. Customer service will be stressed every day of every year. We need one more experienced person in this department and expect to have that person on board by September, year 28.

8. All personnel will sign confidentiality contracts for appropriate periods.

9. We have prepared detailed program evaluation reviews for each of our preceding strategies for years 28 and 29. Task assignments, task expenses, task income, people costs, time, and cash-flow budgets required to guide day-to-day activities through years 28 and 29 have been completed. These detailed programs are available for review. Included in this business plan is the top-level summary of the Chem-Pelleter program. Similarly, structured tactics and budgets were prepared to assure and control attainment of our

other two goals: developing the Chem-Mill and opening the West Coast Sales Service Center.

Because of process changes in the plastics industries, the Chem-Pelleter has been in need of a major modification for some time to make it more competitive.

Chem-Pelleter Modification
(Summary of Tactics)
Impact Statement

Goal: To increase market share by 12 percentage points by year 30 (from 20 to 32 percent of the plastics industry) by modifying and repricing the Chem-Pelleter. This will increase sales by just over $1.8 million in total for years 29 and 30. A secondary goal is to reduce high unit costs of production.

Prime Responsibility: Marketing.

Estimated Cost: $55,000.

Expected Results: Sales of $3.0 million by year 30, up from an estimated $2.4 million in year 27. Revenues are expected at the earliest by the third quarter of the second year. Profitability is expected to be above average for Chem-A-Lot machines.

Time: Three years.

Year	Task	Department Responsible	Task Description	Estimated Quarter	
				Start	*Completion*
28	1	Sales, market research, product D&D	Determination of Chem-Pelleter modification required by plastics industry	28–1	28–2
	2	Sales, engineering, manufacturing	Chem-Pelleter modification	28–2	29–1
29	3	Sales, pricing, market research	Determination of price	29–1	29–1
	4	Sales, advertising	Ad campaign directed	29–1	29–2
30	5	Sales, manufacturing	Reaching sales forecasts and meeting production schedules	29–2	30–4

The responsibility for Task 1 in the summary is outlined here together with estimated costs and completion dates. In addition, actual costs and completion dates will be shown as they become available through our project control system.

CHEM-PELLETER MODIFICATION
DESIGN AND DEVELOPMENT INVESTMENT
(Task 1)

Department Responsible	Function Performed	Estimated Completion		Actual Completion	
		Date	Cost	Date	Cost
Sales	Provide information on customer complaints known to sales engineers, and other pertinent facts, to those working on the task	1/15/28	$ 500	_____	$ ____
Market Research	Surveys of the plastics industry to determine the extent and nature of the modifications required and the impact on sales of making or not making the modifications	2/30/28	$3,000	_____	$ ____
Product D&D	Study of typical applications as identified by market research to determine exact needs of the plastics industry	4/15/28	$4,000	_____	$ ____
			$7,500		$

A complete program of all tasks is maintained by the president and reported on at monthly management meetings.

Manufacturing

Although we may no longer be the lowest-cost producer in the industry, we will regain that position by year 30. Our quality will improve and our production equipment will be modernized on a cost-effective basis.

Our tactics include:

1. Increasing quality control at every production cost center, aided by monthly awareness seminars.

2. Scheduling on- and off-the-job training sessions for all production personnel.

3. Investing approximately $1.8 million in state-of-the-art, but well-tested, production equipment and a warehouse and storeroom renovation over the next two years.

4. Holding plant wage and salary pay-rate increases to within 5 percent of present levels per year.

5. Holding vendor material costs to current prices in year 28 and no more than a 5 percent increase—and hopefully less—in year 29; having all vendors deliver ordered items on time and meet our quality standards. (Each major vendor will be visited within the next quarter by two members of our management team. The purpose of the visit will be to obtain commitments for quality materials at the lowest appropriate prices.)

6. Completing installation of a material requirements planning system next year.

7. Improving inventory turns to 3.0 times per year by the end of year 29.

8. Stepping up on-time shipment of orders to the 90 percent level in year 28 and to 95 percent in year 29.

9. Making subassemblies and other parts ourselves rather than buying them from reputable outside vendors will be studied in detail for 50 percent of our products in year 28 and the remainder in year 29.

Design and Development

Our lack of innovation during the past decade, combined with the retirement of several engineers who designed a number of our "old standards," has left us with a fairly mature series of product offerings. We will become a leading manufacturer of niche products for conditioners, formulators, and conveyors in the process industries. Design engineering strategies to move toward that objective are:

1. Redesign Chem-Pelleter to increase its efficiency and to expand the number of applications for which that equipment can be used.

2. Completely design a new machine (Chem-Mill) to be used in the flour processing industry. Detailed specifications based on market intelligence have been received from the marketing/sales department. Completion is scheduled for year 29; at that time, initial sales are estimated to be in the half-million-dollar range.

3. Total expenditures to complete designs will not exceed $140,000.

4. One experienced design and development engineer will be employed in year 28.

5. We will continue to support marketing and sales personnel in responding to customer needs for improvement to our current product lines.

6. All products will be reviewed from a value-engineering standpoint to reduce their costs while ensuring the highest quality standards.

Administration

No additional personnel will be needed to staff the workload related to this business plan. Specific strategies and tactics being implemented are as follows:

1. Continue emphasis on expense control within the general and administrative area. New areas to be studied for savings include: revised fringe benefits and a clerical efficiency study.

2. Assist manufacturing in completing the installation of the material requirements planning system of controls and reporting in year 29.

3. Produce and issue on a timely basis all reports agreed to for all departments.

4. Meet monthly with manufacturing, design and development, and marketing/sales personnel to review financial results of operations compared to budget and this business plan so that immediate action can be taken on cost or expense overruns.

5. Continue to refine the variable budgeting and cost accounting records and reports, and hold joint training and analysis meetings with manufacturing personnel on this subject.

6. Continue to assist our outside auditors so that audit fees are controlled.

7. Maintain high credit and collection effort to bring accounts receivable days outstanding down from 60 plus days to about 55 days during the next two years, with a target of 52 days in year 30. Telephone collection efforts will be increased, and a collection service used when appropriate.

8. Pay vendors, except those with special needs, in 55 days on average.

9. Assist manufacturing in the make-versus-buy study.

SECTION E—HUMAN RESOURCES

Our employees are motivated, and they enthusiastically support this business plan. With their help, dedication, and support, we will attain our objective. Based on our forecasts, the following personnel are needed:

Personnel	Year		
	27	28	29
President	1	1	1
Secretary	1	1	1
	2	2	2
Manufacturing			
Administration	2	2	2
Purchasing	2	2	2
Engineering	10	10	11
Design & Development	2	3	3
Quality Control	3	4	4
Information Systems	3	3	3
Production Scheduling	2	2	2
Storeroom	3	3	3
Inventory Control	4	4	4
Shop Supervisors	8	8	8
Receiving	2	2	2
Warehouse & Shipping	5	5	5
Total Indirect	46	48	49
Repairs, Parts, and Other			
Direct Labor	131	146	140
Total Manufacturing	177	194	189
Sales/Marketing			
Sales Vice-President	1	1	1
Secretary	1	1	1
West Coast Sales Manager & Staff	2	4	4
Headquarters Sales Manager & Staff	2	2	2
Marketing & Advertising	1	2	2
International Sales Manager & Staff	3	3	3
Director of Agents & Secretary	2	2	2
Field Sales	11	11	11
Sales Administrator & Customer Service	3	4	4
Total Sales/Marketing	26	30	30
General/Administrative			
Controller	1	1	1
Secretary	1	1	1
Assistant Controller & Secretary	2	2	2
Accounting Department	8	8	8
Tax Department	3	3	3
Treasurer	1	1	1
Internal Audit	2	2	2
Cash Receipts, Disbursements, & Payroll	8	8	8
Total General/Administrative	26	26	26
Total Personnel	231	252	247

The budget will assign payroll and fringe-benefit costs specifically to each department. Presently, we believe our hourly employees will receive a pay increase of between 4 and 5 percent. Salaried employees will average 4.5 percent increases, although merit increases for some will reach higher percentages (none over 8 percent).

The same incentive bonus systems will be continued for all employees. Also, the medical and other fringe-benefit programs will continue.

Training programs are being accelerated almost across the board. In addition, joint meetings of hourly and salaried employees will be held quarterly to communicate our progress, our shortcomings, the general results of operations, and our needs. At these meetings, each manager, including department shop floor supervisors, will present a status report on the progress made toward achieving his or her department's goals for the year.

Turnover of employees is now quite low, except for planned retirements.

In the manufacturing area, we have added one design engineer this year and plan to add another in year 28. We also plan to promote another person to the quality function and hire a replacement. Sales and marketing will increase by four people because of the opening of the new West Coast office and additions to strengthen our customer service and marketing/advertising departments. Once this new personnel is added, we should be able to handle at least $48 million in sales. No people increases are planned in the administrative offices.

In summary, we have a good base of technically qualified people today, and we are adding more people and providing additional training and development to all.

SECTION F—CRITICAL ISSUES

The following are critical issues facing Chem-A-Lot:

1. U.S. and world economies are always unpredictable. A measurable decline in orders, especially from domestic customers, would be a real problem. Our break-even operating level is about $27 million in sales.
2. Competitors are on the move! We believe we know their objectives and strategies and are working to retard their progress.
3. Productivity depends on people and plant equipment. Our people are at least adequate. Our production equipment is not up to modern standards. We plan to upgrade over a relatively short period.
4. We need at least one new design engineer to speed up the Chem-Mill and Chem-Pelleter projects and to move forward from there.
5. Our customers must perceive recent changes in management and direction as being beneficial over the long-term, not just another short-term switch in direction.
6. Our new pricing policies must work.

SECTION G—FINANCIAL HIGHLIGHTS

Just prior to completing the business plan, a careful analysis of the relationship between Chem-A-Lot sales and the economy was conducted using the 12/12 pressure technique. The findings were verified by our sales engineers and key customers. After that, the base forecast for the strategy plan was revised as follows for the business plan.

SALES, COSTS, AND INCOME BASE BUSINESS FORECASTS FOR PLAN YEARS 28 THROUGH 30
(Dollars in Thousands)

Year	Earlier Sales Forecasts	Revised Sales Forecasts	Fixed Costs	Variable Costs	Operating Income Amount	%
27	$33,000	$33,900	$ 9,510	$21,690	$2,700	8%
28	38,300	39,500	10,546	24,284	4,670	12
29	40,600	35,700	10,982	21,272	3,446	10
30	46,000	42,000	12,078	25,747	4,175	10

The base business sales forecast plus new strategies to increase market share are now anticipated to result in the following:

BASE BUSINESS FORECASTS PLUS NEW STRATEGY INITIATIVES FOR YEARS 28 THROUGH 30
(Dollars in Thousands)

Year	Earlier Sales Forecasts	Revised Sales Forecasts	Fixed Costs	Variable Costs	Operating Income Amount	%
27	$33,000	$33,900	$ 9,510	$21,690	$2,700	8%
28	38,300	39,500	10,546	24,284	4,670	12
29	44,000	38,200	11,321	22,772	4,107	11
30	49,800	48,060	12,417	28,631	7,012	15

We now forecast a cyclical sales decline in our base product lines in year 29 to $35.7 million from the $39.5 million level forecasted for the previous year. Nevertheless, the efforts of our overall strategy plan will start to bear fruit in year 29, adding $2.5 million in sales and, hopefully, another $6.1 million in year 30 due to product line modifications, additions, and the increase in market share from the efforts of our new West Coast Service Center.

The investment in years 28 and 29 in marketing, redesign of the Chem-Pelleter, development of a new Chem-Mill, and expenses of a new West Coast sales/service center will have no impact on sales in budget year 28.

When sales from these investments do start in year 29, associated variable and fixed costs and the overall projected operating income should approximate the following data:

STRATEGY IMPACT ON BASE BUSINESS
FOR YEARS 28, 29, AND 30
YEAR 28 BUSINESS PLAN
(Dollars in Thousands)

	Year			
Account	27	28	29	30
Category	(Current)	(Budget)	(Estimate)	(Goal)
Sales—Base Forecast	$33,900	$39,500	$35,700	$42,000
Strategy Plan Sales Forecast				
Chem-Pelleter Modification	—	—	400	1,410
New Chem-Mill	—	—	700	2,050
West Coast Service Center	—	—	1,400	2,600
Strategy Sales	—	—	2,500	6,060
Total Sales	33,900	39,500	38,200	48,060
Variable Costs—Base Forecast	21,690	24,284	21,272	25,747
Strategy Plan Variable Costs Forecast				
Chem-Pelleter Modification	—	—	700	1,154
Other Strategy Tactics	—	—	800	1,730
Strategy Variable Costs	—	—	1,500	2,884
Total Variable Costs	21,690	24,284	22,772	28,631
Contribution Margin	12,210	15,216	15,428	19,429
Fixed Costs—Base Forecast	9,510	10,546	10,982	12,078
Strategy Plan Fixed Costs Forecast				
Chem-Pelleter Modification	—	—	220	200
Other Strategy Tactics	—	—	119	139
Strategy Fixed Costs	—	—	339	339
Total Fixed Costs	9,510	10,546	11,321	12,417
Operating Income	$ 2,700	$ 4,670	$ 4,107	$ 7,012

The following is a summary of the financial condition projected for the next two years:

SUMMARY OF PROJECTED FINANCIAL CONDITION
(Dollars in Thousands)

	Year		
	27 (Current)	28 (Budget)	29 (Estimate)
Current Assets	$15,373	$16,076	$15,538
Current Liabilities	5,351	5,962	5,317
Working Capital	10,022	10,114	10,221
Net Property, Plant, and Equipment	1,713	1,993	2,845
Other Assets	500	500	500
Less Long-Term Loans	(1,200)	—	—
Shareholders' Equity	$11,035	$12,607	$13,566

GENERATED CASH FLOW AND DISPOSITION ESTIMATES
(Dollars in Thousands)

	Year	
	28	29
Net Income	$2,926	$2,575
Depreciation & Amortization	271	358
Cash Generated by Operations	3,197	2,933
Add (Deduct)		
—Change in Receivables	(727)	900
—Decrease in Inventories	215	1,032
Deduct (Add):		
—Change in Current Liabilities	611	(645)
Deduct—Capital Expenditures	(550)	(1,210)
—Dividends	(1,355)	(1,616)
—Repayment of Loan	(1,200)	—
	191	1,394
Cash on Hand:		
—Beginning of Year	500	691
—End of Year	$ 691	$2,085

EXPECTED PERFORMANCE OVERVIEW

(Dollars in Thousands)

| | Year 27 (Current) | | Year 28 (Budget) | | Year 29 (Estimate) | |
Overview Categories	$	%	$	%	$	%
Market:						
Conditioners						
—Size	$70,000		$79,000		$74,000	
—Share	21,000	30%	24,500	31%	23,700	32%
Formulators						
—Size	50,000		54,800		52,400	
—Share	10,000	20%	11,500	21%	11,000	21%
Transporters						
—Size	11,600		13,500		13,500	
—Share	2,900	25%	3,500	26%	3,500	26%
Manufacturing/Service:						
Sales	$33,900		$39,500		$38,200	
Variable Costs	21,690		24,284		22,772	
Contribution Margin	12,210		15,216		15,428	
Fixed Costs	9,510		10,546		11,321	
Break-Even Point	26,417		27,392		28,302	
Operating Income	2,700		4,670		4,107	
Net Income	1,700		2,926		2,575	

(Continued)

345

EXPECTED PERFORMANCE OVERVIEW (Continued)

(Dollars in Thousands)

Overview Categories	Year 27 (Current) $	%	28 (Budget) $	%	29 (Estimate) $	%
Investment:						
Plant and Equipment	—		550		1,210	
Market/Product D&D	132		155		135	
Number of Employees	231		252		247	
Performance Ratios:						
Gross Profit		33.9%		37.9%		36.9%
Return on Sales		4.7%		7.4%		6.8%
Return on Average Shareholders' Equity (After-Tax)		15.8%		24.8%		19.7%
Return on Average Investment (After-Tax)		13.4%		22.3%		18.7%
Working Capital as Cents/$1 Sales		.30		.26		.27
Debt to Equity Ratios		17.2%		5.68%		5.2%

SECTION H—CONTINGENCY PLAN

In connection with the preparation of our annual budget, we will provide a contingency or crisis plan.

In general, if our incoming sales order rate falls below budget by as much as 15 percent, our fixed costs will remain about the same (approximately $10.3 to $10.5 million). However, we can reduce controllable expenses in all departments a minimum of 16 and possibly 20 percent, depending on the severity of the condition and the estimated recovery period. Operating income would tumble, more or less, by about $350,000 for each $1.0 million of sales shortfall, from a level of $38 to $40 million.

If sales drop more than 15 percent below those projected in our business plan, much more drastic measures might be taken. Again, depending on the estimated length of the recession, our crisis plan involves added pressure for the lowest possible prices from suppliers, deferral or delay in our capital equipment expenditures, wage and salary pay-rate reductions, and possible employee terminations. We can defer some design and development expenditures but would leave those for last since our future survival and growth depend on product innovations.

CHAPTER 27

CHEM-A-LOT
BUDGET PACKAGE

CONTENTS

Note: The President's letter summarizing the budget package is not reproduced herein. See Chapter 18 for excerpts.

BUDGET FORM 1
INCOME STATEMENT—ANNUAL
(Dollars in Thousands)

	Current Year 27				Year 28		Following Year	
	Budget		Estimated Actual		Budget		Forecast	
Sales	$35,000	100.0%	$33,900	100.0%	$39,500	100.0%	$38,200	100.0%
Cost of Sales	22,750	65.0	22,400	66.1	24,530	62.1	24,093	63.1
Gross Profit	12,250	35.0	11,500	33.9	14,970	37.9	14,107	36.9
Selling Expenses	4,200	12.0	4,268	12.6	4,995	12.6	4,865	12.7
Gen'l Admin. Expenses	4,450	12.7	4,400	13.0	5,150	13.0	5,000	13.1
Design & Development	145	0.4	132	0.4	155	0.4	135	0.4
Total Expenses	8,795	25.1	8,800	26.0	10,300	26.1	10,000	26.2
Operating Income	3,455	9.9	2,700	7.9	4,670	11.8	4,107	10.7
Sale of Capital Assets	—		—		—		—	
State Income Taxes	110	0.3	135	0.4	236	0.6	205	0.5
Other	—		—		—		—	
Total	110	0.3	135	0.4	236	0.6	205	0.5
Profit before Federal Taxes	3,345	9.6	2,565	7.5	4,434	11.2	3,902	10.2
Federal Tax Provison	1,245	3.6	951	2.8	1,508	3.8	1,327	3.5
Net Income	$ 2,100	6.0%	$ 1,614	4.7%	$ 2,926	7.4%	$ 2,575	6.7%
Average Shareholders' Equity Investment			$11,000		$11,821		$13,086	
Operating Income ROI			24.6%		39.5%		31.4%	
After-Tax ROI			14.7%		24.8%		19.7%	

BUDGET FORM 2
QUARTERLY INCOME STATEMENT

(Dollars in Thousands)

	1st Quarter	2nd Quarter	3rd Quarter	4th Quarter	Total
Sales	$8,394	$11,292	$10,246	$9,568	$39,500
Cost of Sales	5,558	6,754	6,225	5,993	24,530
Gross Profit	2,836	4,538	4,021	3,575	14,970
Selling Expenses	1,204	1,336	1,206	1,249	4,995
Gen'l Admin. Expenses	1,237	1,347	1,281	1,285	5,150
Design & Development	25	35	40	55	155
Total Expenses	2,466	2,718	2,527	2,589	10,300
Operating Income	370	1,820	1,494	986	4,670
Sale of Capital Assets	–	–	–	–	–
State Income Taxes	20	91	76	49	236
Other	–	–	–	–	–
Total	20	91	76	49	236
Profit before Federal Taxes	350	1,729	1,418	937	4,434
Federal Tax Provison	120	588	482	318	1,508
Net Income	$ 230	$ 1,141	$ 936	$ 619	$ 2,926

BUDGET FORM 3
GROSS PROFIT BY PRODUCT LINE[1]
(Dollars in Thousands)

| | Quarter 1 | | | | Quarter 2 | | | |
| | Sales | | Gross | G.P. | Sales | | Gross | G.P. |
Product Lines	Amount	Units	Profit	%	Amount	Units	Profit	%
Base Business Forecast								
Conditioners[1]								
Kraker	$1,769	20	$ 812	45.9%	$ 3,096	35	$1,684	54.4%
Pelletizer	522	17	78	14.9	645	21	154	23.9
Sifter	239	18	88	36.8	399	30	178	44.6
Dryer	404	17	115	28.5	593	25	237	40.0
Cooler	1,026	65	278	27.1	1,263	80	442	35.0
Washer	214	40	55	25.7	268	50	80	30.0
Total Conditioners	4,174	177	1,426	34.2	6,264	241	2,775	44.3
Total Formulators	2,293	140	603	26.3	2,785	170	869	31.2
Total Transporters	627	20	117	18.7	940	30	202	21.5
Total Machines	7,094	337	2,146	30.3	9,989	441	3,846	38.5
Total Repairs/Parts	1,300	–	690	53.1	1,303	–	692	53.1
New Products, Etc.[2]	–	–	–	–	–	–	–	–
Total	$8,394	337	$2,836	33.8%	$11,292	441	$4,538	40.2%

(Continued)

BUDGET FORM 3 (Continued)
GROSS PROFIT BY PRODUCT LINE[1]

(Dollars in Thousands)

Product Lines	Quarter 3				Quarter 4				Total			
	Sales		Gross Profit	G.P. %	Sales		Gross Profit	G.P. %	Sales		Gross Profit	G.P. %
	Amount	Units			Amount	Units			Amount	Units		
Base Business Forecast												
Conditioners[1]												
Kracker	$ 2,654	30	$1,420	53.5%	$2,034	23	$ 981	48.2%	$ 9,553	108	$ 4,897	51.3%
Pelletizer	583	19	128	22.0	584	19	128	21.9	2,334	76	488	20.9
Sifter	319	24	133	41.6	345	26	147	42.6	1,302	98	546	41.9
Dryer	499	21	188	37.7	451	19	160	35.5	1,947	82	700	36.0
Cooler	1,231	78	430	34.9	1,105	70	376	34.0	4,625	293	1,526	33.0
Washer	252	47	73	28.9	279	52	86	30.8	1,013	189	294	29.0
Total Conditioners	5,538	219	2,372	42.8	4,798	209	1,878	39.1	20,774	846	8,451	40.7
Total Formulators	2,604	159	784	30.1	2,735	167	853	31.2	10,417	636	3,109	29.8
Total Transporters	784	25	165	21.0	721	23	146	20.2	3,072	98	630	20.5
Total Machines	8,926	403	3,321	37.2	8,254	399	2,877	34.9	34,263	1580	12,190	35.6
Total Repairs/Parts	1,320	—	700	53.0	1,314	—	698	53.1	5,237	—	2,780	53.1
New Products, Etc.[2]	—	—	—	—	—	—	—	—	—	—	—	—
Total	$10,246	403	$4,021	39.2%	$9,568	399	$3,575	37.4%	$39,500	1580	$14,970	37.9%

[1]Only the conditioner line is detailed herein for illustrative purposes.
[2]New product introductions are scheduled for years 29 forward.

BUDGET FORM 4
COST OF SALES SUMMARY BY COST ELEMENT[1]
(Dollars in Thousands)

Product Line	Material[2]			Direct Labor/Fringes[3]			Overhead			Total Manufacturing Costs		
	Budget Amount	Budget % of Sales[4]	Current % of Sales	Budget Amount	Budget % of Sales[4]	Current % of Sales	Budget Amount	Budget % of Sales[4]	Current % of Sales	Budget Amount	Budget % of Sales[4]	Current % of Sales
Conditioners[1]												
Kracker	$2,041	21.4%	21.3%	$ 887	9.3%	9.0%	$ 1,728	18.1%	19.6%	$ 4,656	48.7%	49.3%
Pelletizer	488	20.9	20.8	334	14.3	14.1	1,024	43.9	42.1	1,846	79.1	78.0
Sifter	266	20.4	20.0	133	10.2	9.9	357	27.4	27.2	756	58.1	57.5
Dryer	399	20.5	20.3	177	9.1	8.9	671	34.5	33.1	1,247	64.0	64.0
Cooler	976	21.1	21.0	555	12.0	11.8	1,568	33.9	33.2	3,099	67.0	66.4
Washer	268	26.5	26.1	133	13.1	13.0	318	31.4	31.9	719	71.0	70.8
Total Conditioners	4,438	21.4	22.0	2,219	10.7	11.4	5,666	27.3	27.9	12,323	59.3	61.1
Total Formulators	2,426	23.3	25.5	1,413	13.6	14.2	3,469	33.3	34.9	7,308	70.2	74.4
Total Transporters	789	25.7	27.0	404	13.2	13.9	1,249	40.7	41.0	2,442	79.5	82.8
Total Machines	7,653	22.3	23.1	4,036	11.8	12.3	10,384	30.3	32.9	22,073	64.4	68.5
Total Repairs/Parts	852	16.3	16.9	453	8.7	9.0	1,152	22.0	22.1	2,457	46.9	47.8
Total	$8,505	21.5%	22.6%	$4,489	11.4%	11.9%	$11,536	29.2%	31.4%	$24,530	62.1%	66.1%

[1] Only the conditioner line is detailed herein for illustrative purposes.
[2] Raw material and supply costs are not budgeted to increase in real terms over year 27.
[3] Labor and related fringe benefits are budgeted to increase 4.5 percent over year 27.
[4] Percentage of sales relates to sales of respective product lines, not total company sales.

BUDGET FORM 5
VARIABLE BUDGET SUMMARY—BREAK-EVEN POINTS

(Dollars in Thousands)

	85% of Plan		100% of Plan	
	Amount	Percent	Amount	Percent
Sales	$33,575	100.0%	$39,500	100.0%
Variable Costs				
Materials	7,229	21.5	8,505	21.5
Manufacturing	10,545	31.4	12,407	31.4
Design & Development	132	0.4	155	0.4
Selling	1,806	5.4	2,166	5.5
General & Admin.	801	2.4	1,051	2.7
Total Variable	20,513	61.1	24,284	61.5
Contribution Margin	13,062	38.9	15,216	38.5
Fixed Costs				
Manufacturing	3,618	10.8	3,618	9.2
Selling	2,829	8.4	2,829	7.1
General & Admin.	4,099	12.2	4,099	10.4
Design & Development	—	—	—	—
Total Fixed	10,546	31.4	10,546	26.7
Operating Income	$ 2,516	7.5%	$ 4,670	11.8%
Break-Even Point[1]	$27,110	80.7%	$27,392	69.3%

> Note: A detailed operating plan has been developed if the budgeted sales do not materialize. These contingency plans trigger at a $36 million sales level, assuming a normal product mix.

[1]Contribution margin equals your fixed costs at the break-even point. Dividing your fixed costs by your contribution margin *rate* will give you the break-even point in dollars. There are other correct methods for deriving your break-even points. Break-even dollars are sales and are expressed also as a percentage of total sales.

BUDGET FORM 6
CONTRIBUTION MARGIN BY PRODUCT LINE
(Dollars in Thousands)

	Conditioner		Formulator		Transporter		Parts		Total	
Sales	$20,774	100.0%	$10,417	100.0%	$ 3,072	100.0%	$ 5,237	100.0%	$39,500	100.0%
Variable Costs										
Materials	4,438	21.4	2,426	23.3	789	25.7	852	16.3	8,505	21.5
Manufacturing	6,155	29.6	3,802	36.5	1,200	39.1	1,250	23.9	12,407	31.4
Design & Dev.	155	0.7	—	—	—	—	—	—	155	0.4
Selling	1,148	5.5	580	5.6	188	6.1	250	4.8	2,166	5.5
General & Admin.	557	2.7	250	2.4	124	4.0	120	2.3	1,051	2.7
Total Variable	12,453	59.9	7,058	67.8	2,301	74.9	2,472	47.2	24,284	61.5
Contribution Margins	$ 8,321	40.1%	$ 3,359	32.2%	$ 771	25.1%	$ 2,765	52.8%	$15,216	38.5%
Fixed Costs										
Manufacturing									3,618	9.2
Selling									2,829	7.1
General & Admin.									4,099	10.4
Total Fixed[1]									10,546	26.7
Operating Income									$ 4,670	11.8%

[1]Some businesses may allocate fixed costs to product lines. Chem-A-Lot does not allocate fixed costs to product lines since there are no clear relationships on which to base such allocations in this particular business.

BUDGET FORM 7
BALANCE SHEETS—QUARTERLY
(Dollars in Thousands)

	Last Year	Quarters—Year 28 1st	2nd	3rd	4th	Forecast Year 29
Current Assets						
Cash and Marketable Securities	$ 500	$ 2,165	$ 687	$ 2,204	$ 691	$ 2,085
Accounts Receivable	5,573	5,350	7,197	6,530	6,300	5,400
Notes Receivable	—	—	—	—	—	—
Inventory	9,300	6,715	8,606	7,926	9,085	8,053
Total Current Assets	15,373	14,230	16,490	16,660	16,076	15,538
Property, Plant, & Equipment	20,000	20,000	20,000	20,550	20,550	21,760
Less Accumulated Depreciation	(18,287)	(18,354)	(18,421)	(18,488)	(18,557)	(18,915)
Capitalized Leases, Net of Amortization	—	—	—	—	—	—
Net Property, Plant, & Equipment	1,713	1,646	1,579	2,062	1,993	2,845
All Other Assets	500	500	500	500	500	500
Total Assets	$ 17,586	$ 16,376	$ 18,569	$ 19,222	$ 18,569	$ 18,883
Current Liabilities						
Loans Payable	$ 700	$ 700	$ 700	$ 700	$ 700	$ 700
Accounts Payable	3,650	3,190	4,102	3,774	3,694	3,449
Income Taxes Payable	951	183	734	1,183	1,508	1,113
Accrued Expenses, etc.	50	50	50	50	60	55
Total Current Liabilities	5,351	4,123	5,586	5,707	5,962	5,317
Long-Term Loans	1,200	1,200	1,200	1,200	—	—
Other Non-Current Liabilities	—	—	—	—	—	—
Total Liabilities	6,551	5,323	6,786	6,907	5,962	5,317
Shareholders' Equity	11,035	11,053	11,783	12,315	12,607	13,566
Total Liabilities & Shareholders' Equity	$ 17,586	$ 16,376	$ 18,569	$ 19,222	$ 18,569	$ 18,883

BUDGET FORM 8
OUTSIDE FINANCING
(Dollars in Thousands)

	Current Balance December 31	Budget Year Activity			Budget Year Balance—December 31	Terms
		Date	Payments	Borrowings		
Short-Term Borrowing[1]	$ 700	2/15	$ (350)	$ —	$700	2% over prime, maximum line of credit $1 million
		3/15		350		
		8/15	(350)	—		
		9/15		350		
Current Portion of Long-Term Debt	—				—	
Long-Term Debt	1,200	12/15	(1,200)	—	—	
	$1,900		$(1,900)	$700	$700	

[1]We may pay off the short-term loan in year 28, but list it as outstanding in the event more capital expenditures, working capital, or dividends are required.

BUDGET FORM 9
STATEMENT OF CASH FLOW
(Dollars in Thousands)

	Quarter 1	Quarter 2	Quarter 3	Quarter 4	Total
Net Income	$ 230	$ 1,141	$ 936	$ 619	$ 2,926
Depreciation and Amortization	67	67	67	70	271
Cash Operating Income	297	1,208	1,003	689	3,197
Additions (Deductions) in Cash Resulting from Changes In					
Accounts Receivable	223	(1,847)	667	230	(727)
Inventories	2,585	(1,891)	680	(1,159)	215
Prepaid Expenses	—	—	—	—	—
Accounts Payable	(460)	912	(328)	(80)	44
Other Accruals	(768)	551	449	335	567
Net Operating Cash Flow	1,877	(1,067)	2,471	15	3,296
Other Receipts (Disbursements)					
Sale of Assets	—	—	—	—	—
Capital Expenditures	—	—	(550)	—	(550)
Borrowing (Loan Repayments)	—	—	—	(1,200)	(1,200)
Other—Dividends	(212)	(411)	(404)	(328)	(1,355)
—Miscellaneous	—	—	—	—	—
Total	$1,665	$(1,478)	$1,517	$(1,513)	$ 191
Cash Beginning of Period	$ 500	$ 2,165	$ 687	$ 2,204	$ 500
Cash End of Period	$2,165	$ 687	$2,204	$ 691	$ 691

BUDGET FORM 10
SELLING EXPENSE
(Dollars in Thousands)

	Previous Year Actual		Current Year Budget		Current Year Estimated Actual		Budget Year	
	Amount	% of Sales	Amount	% of Sales	Amount	% of Sales	Amount	% of Sales
Total Selling Expenses	$2,958	14.3	$4,200	12.0	$4,268	12.6	$4,995	12.6

Expense Items	Estimated Year 27	Budget Year 28	Explanation of Significant Changes
Salaries and Wages	$1,400	$1,825	5% increase in compensation levels, two people added during year for West Coast sales office, one person added in marketing/advertising, and an additional customer service person, plus $230 estimated bonuses based on increased profits
Freight Out	700	790	N/A
Rent	220	220	
Office Expense	530	613	In line with 16.5% budgeted increase in sales
Insurance	88	110	Insurance premiums raised 25%
Conventions & Trade Shows	90	100	
Advertising & Promotional	300	350	In line with budgeted sales increase
Travel & Entertainment	220	257	In line with budgeted sales income
Maintenance	88	103	Normal items plus $9.2 to redecorate sales offices
Utilities	120	135	
Dues & Subscriptions	30	50	
Depreciation	12	13	N/A
Other	470	429	Increase in commissioned sales ($79) and other miscellaneous expenses less than sales increases
Total	$4,268	$4,995	

Note: Separately list any item equaling 5 percent or more of total budgeted selling expense; list remaining expenses under caption "Other."

BUDGET FORM 11
GENERAL AND ADMINISTRATIVE EXPENSE

(Dollars in Thousands)

	Previous Year Actual		Current Year Budget		Current Year Estimated Actual		Budget Year	
	Amount	% of Sales	Amount	% of Sales	Amount	% of Sales	Amount	% of Sales
Total G & A Expenses	$3,050	14.7	$4,450	12.7	$4,400	13.0	$5,150	13.0

Expense Items	Estimated Year 27	Budget Year 28	Explanation of Significant Changes
Salaries and Wages	$1,285	$1,545	5% increase in compensation levels, plus $200 bonuses due to increased profits
Office Expense	705	760	Normal inflation increases
Rent	100	100	
Insurance	320	440	50% increase in product liability and casualty insurance ($100) plus increase in all other premiums
Travel & Entertainment	220	230	Normal inflation increases
Professional Fees	540	650	Consultants for new cost and production control system ($30) plus increased legal fees on patent suit ($80)
Utilities	200	225	
Taxes—Non-Income Based	100	100	
Maintenance	256	424	Repair roof and all internal office walls and repaint all offices
Contributions	150	160	
Dues & Subscriptions	50	50	
Director Fees	90	90	
Depreciation	24	26	N/A
Other	360	350	N/A
Total	$4,400	$5,150	

Note: Separately list any item that is 5 percent or more of total budgeted G & A expense; list remaining expenses under caption "Other."

BUDGET FORM 12
DESIGN AND DEVELOPMENT PROJECTS
(Dollars in Thousands)

Number	Project Description	Total Cost	Amount to Be Spent in Budget Year	Estimated Completion Date
28–1	Design and produce modified Chem-Pelleter chemical process unit	$ 51	$ 51	June 30, Year 29
28–2	Design and produce new Chem-Mill unit	104	104	October 1, Year 29
	Total for Operating Budget	$155	$155	

BUDGET FORM 13
DETAIL OF OTHER INCOME (EXPENSE)
(Dollars in Thousands)

	1st Quarter	2nd Quarter	3rd Quarter	4th Quarter	Total
Gain (Loss) on Sale of Capital Assets (Detail)	$–	$–	$–	$–	$–
State Tax (Expense)[1]	20	91	76	49	236
Other Income (Expense)—(Detail)	–	–	–	–	–
Total Other Income	$20	$91	$76	$49	$236

[1] State income tax rate approximates 5 percent.

BUDGET FORM 14
FEDERAL/FOREIGN INCOME TAX PROVISION
(Dollars in Thousands)

	Quarter 1		Quarter 2		Quarter 3		Quarter 4		Total
	Taxable Income	*Tax Liability*	*Taxable Income*	*Tax Liability*	*Taxable Income*	*Tax Liability*	*Taxable Income*	*Tax Liability*	*Tax Liability*
Profit before Taxes	$350		$1,729		$1,418		$937		$4,434
Add (Deduct) Reconciling Items	—		—		—		—		—
Non-Deductible Expenses									
	$350		$1,729		$1,418		$937		$4,434
Taxable Income Calculation:									

	Rate		Quarter 1		Quarter 2		Quarter 3		Quarter 4		Total
Ordinary Income	34%	×	$350 =	$120	$1,729 =	$588	$1,418 =	$482	$937 =	$318	$1,508
Capital Gain	%	×	— =	—	— =	—	— =	—	— =	—	—
Foreign	%	×	—	—	—	—	—	—	—	—	—
Other (Specify)	%	×	— =	—	— =	—	— =	—	— =	—	—
			$350	$120	$1,729	$588	$1,418	$482	$937	$318	$1,508
Less: Investment Tax Credit on											
Qualified Property 10%				(0)		(0)		(0)		(0)	(0)
Other Credits				(0)		(0)		(0)		(0)	(0)
Foreign Tax Credit				(0)		(0)		(0)		(0)	(0)
Total Provision for Income Taxes				$120		$588		$482		$318	$1,508

BUDGET FORM 15
CAPITAL EXPENDITURES REPORT SUMMARY
(Dollars in Thousands)

Classification	Carryover from Prior Year(s)	Current Year	Total	Expenditures by Quarter				Total Expenditures	Carryforward to Future Year(s)
				First	Second	Third	Fourth		
N—New Item for Capacity	$0	$0	$0	$0	$0	$ 0	$0	$ 0	$0
E—Environmental									
R—Replacement		0		0	0	550	0	550	0
O—Other									
Total	$0	$0	$0	$0	$0	$550	$0	$550	$0
Investment Tax Credit	$0	$0		$0	$0	$0	$0	$ 0	

Budget Item	Description	Classification	Future Years	Total Budget Year	Expected DCF[1] Return
28–1	Computer-controlled lathe	R	0	215	18%
28–2	Boring mill	R	0	275	22%
28–3	Additions and renovations in storeroom and warehouse	R	0	60	15%

[1] Discounted Cash Flow.

BUDGET FORM 16
CAPITAL EXPENDITURE BUDGET
CARRY OVER FROM PRIOR YEAR(S)

(Dollars in Thousands)

Item #	Description	Classification	Total Authorization Approved	Amount Spent before Budget Year	Authorized Amount Remaining	Amount to Be Spent in Budget Year	Amount to Be Spent in Future Year(s)
				None			
		Total	$	$	$	$	$

BUDGET FORM 17
BUDGET ASSUMPTIONS

Accounts Receivable Days Outstanding	58 days
Inventory Turns	2.7 times
Accounts Payable Days Outstanding	55 days
Sales Price Change	0%
Raw Material and Supply Cost Inflation	0%
Wage, Salary, and Benefits Increase	4.5%
Bank Average Prime Loan Rate	8%
State Income Tax Rate	5%
Federal Income Tax Rate	34%
Sales Backlog—Beginning of Year	$9.4 million
—End of Year	$8.1 million

BUDGET FORM 18
PERSONNEL

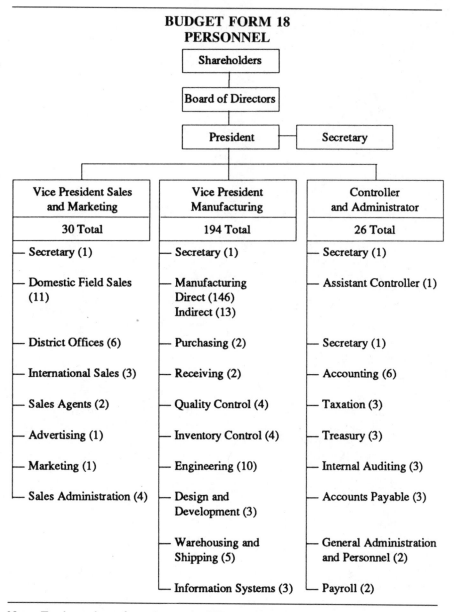

Note: Total number of employees is 252; numbers in each department are given above in parenthesis for departments with more than one person.

PART SEVEN

THE CHEM-A-LOT MANAGEMENT TOOL KIT (MORE THAN AN INDEX)

The first part of the kit lists and explains the use of each diagnostic and control tool employed in the story of Chem-A-Lot together with page references as to where each tool can be found in its appropriate context. The second part of the kit lists the pages where aspects of each management concept are discussed.

DIAGNOSTIC TOOLS

Appropriateness for the task at hand determined whether or not a tool was selected for use at Chem-A-Lot. Those tools that were not selected should also be in every manager's tool kit. This kit can serve only as an introduction to some of the more useful tools. To learn more about each of them, consult good texts on statistics and management. Tools are arranged alphabetically by name. Page references in boldface refer to main entry for the item discussed.

• Break-Even Charts

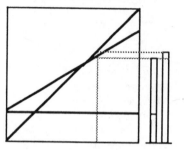

Type: Combination line and bar.
Scales: Arithmetic.
Use: To estimate costs, revenues, and profits for different levels of sales.
Pages: 149, 150, **153**, 280

• Break-Even Point

Formula, calculation: Page: 151

• Cause and Effect Charts

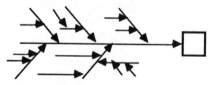

Type: Fishbone.
Use: To trace muddled problem causes and effects. Not shown directly for Chem-A-Lot.

• Combination Chart/Tables

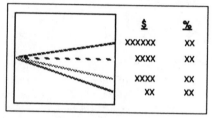

Type: Size, growth, or rate comparison charts with tables.
Scales: Arithmetic or logarithmic.
Use: To help clarify chart and table.
Pages: 58, **59**, 60, 61, 62, **63**, 67, 68, **104, 283**, 288, 289, 290, 291, 292, 293, 297, 298, 299

• Control Charts

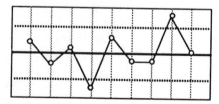

Type: Line.
Scales: Arithmetic.
Use: To monitor and control deviations from norms against set limits. One use measures effectiveness of a production system. Not discussed for Chem-A-Lot.

- **Critical Path Charts**

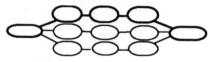

Type: Project analysis.

Use: To determine the path through critical tasks that put a time limit on project completion.

Pages: **183**, 194, 195

- **Distribution Charts**

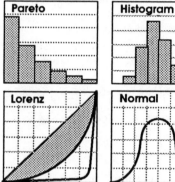

Pareto Type: Column.

Scales: Arithmetic.

Use: To determine problem priorities through column height. The top-priority item could be "Paretoed" again to determine primary cause of problem.

Lorenz Type: Curvilinear.

Scales: Arithmetic.

Use: To determine the deviation from absolute equality of one or more data distributions. The straight diagonal line represents absolute equality. The grey area simply highlights the degree of inequality for one of the two distributions shown.

Histogram Type: Column.

Scales: Arithmetic.

Use: To determine the shape of clustered measurements around a mean (average).

Normal Type: Curvilinear.

Scales: Arithmetic.

Use: This bell-shaped curve represents what is considered to be a normal distribution around a mean. With the emphasis on long-range planning these four charts were not specifically shown for Chem-A-Lot.

- **Elasticity of Demand**

Equation: Page: 123

- **Elasticity of Supply**

Equation: Page: 136

- **Flow Charts**

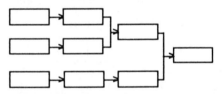

Type: Flow, one of many.

Use: To display dependencies that occur prior to a final result. For example, to summarize financial relationships or illustrate strings of tactics.

Pages: 190–191 (Financial), 194 (Tactical)

- **Forecasting Model Types**

Types: Naive, time series, causal, learned behavior, and barometric models, which are classified as quantitative types, and another group of models, which are classified as qualitative types.

Pages: 120–121

- **Geographic Distribution Maps**

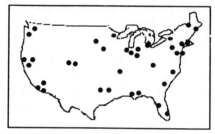

Type: Cluster.
Use: To display and compare territories and a variety of data or small charts by geographic area.
Page: 101 (Geographic boundaries only)

- **Index Derivation**

Single products: Pages: 288–294

Multiple products: Pages: 294–300

- **Interrelationship Charts**

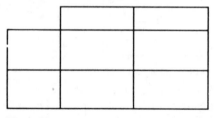

Type: Grid.

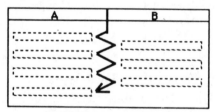

Type: Sequence.
Use: To define interrelationships between people or things. A complex grid example would be the Industry or Input/Output grid for the United States.
Pages: 41 (Grid), 98 (Sequence)

- **Leadership Charts**

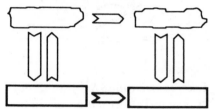

Type: Concept Clarification.
Use: In this instance to illustrate how a leader's beliefs about the present and valuations about the future of a business relate to motives of workers in the achievement of economic results. Helpful in understanding business dynamics.
Pages: 35, 178, **250**, 266

- **Moving Average Formula**

Centering procedure, formula, and calculation: Page: 105

- **Organization Charts**

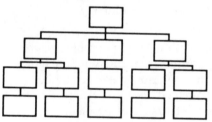

Type: Traditional.
Use: To identify the authority structure. A variety of other structures are possible.
Personnel version: Page: 365

- **Percentage Charts**

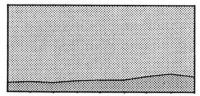

Type: Area.

Scales: Arithmetic.

Use: To show simple comparisons over several years. With too many data series, these charts become difficult to interpret.

Page: 72

- **Percentage Tool(%)**

Pages: 276–278

- **Performance Charts**

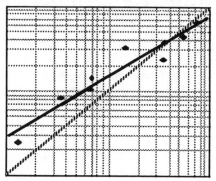

Type: Combined scatter and line.

Scales: Log-log (both logarithmic).

Use: To compare, *fairly*, performance data of vastly differing amounts for a single time period. Fair because size no longer dominates the measure of performance. Charts with arithmetic scales fail in this respect.

Pages: 115, 116, 285

- **Pie Charts**

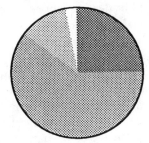

Type: Area.

Scales: Circular arithmetic.

Use: To make simple size comparisons for a single year. Two or more pies can show proportionate changes in the same items for different years.

Pages: 107, 280

- **Pressure Charts**

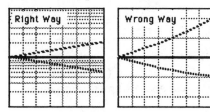

Type: Line.

Scales: Arithmetic.

Use: To provide advance warning of economic changes. Useful in sales forecasting when a leading indicator can be found.

Page: 126

- **Rate Comparison Charts**

Right Way   Wrong Way

Type: Line.

Scales: Semi-log (Logarithmic vertical and arithmetic horizontal).

Use: To show clearly proportionate growth or decline among several data series over a number of years.

For example: The semi-log chart on page 63 contains a price growth line and a quantity decline line. If the angles formed by these lines with the sales line had been identical above and below the base line (100), we could have said that unit elasticity of demand prevailed on average throughout the eight years shown. That is, the quantity decrease would have exactly offset the price increase, and the growth in sales would have been precisely zero. Because such a change would have been so slight, the rounded annual average percentages for price growth and quantity decline would not have changed. Arithmetic charts are wrong for this purpose. Semi-log lines would appear curved with unequal angles above and below the base line. Arithmetic charts are, on the other hand, appropriate for showing size trends.

Pages: 59, 60, 61, 62, **63**, 67, **68**, 104, 275

- **Rate-of-Change Charts**

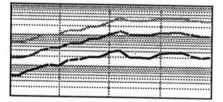

Type: Line.
Scales: Semi-log (logarithmic vertical and arithmetic horizontal).

Use: To show proportionate growth or decline between several data series. Average rate-of-change lines can be added. Avoid bars or columns on semi-log charts because they visually mix size with proportion.

Pages: **49**, **87**, 104, 281, 282, 287

- **Rate-of-Change Formula**

Formula and calculation: Pages: 102, 284

- **Rate-of-Change Trend Charts**

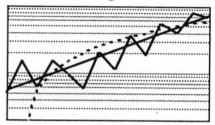

Type: Line.
Scales: Semi-log (logarithmic vertical and arithmetic horizontal).

Use: To demonstrate that a straight rate-of-change line shows a constant average annual growth (or decline) for a data series. The dotted size trend line for the same data has been added to demonstrate how it would appear plotted on a semi-log chart.

Pages: 51, 54, **55**, 58, 79, **244**, 275, 282, **283**, 286, 311

- **Return on Investment (ROI)**
  Return on Assets (ROA)

Formulas and calculations:
Pages: 163–165

- **Sales Geology Charts**

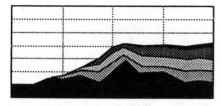

Type: Area.

Scales: Arithmetic.

Use: To show how unit or dollar sales of products with different growth profiles stack up to total sales over a period of years. Charts could also be used for costs.

Pages: 80, 279

- **Size Comparison Charts**

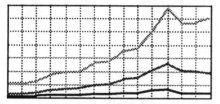

Type: Line.

Scales: Arithmetic.

Use: To compare *size* among three or more data series over many years.

Pages: **14**, 25, 28, 30, 49, **53**, 66, 100, 281

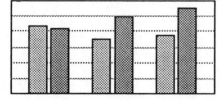

Type: Column.

Scales: Arithmetic.

Use: To compare the size of one or two data series covering a few years.

In combination on pages: 149, **153**, 280

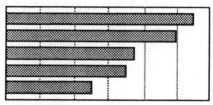

Type: Bar.

Scales: Vertical item list with horizontal arithmetic scale.

Use: To compare the size of a number of items within one year.

Modified version: Pages: 195, 196, 280

- **Size Trend Charts**

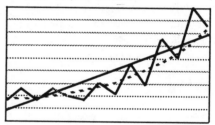

Type: Line.

Scales: Arithmetic.

Use: The straight trend line shows the *size* increase or decrease of a data series. *Caution:* This size trend line will have varying percentage changes between any two different segments along its entire length. The dotted growth line for the same data has been added to demonstrate how a constant average annual rate-of-change line would appear plotted on an arithmetic scale. Absolute size grows exactly like money on compound interest.

- **Supply and Demand Charts**

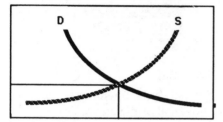

Type: Line.

Scales: Arithmetic.

Use: Traditional supply and demand charts are helpful in understanding how the quantity of a product demanded is related to the quantity supplied at a price in the marketplace.

- **Tables**

	$	%
Sales	xxxx	xxx
Cost of Goods Sold	xxx	xx
Gross Profit	xxxx	xx
Operating Expenses:		
Operating and Selling	xx	xx
General and Admin.	xx	xx
Total Operating Exp.	xx	xx
Pre-tax Income	xx	xx

Type: A wide variety.

Use: Whenever a detailed look at underlying data is required, tables are essential. Chapters 25, 26, and 27 (pages 307–365) consist of a complete cycle of plan packages: Strategic Plan, Business Plan, and Budget. These plan packages are self-contained and can be adapted to other businesses. Chapter 27 details the forthcoming year for Chem-A-Lot in an interrelated set of 17 accounting tables. These tables represent the culmination of the proper use of long-term management tools and concepts.

- **Time Charts**

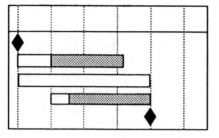

Type: Modified bar.

Scale: Horizontal arithmetic scale with vertical list.

Use: To keep track of time required for work assignments, production schedules, R&D, etc.

Pages: 195, 196

- **Trend Equations**

Use: To calculate the best fit for a line to represent scattered data points. (See a statistics text for information on arithmetic and logarithmic regression calculations as well as for standard errors of estimate and statistical coefficients.)

Page: 116 (logarithmic)

- **Turning Points**

Pages: 281–285

- **Weight Calculation**

Page: 295

All of the charts and tables in the tool kit were created on a desktop personal computer. Difficult statistical calculations for charts were done and plotted automatically from data spreadsheets entered in the computer memory.

Not so long ago, it was very tedious work indeed to do the calculations and then choose the appropriate chart to display just one numerical result. And often, upon completing the work, you had the nagging feeling that there might have been a better way to present the information. Many times the effort was never even made to find out.

With a personal computer, you can speed up calculations and in seconds view a variety of ways of displaying the results for maximum communication. Thus, it becomes feasible to integrate masses of information and really see how to analyze an entire business from an integrated accounting and economic perspective.

MANAGEMENT CONCEPTS

Listed here are page references to concepts needed to prepare professional plans. Chem-A-Lot's strategy plan, business plan, and budget are stand-alone example packages—complete with the descriptive documents and numerical data a competent CEO would submit for board approval. Each package has a separate table of contents shown on pages 307, 328, and 348, respectively.